SPACE, REGION & SOCIETY

GEOGRAPHICAL ESSAYS
IN HONOR OF
ROBERT H. STODDARD

Edited by

MICHAEL R. HILL

Zea Books • Lincoln, Nebraska
2016

Copyright © 2016 by Michael R. Hill

ISBN 978-1-60962-103-2 paperback

The text is set in Times New Roman.

Zea Books are published by the University of Nebraska–Lincoln Libraries

Electronic (pdf) edition available online at http://digitalcommons.unl.edu
Print edition available from http://www.lulu.com/spotlight/unlib

UNL does not discriminate based upon any protected status.
Please go to unl.edu/nondiscrimination

Nebraska
UNIVERSITY OF
Lincoln

As an expression of their friendship and
esteem, the authors dedicate these essays to

ROBERT H. STODDARD

in honor of his many years of exemplary service
to the people of Nebraska, the World, and the
discipline of Geography.

Robert H. Stoddard

Preface

This volume was a collective effort. Tom Doering and the late Steve Kale signed on immediately. The late Dick Lonsdale provided welcome encouragement. Sally Stoddard suggested contacting two colleagues who worked closely and meaningfully with Bob over the past several years: Surinder Bhardwaj and Carolyn Prorok. This duo responded immediately with the highest possible praise for Bob's work and collegiality. The editor extends his deepest apologies to those who had every right and reason to see the completion of the volume at a much earlier date.

This volume includes two significant "prologue" pieces. First, Carl Ritter's prescient 1828 essay on quantification in geography is an uncanny precursor to many ideas systematically developed in Bob's subsequent teaching and research. Second, the prize-winning 1935 essay by Mrs. Hugh P. Stoddard (Bob's mother) about Martha Jane Harshman Aldrich (Bob's great-grandmother), sets the stage for Bob's upbringing *in* — and subsequent master's thesis *on* — Nemaha County, Nebraska.

Finally, and most important, this volume features one of Bob's writings that he personally considers among his most satisfying work. The immediate problem for the editor was how to identify such an essay and wrangle this information out of Bob without alerting him that a *Festschrift* was in the works. Sally Stoddard took on this delicate chore, discovering that Bob's essay on regionalization in Sri Lanka is one of his special favorites. Sally forwarded her finding to me (along with a copy of Bob's resume and a selection of photographs). It remained only to obtain a copy of Bob's unpublished manuscript from him, and for this the editor resorted to a plausible subterfuge for which he hopes to be forgiven.

Bob's essay melds his expertise with high-order regionalization techniques, on the one hand, with his regional focus on Asia, on the other. In this study, Bob astutely demonstrates how the problem of defining a Tamil homeland in Sri Lanka becomes increasingly difficult as one obtains greater detail and regional specificity. Presented in 1986 to the15th Annual Conference on South Asia, Bob's paper is a prescient exemplar of Ray Hudson's (1990: 296) note on the centrality of scale in geographical analysis:

> Scale is an important consideration in nearly all geographical studies. Careful selection of appropriate scales in space and in time is required to formulate and answer meaningful geographical questions. Because trends discernable at one scale are often invisible at another, geographers commonly use a range of scales to insure that the conclusions drawn from a study are well matched to the economic,

social, and physical processes known to underlie observed patterns. A map can effectively portray a geographer's thesis when an appropriate scale is chosen. A geographer's skills in constructing a map that shows only the relevant information resemble the crafting of a well-argued point in a debate, and when the map argument succeeds, a geographical thesis is substantiated.

The sequence of maps in Bob's presentation is a forceful "map argument" that successfully explicates the entangled spatial difficulties of any attempt to rationalize ethnicity and regionalization in Sri Lanka. As Bob was given no opportunity to revise his "contribution" before the publication of this volume, any errors must be laid at the editor's doorstep.

It is one of my deepest honors to be listed among Bob Stoddard's many students and colleagues. His accomplished professional demeanor, breadth of knowledge, and enduring personal integrity are exemplars to which many of us strive but rarely achieve. In sum, this small tribute to Professor Stoddard in no way captures the extraordinary measure of his influence on us all. He unquestionably joins the ranks of Nebraska's distinguished early faculty: Charles Bessey, George Howard, Roscoe Pound, Hattie Plum Williams, and their like-minded, often selfless co-workers.

The editor directs special thanks Mary Jo Deegan, John Hudson, the late Dick Lonsdale, Paul Royster, Gerard Rushton, and Sally Stoddard for making helpful suggestions during the conception, evolution and preparation of this volume.

Permission from David Bristow of *Nebraska History* to reprint "The Biography of a Builder of Nebraska: Martha Jane Harshman Aldrich," by Nainie Lenora Robertson Stoddard, is gratefully acknowledged.

Permission from Alyson Greiner of the *Journal of Cultural Geography* to reprint "Non-Hajj Pilgrimage in Islam: A Neglected Dimension of Religious Circulation," by Surinder M. Bhardwaj, is also gratefully acknowledged.

— MRH

Reference

Hudson, John C. 1990. "Scale in Space and Time." Pp. 280-297 in *Geography's Inner Worlds: Pervasive Themes in Contemporary American Geography*, edited by Ronald F. Abler, Melvin G. Marcus, and Judy M. Olson. (Occasional Publications of the Association of American Geographers, No. 2). New Brunswick, NJ: Rutgers University Press.

Contents

A CLASSIC EXEMPLAR

BIBLIOGRAPHIC APPENDICES

List of Illustrations, Maps, and Tables

1

ROBERT H. STODDARD:
A GEOGRAPHER'S JOURNEY
FROM AUBURN TO LINCOLN

Michael R. Hill

Robert H. Stoddard was born in Auburn, Nebraska, on August 29, 1928, the son of Hugh Pettit Stoddard and Nainie Lenora Robertson Stoddard.[1] Bob's ancestors were members of pioneering Nebraska families in Nemaha County. Their openness to African Americans was then well above the norm (Kennedy 2001) and they displayed a wide range of intellectual and literary interests. Bob's great grandparents, Benton and Martha Jane Harshman Aldrich, established the Clifton Public Library, "the first public library in Nemaha County" (N.L.R. Stoddard, 1935). Of this activity, J.H. Dundas (1902: 24) noted: "Probably no more successful reading circle or library association has ever been conducted in the state than was the Clifton Library association." It was a good beginning — that early library collection included many geographical works.

On December 10, 1955, Bob married Sally E. Salisbury and together they raised three children: Martha, Andrew, and Hugh.

With the above obligatory biographical data as preamble, the remainder of this chapter focuses on Bob's life in higher education. The main facts are these: after earning the BA at Nebraska Wesleyan (1950), an MA at the University of Nebraska (1960), and the PhD at the University of Iowa (1966), he taught for some forty combined years at Nebraska Wesleyan University (1961-67) and the University of Nebraska-Lincoln (1967 to the present, where he is now Professor Emeritus). He also taught high school in India (1952-57), and was Visiting Professor at Tribhuvan University in Kathmandu, Nepal (1975-76), and the University of Columbo in Sri Lanka (1986). In addition to much productive research, many scholarly publications (notably *Field Techniques and Research Methods in Geography*, 1982), and

---

[1] Hugh Pettit Stoddard (1899-1967) was the son of Nella Aldrich and Collins DeWayne Stoddard. In her turn, Nella Aldrich was the daughter of Martha Jane Harshman Aldrich. Martha is the subject of the prize-winning biographical essay by Nainie Lenora Robertson (Mrs. Hugh P. Stoddard) reproduced below, as Chapter 3.

unstinting university service, he also served his local community as a member of the Lincoln-Lancaster Planning Commission (1974-78). In 1992, the National Council for Geographic Education bestowed its Distinguished Teaching Achievement Award on Dr. Stoddard.

No simple factual summary can capture the life of an active scholar, and this is especially true in Bob Stoddard's case — albeit he might well consider it description enough.[2] My purpose here is to expand the paragraph above. The principal contours of Bob's academic journey are charted below in greater detail.[3] In so doing, however, much is omitted: Bob's inner thoughts and the specifics of his political and religious beliefs (he is an active Unitarian), his decision to become an academic, his deep affection for India and Nepal, his foibles, his avocations and pet peeves, his public service, his private struggles and personal triumphs, his childhood, the influence of his history-loving parents,[4] his obvious delight in his children and his great, egalitarian love for his erudite life-partner and steadfast helpmeet, Sally[5] — all these await amplification and discussion by a full-fledged intellectual biographer.

Undergraduate Training

In 1947, Auburn, Nebraska, was a classic "central place," a county seat town. From Auburn, Bob traveled to Lincoln, Nebraska's capital city and the home of Nebraska Wesleyan University, a school with strong Methodist affiliations. During his undergraduate years at Wesleyan, Bob became an active member of the Barbs, a racially integrated organization of some ninety women and men:

> composed of unaffiliated students who are working together to further the good of the university, to foster and maintain wholesome school spirit, and to sponsor social activities for members of the group. Participation in extra-curricular activities is but one of the

---

[2] See for example, the brief *Who's Who* entry: "Stoddard, Robert H." (1999: 4751).

[3] In drawing this account, I relied primarily on published materials, archival sources (cf., Hill 1993), correspondence with colleagues, and my own recollections.

[4] *See*, for example, Hugh P. Stoddard and Mrs. Hugh P. Stoddard (1967) on the history of Nemaha County, and Mrs. Hugh P Stoddard's (1935) essay on a pioneering Nebraska woman, Martha Jane Harshman Aldrich. As previously noted, the latter essay, by Bob's mother, won first prize in a contest sponsored by *Nebraska History Magazine* and is reprinted below as Chapter 3.

[5] Sally, an accomplished photographer and fellow traveler on Bob's Asian adventures, completed her doctoral dissertation (1984) in the Department of English at the University of Nebraska.

means though which the Barbs fulfill their purpose. High scholastic standards and qualities of leadership are also emphasized.[6]

Bob served on the Barb cabinet and worked on the weekly paper, the *Barb-Wire* (Figure 1.1). Bob was also an active participant in the International Relations Club and, as a top student interested in the social sciences, he was selected for membership in Pi Gamma Mu honorary society.

Figure 1.1. Bob Stoddard (leftmost male), student reporter.
Archives, Nebraska Wesleyan University.

The resident geographer at Wesleyan during this era was Professor Dale Edward Case. Professor Case earlier completed the S.M degree in geography at the

---

[6] *The Plainsman*, Vol. 48 (Lincoln: Nebraska Wesleyan University, 1950: 132).

University of Chicago (Case 1938), and later finished the Ph.D., five years after leaving Wesleyan, at the University of Tennessee (Case 1955) under the tutelage of the noted agricultural geographer, Loyal Durand, Jr.

Bob graduated from Wesleyan with the B.A. degree in 1950 and subsequently taught high school in India for five years (1952–1957).

MA Thesis at Nebraska

Returning to Nebraska, Bob completed his 1960 master's thesis, "The Geography of Churches and Their Rural Congregations in Nemaha County, Nebraska," under the supervision of then Assistant Professor C. Barron McIntosh[7] in the Department of Geography at the University of Nebraska. At that time, the Head of the Department and the Chair of the Graduate Committee in Geography was Leslie Hewes, an Oklahoman with a Ph.D. from the University of California-Berkeley where he had been a student of the legendary Carl O. Sauer. McIntosh (1955) was still a relatively new Ph.D.[8] from Nebraska who had studied with Robert G. Bowman (another Ph.D. from California-Berkeley — and the son of the noted geographer, Isaiah Bowman).[9]

---

[7] In an annual report to the university administration describing his activities during this era, McIntosh noted that Stoddard's thesis, and one other, "were turned over to me for the final stages of writing." McIntosh also chaired Stoddard's oral examination. This was the beginning of a period of great personal challenge for McIntosh. His wife, Ruby, entered the hospital in 1959, leaving him in sole charge of their small children. She died in 1961. Following a long period of increasing blindness, Mac died in 2007.

[8] In addition, McIntosh (1951) earlier completed his master's thesis on "Diurnal Amplitude of Temperature in Nebraska," under the guidance of Robert G. Bowman. McIntosh's lively accounts of his adventures as a 1950s night clerk in a Lincoln hotel, where he earned just enough money to put himself through graduate school, are models of risque storytelling at its outrageous best. In subsequent years, he published a series of interrelated studies, culminating in his magnum opus, *The Nebraska Sand Hills: The Human Landscape* (McIntosh 1996).

[9] Bowman, an A.B. from Dartmouth, earned the Ph.D. at the University of California-Berkeley (Bowman 1941). Prior to his arrival at Nebraska in 1949, he was Associate Professor of Geography at the University of Iowa (1946-1949). He attained local prominence, including the presidency of the Nebraska Academy of Sciences (Bowman 1959), but labored under the extraordinary shadow — and resultant expectations — cast by his far more famous father (cf. Carter 1950). With Bowman as chair, Professors Leslie Hewes and Colbert C. Held completed McIntosh's dissertation committee. Held subsequently left Nebraska for an extended sojourn with the U.S. Department of State in the Middle East. He returned in 1968, taking charge of the Nebraska department, but did not long resist the call of foreign diplomacy and soon boomeranged back to government service.

4

Figure 1.2. Robert H. Stoddard, teaching mathematics, circa 1956.

This was an era of continuing transition within the Lincoln department. Shortly after 1958-59, longtime Assistant Professor Esther S. Anderson (a Ph.D. from Clark University), who had been a member of the Graduate Faculty, became emeritus. Professor Nels A. Bengtson (also a Ph.D. from Clark University) was already emeritus.[10] Assistant Professor James E. Vance, Jr. (then a young urban geographer and yet another Ph.D. from Clark University) had been an Associate Member of the Graduate Faculty but moved to the University of California-Berkeley in 1958. By 1960, the core Graduate Faculty of the Department of Geography was composed of Professors Leslie Hewes, Robert Bowman, John C. Weaver (a Ph.D. from the University of Wisconsin and Dean of the Graduate College),[11] and Assistant Professor McIntosh.[12] The influence of Clark University waned whereas input from California-Berkeley increased by default.

---

[10] Blouet and Stitcher (1981: 335) report that the Nebraska department was formally established in 1908 with the "appointment of N.A. Bengtson as instructor in the Department of Geography." Bengtson (1879-1963), a young Swede who immigrated to Nebraska with his parents, graduated from Peru (Nebraska) State Normal School with a two-year degree in 1902, earned the AB degree at the University of Nebraska in 1907, and, in short order, Nebraska awarded the AM in 1908. He did not receive the Ph.D. from Clark until 1927. Bengtson was Professor of Geography at Nebraska from 1908 to 1940, and served as Vice-President of the Association of American geographers in 1923 and 1942. As to the origins and founding of the department, William Van Royen (1968: 601-602) provided the following sequence of events:

> After obtaining his M.S. in 1908 [Bengtson] was asked to accept a position of Instructor in the Department of Geology of the University of Nebraska as assistant to Dr. George E. Condra. Until 1912 geography was given in an autonomous part of the department, entitled "Geography and Economic Geology." A few years later a separate Department of Geography and Conservation was created, with Dr. Condra at its head . . . . In 1915, Nels Bengtson was appointed full professor . . . . In 1927 Bengtson obtained his Ph.D. degree in geography from Clark University, and in 1929 a separate Department of Geography was established under his chairmanship . . . . Nels . . . was the creator of the Department of Geography at the University of Nebraska.

[11] Weaver moved in subsequent years to the Department of Geography of the University of Southern California.

[12] Professor Nels Bengtson and Assistant Professor Esther Anderson, both emeritus, remained technically on the Graduate Faculty. Also present in the department, and an Associate Member of the Graduate Faculty, was Rayfred L. Stevens (Doctor en Geograpfia, National University of Mexico), an authority on Alexander von Humboldt.

6

Bob's master's thesis is a carefully documented, 150-page empirical study involving triangulated data collection.[13] In addition to McIntosh, Bowman and Hewes "provided guidance at various stages of the research" (p. ii). This was quintessential academic guild work; Bob was the apprentice who a half decade later, after testing, tempering and honing his mettle at Iowa, joined the Nebraska faculty with McIntosh, Bowman, and Hewes as full colleagues.

The thesis reveals several guiding principles and themes that are manifest throughout Bob's subsequent geographical work:

(a) Fundamental concern to describe and explain spatial patterns. For example, the thesis "deals specifically with the description and interpretation of the variable character of religious institutions and their functions over the surface of part of the earth," (p. 3),

(b) Direct confrontation of complexity in empirical reality: "No phenomenon occurs in isolation but in complex relationship with numerous others," (p. 1),

(c) Openness to interdisciplinary scholarship and multiple methodologies. For example, "The observations by sociologists concerning the movements and actions of church and rural groups have been helpful," (p. 3),[14]

(d) Appreciation of the temporal dimensions of human phenomena: "The search for data relative to the geography of the churches and their functional areas of former times involved utilization of historical records," (p. 4), and, perhaps most important,

(e) Recognition that, "The church is an important institution . . . [it] is a human organization yet it embodies that which is greater than man himself. As such its importance is as great as life and the goals that make life important," (p. 1).

---

[13] For an MA thesis, this was a particularly popular work. Between 1962 and 1984, multiple interlibrary loan requests for the thesis were made by geographers from a surprising number of universities, including: California State University at Northridge, Northwestern University, Ohio State University, San Diego State University, Syracuse University, University of Akron, University of Calgary, University of Iowa, University of South Carolina, University of Tennessee, and Western Washington State College.

[14] Stoddard specifically notes, commends, and utilizes the sociological study of rural communities in eastern Nebraska by A.B. Hollingshead, whose classic dissertation was completed at the University of Nebraska in 1935.

Bob selected Nemaha County, Nebraska, the county of his birth, as the study site for his master's research (Figure 1.3). This decision facilitated local data collection, including the making of documentary photographs. As a "local," he

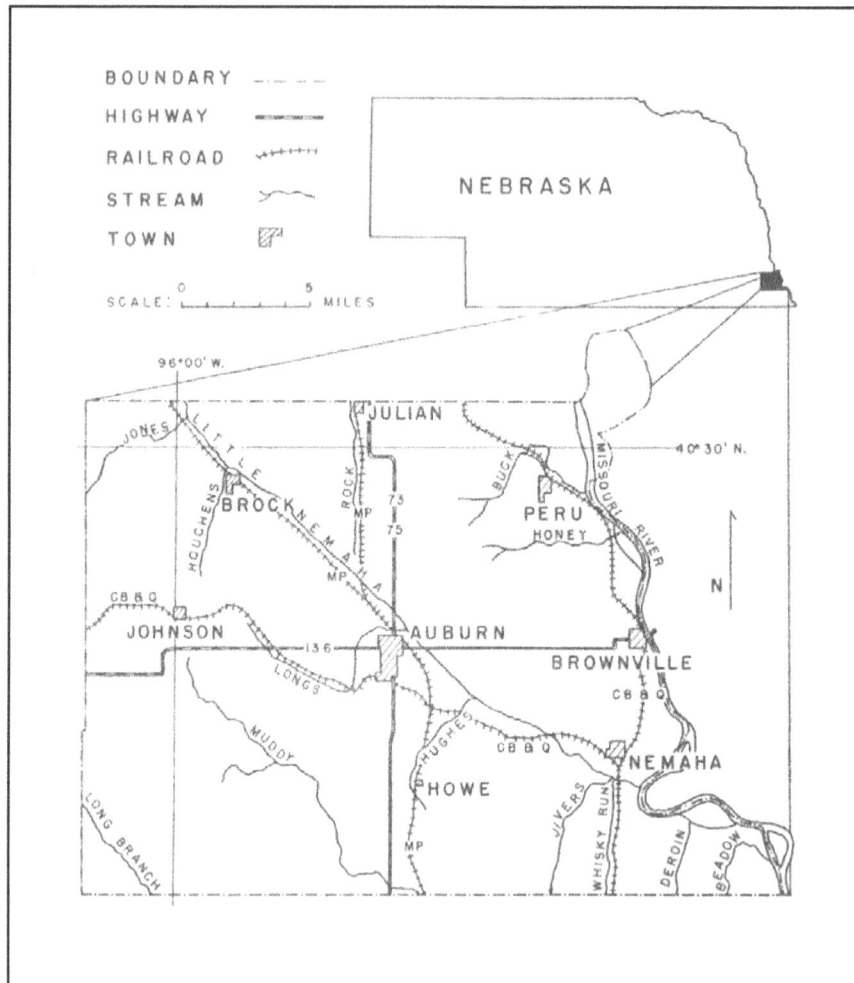

Figure 1.3. Nemaha County, Nebraska.
Source: (Stoddard 1960: 8).

benefitted from "the kindness of . . . many persons in Nemaha County who aided in the collection of historical data and provided valuable information about church congregations" and could count on his father, Hugh P. Stoddard, who provided "assistance during the periods of research in the county" (p. ii). The scope of the study is explicated in Bob's summary statement:

> Church buildings and their areal extensions through rural congregations are distributed unevenly in Nemaha County. These distributions possess a dynamic quality because they differ in their chrographical arrangements for the years 1894, 1913, 1935, and 1959. In addition, they are areally associated with the other landscape features in varying patterns which change unevenly through time. Many of these features associated by proximity are causally related with others merely occupying the same region. Conversely, other features separated by space and time possess a close relationship with each other and with other features in various complexes. The other landscape features considered in the study are topographic variations, concepts of land capability, towns and their spatial positions, transportation routes, school buildings and districts, cemeteries, the distribution of population, population characteristics, and groupings of population by functional situations. (p. 133).

Thus, with a declared and demonstrated interest in documenting and explaining the spatial distribution of religious phenomena, and after five years of collegiate teaching at Nebraska Wesleyan, Bob elected to pursue graduate studies in Iowa City.

Doctoral Studies

In 1966, Bob completed his doctoral dissertation, "Hindu Holy Sites in India," at the University of Iowa under the direction of Professor Clyde F. Kohn. Bob now entered the academic market place as a bona fide member of the "Iowa school" of quantitative geography. Kohn (1911-1989) was a Midwesterner who earned the Ph.D. in his home state at the University of Michigan in 1940. He taught briefly at Harvard University and then settled at Northwestern from 1945 to 1958. He moved finally to the University of Iowa where he remained until 1980, serving as department chair from 1966 to 1977. Kohn was President of the Association of American Geographers for 1867-68, and edited the NCGE Pacesetter series in which Bob's *Field Techniques and Research Methods in Geography* appeared in 1982.

Clyde Kohn had instrumentally and progressively shaped the Iowa department in which Bob enrolled for doctoral studies. According to Michael McNulty (1990: 299):

> At the University of Iowa, together with H.H. McCarty, Clyde helped to fashion a strong graduate research program that gained a national reputation as a major center of quantitative geographic research.

Moreover, Kohn became "one of the most outstanding advocates of geographic education in the nation" (McNulty 1991: 698), and he was:

> adamant about the fact that sound geographic education needs to be based on solid scholarship. Through his own work, and through the support and promotion of others' research, he sought to reinforce that vital link between research and teaching (McNulty 1991: 699).

These same traits characterize Bob Stoddard's tandem commitment to education and research and make understandable his years of selfless service to the Nebraska Chapter of the National Council on Geographic Education.

At Iowa, Bob became part of a hard-working cohort of serious and productive students. John C. Hudson[15] recalls that "Bob Stoddard, Doug Amedeo, and I were all graduate students in the Geography Department at the University of Iowa (then called the State University of Iowa) in the mid-1960s." Hudson recalled:

> Bob was very smart, he was a hard worker (spent all day at his cubicle office in the Old Armory), and was a dedicated family man. He and Sally had been missionaries, as I recall, and whether from that experience or just their own backgrounds, growing up in rural Nebraska, they were quite frugal. My favorite Bob Stoddard story concerns a used air conditioner that I purchased from a family who ran an ad in the Iowa City newspaper. My wife was pregnant with our first child and the summers in Iowa city were hot, by any standard. We decided we could afford it, so I decided to go pick the thing up. It was very heavy, of course, and I really couldn't do it myself, nor was I about to ask my pregnant wife for help. So I went

---

[15] John C. Hudson completed his 1967 dissertation on "Theoretical Settlement Geography." He edited the *Annals* of the Association of American Geographers from 1975 to 1982.

down to the Old Armory, where all the geography grad students were, to see if somebody could help me move this thing. The only person there was Bob, who willingly went along. We managed to load it in to the back seat of my VW "bug," and then got it to my house and slid it into the window. But Bob was somewhat somber, I thought. I was exclaiming how nice it would be, to have at least one cool room, but Bob sort of looked sober and said, "well, I don't know . . . the pioneers got along without air conditioning and I don't see why we need it today."[16]

Purposeful, helpful, and frugal — these traits have served Bob well, earning him lasting friendships and deep respect. His extraordinary thriftiness and self-deprecation are legendary, as are his equally renowned and opposite traits of enormous interpersonal generosity and encouraging supportiveness. As John Hudson notes, "I had then — and still have today — the highest regard for Bob Stoddard as a geographer and as a friend." Such qualities also permeate Bob's doctoral research and writing: scientific determination, respect for others, and spare, direct prose.

Economical empiricism and the forthright quantitative analysis of the spatial properties of religious phenomena are central to Bob's doctoral work on India, work best summarized by his own abstract (Stoddard 1966):

This study in the geography of religion deals with Hindu holy sites in India. These sacred places, although dependent upon the spiritual beliefs held by a given population, occupy precise positions on the earth's surface and are the destinations of religious pilgrimages. Notwithstanding the manifest spatial implications associated with these religious phenomena, they have been analyzed infrequently by geographers. This study attempts to contribute toward the understanding of the distribution of the holy sites and their areal relationships with other phenomena.

Three relationships are hypothesized between the distribution of holy sites and other phenomena. The first pertains to the arrangement of holy sites relative to the distribution of the Hindu population. The geographic relationship is hypothesized on the basis of the functional interaction between places nourishing the Great

---

[16] Personal communication (September 18, 2003).

11

Traditions and the Hindu population. Specifically, it is hypothesized that the major Hindu holy sites are distributed relative to the Hindu population so that the aggregate travel distance is minimized. The primary method for testing the hypothesis relies upon comparisons between the distribution of the actual holy sites with the distribution of theoretical sites that satisfy the hypothesized relationship.

The locations of the theoretical sites are determined cartographically by utilizing map transformations. Several techniques are employed to achieve maps of uniform population density from which the locations are determined; the most successful one is based upon representing the distribution of population by a network of hexagonal cells that enclose a given number of persons. The distributional characteristics of the sites generated from these transformations are compared to the locations of the actual holy sites by employing several spatial measurements. It is concluded that the distribution of theoretical sites is significantly different from the distribution of holy places; thus, the first hypothesis is rejected. Nevertheless, the theoretical sites predict the actual sites significantly better than expected under random conditions, a fact which lends encouragement for future research based upon this relationship of minimal travel distances.

The second hypothesis is based upon the geographic relationship that exists between major Indian cities and the population distribution. Specifically, the hypothesis states that the distribution of major holy sites is similar, but not coincident, to that of the largest urban centers. Again measurements that compare selected properties of the two distributions are used for testing. These measurements indicate that the two distributions are significantly different; thus, the second hypothesis is rejected.

The third hypothesis concerns the relationships between the areal variations in selected social characteristics of the population and the distribution of holy sites. The null hypothesis states there is no significant difference between two classes of social variables when one class consists of only those districts containing a holy site and the other class is composed of only districts that do not contain a holy site. The specific variables divided into the two classes are the per cent of caste Hindus, female literacy rate, and sex ratio per district. Both analysis of variance and analysis of covariance, the latter being utilized to hold constant the degree of urbanization per district, lead to the conclusion that there is no significant difference between the two classes.

The results indicate that neither the last two hypotheses provide an encouraging foundation for future research; however, the relationship first hypothesized presents a useful base for subsequent investigation. It is suggested that data about actual patterns of pilgrimage movement might furnish considerable insight into the geographic relationships between a given population and its sacred places.

Bob submitted the results of his study to the 1967 meeting of the Association of American Geographers in St. Louis. The 200-page dissertation generated considerable interest, and copies now reside not only at the University of Iowa, but also rest on library shelves at Georgia State University, Oregon State University, University of California-Berkeley, University of Chicago, University of Michigan, University of Minnesota, University of Washington, Syracuse University, Western Illinois University, and Wright State University. It is exceptional that so many libraries responded to the needs of their students and faculties by ordering copies of Bob's dissertation for their collections.

The new "Iowa school" geography became an important intellectual current at Nebraska. The first "Iowan" in the department was Stoddard, in 1967,[17] followed by Douglas Amedeo in 1973, and J. Clark Archer in 1985. At a General Seminar in October, 1967, Bob sketched (using a Venn diagram, of course!) the relationships between the various components (earth sciences, social sciences, and geometrical sciences) of the "Iowa approach" to geographic thinking (Figure 1.4). This was closest, Bob observed, to the description of "spatial geography" identified by Robert McNee (1967: 7).[18]

---

[17] In answer to my youthful questions about the program at Nebraska, Leslie Hewes wrote: "It is our intention to . . . add someone with competence in quantification" (personal communication, December 13, 1966).

[18] "Spatial geography," according to McNee, now focuses "on location theory in urban-economic-transportation geography but deriving [from] a very ancient geometric concern in geography and now spreading to diffusion theory in cultural geography, spatial political geography, and a general concern for revealing the spatial dimensions of society as a whole."

According to Bob's presentation, the introductory course at Iowa in the mid-1960s focused on the following primary topics:

1. The concept of location,
2. Distributions and surfaces:
    A. Ways to represent distributions (e.g., maps, tables indices of position, equations of distributions),
    B. Properties of distributions (e.g., density, patterns, etc.),
    C. Sampling,
    D. Types and distributions of surfaces (e.g., air masses, economic fronts, drainage basins, etc.), and
3. Spatial factors and interaction:
    A. Flow diagrams,
    B. Transportation networks,
    C. Migrations,
    D. Gravity and potential models,
    E. Diffusion, and
    F. Central place theory.

The Iowa graduate program *per se* had at that time three major phases: (I) Foundation knowledge of the field, including physical, economic, social, and political aspects, (II) Quantitative methods and competency in a specialized field (obtained via courses in related sciences, completing tool requirements — including advanced statistics and either math or a foreign language — and passing written and oral comprehensive examinations, and (III) Dissertation research and writing.

Bob located the intellectual roots of the specifically quantitative emphasis at Iowa in the work of Harold H. McCarty, Edwin Thomas, and Neil E. Salisbury. Leslie King (1979: 125), who went to Iowa to study specifically with McCarty, later observed that:

> The appointment of Edwin Thomas to the department's faculty in 1958 was the catalyst in the accelerated and formal development of quantitative work in the department. Thomas not only brought a level of expertise in statistical analysis then unmatched by that of any of his colleagues but, more importantly, his past association with William Garrison at Northwestern meant that the Iowa group now had a fairly direct link through him to the work of the cadre of young scholars that Garrison and his colleagues had attracted to the University of Washington in Seattle. The seminal discussion papers

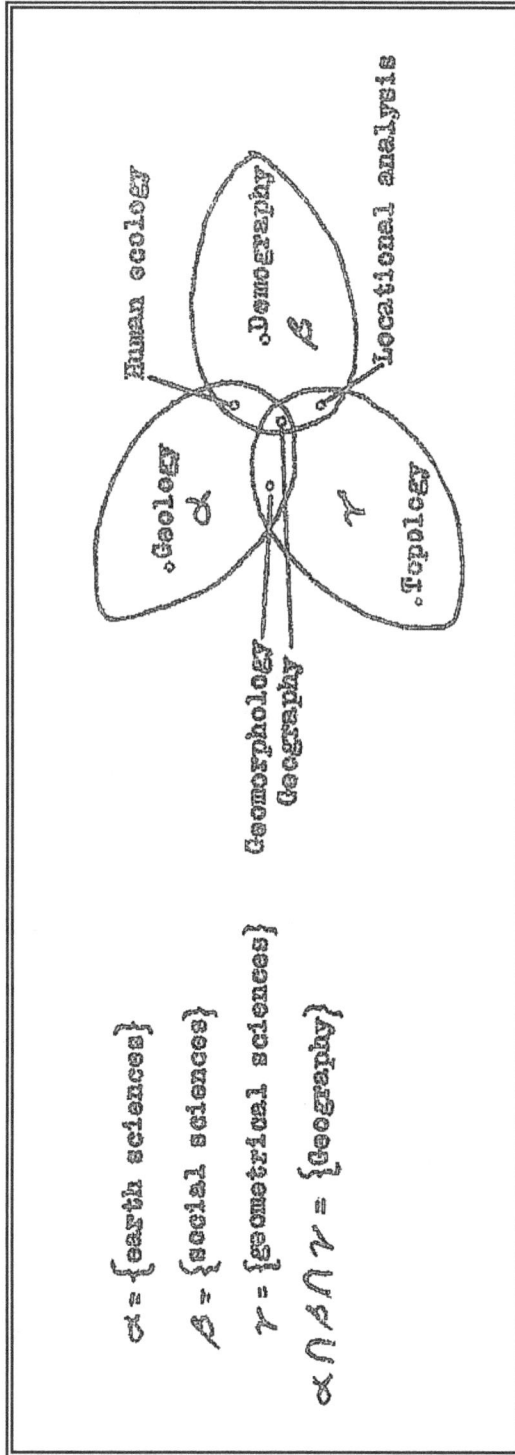

Figure 1.4. The Iowa School of Geography

15

of the Washington group, which were issued first in March, 1958, usually formed the subject of Iowa seminars a week or so after they had been distributed . . . .

Stoddard noted a pattern of increasing spatial and quantitative focus in a series of Iowa Ph.D. dissertations dating from 1954 onward. From 1965 to August 1967 (a period that roughly defines the overlapping years of Bob's graduate school cohort) the "Iowa approach" produced more than a dozen intellectually compatible dissertations (Figure 1.5).

Intellectually, Bob Stoddard was part and parcel of large, inexorable forces that were transforming the discipline of geography. Clyde F. Kohn (1970: 212), Bob's dissertation chair, summarized the situation thus:

> Following World War II, and especially in the early 1950's, there was a growing sense, restricted at first to relatively few in the geography community, that the then existing paradigm for geographical research was not adequate in explaining how physical, economic, social, and political processes are spatially organized, ecologically related, or how outcomes generated by them are evidenced at given times and in particular places. There was inaugurated, therefore, a new model for geographical research and instruction, new not only in terms of its fundamental research goals, but new also in the methods of investigation used to attain these goals. A more abstract, theoretical approach to geographical research emerged, involving the analytical method of inquiry.

Bob's decision to study at Iowa, combined with his inherent penchant for logical analysis and his deep respect for careful empirical research, placed him at precisely the right place at a most opportune time.

Teaching at Nebraska

When Bob returned to Nebraska, now as an Assistant Professor, in 1967, he introduced his students and colleagues to the vast changes then transforming the discipline under the appellation of "the quantitative revolution in geography." I was privileged to be among his first students on the Nebraska campus. This was, for many, a difficult transitional era, one that moved from the traditional geography then represented predominantly at Nebraska by Leslie Hewes, to a logically rigorous vision of scientific geographical thinking, then freshly represented at Nebraska by Stoddard (and, at the time, by a visiting British geographer, Gwyn Rowley). It was primarily through Bob's Field Methods course and subsequent Quantitative Methods course that Nebraska graduate students learned about the "new" geography.

16

**PH.D. DISSERTATIONS,
DEPARTMENT OF GEOGRAPHY, UNIVERSITY OF IOWA, 1965-1967**

Mukherjee, B. (1965), *Economic Structure of the Specialized Educational Centers of the U.S.A.*

Golledge, R.G. (1965), *A Probabilistic Model of Market Behavior.*

LaValle, P. (1965), *Areal Variation of karst Topography in Southcentral Kentucky.*

Johnson, P.T. (1966), *An Analysis of the Spread of the Church of Jesus Christ of Latter-Day Saints from Salt Lack City, Utah, Utilizing a Diffusion Model.*

Roberts, M..C. (1966), *The Spatial Variation of Slopes and Associated Climatic and Watershed Variables.*

Goranson, L.D. (1966), *An Analysis of the Location and the Spatial Arrangements of the United States Beet Sugar Industry.*

Stoddard, R.H. (1966), *Hindu Holy Sites in India.*

Kimani, S.M. (1966), *Application of Location Theory to Commuting Patterns in Iowa.*

Amedo, D.M. (1967), *Analysis of the Distribution of Farm Operator Levels of Living: 1950-1959.*

Cumings, L.P. (1967), *The Structure of Networks and Network Flows.*

Keinath, W.F. (1967), *The Spatial Concentration of Manufacturing Industries in the American South.*

Hudson, J.C. (1967), *Theoretical Settlement Geography.*

Maxfield, D.W. (1967), *A Change in the Locational Pattern of Production Sites: A Change in Transportation Rates as Applied to Wheat Export Sites.*

Stephenson, R. (1967), *The Spatial Variation of Streamflow and Related Hydrologic Characteristics in Selected Basins of the Southern*

Figure 1.5. Doctoral Dissertations Written by Members
of Robert Stoddard's Graduate School Cohort at Iowa

This was a time of strong tensions and occasional conflict between old and new geographers — not only at Nebraska, but also nationally and internationally. Four years earlier, Ian Burton (1963: 151) declared from Toronto:

> In the past decade geography has undergone a radical transformation of spirit and purpose, best described as the "quantitative revolution." The consequences of the revolution have yet to be worked out and are likely to involve the "mathematization" of much of our discipline, with an attendant emphasis on the construction and testing of theoretical models. Although the future changes will far outrun the initial expectations of the revolutionaries, the revolution itself is now over.

Over? Burton, obviously, had not been to Nebraska.[19]

If the parting revolutionary salvos had already been fired elsewhere, their echoes still reverberated loudly in Lincoln. Here, for example, Leslie Hewes (1966) argued for the center stage of world maps in geographic education, concluding: "Herein is a challenge to get on with the job instead of each insisting on the distinctiveness of his particular variety of geography." In one important sense, Hewes was right (most undergraduates then and now remain woefully ill-informed when it comes to rudimentary place-name geography and basic geopolitical relationships), but he confounded his argument in practice by insisting on the superiority of *his* geographical tradition. In his last year as department chair, 1967-68, Hewes actively

---

[19] In 1966, as I cast about for graduate schools, I received tentative acceptance (and the offer of a residence hall directorship) in the (as I then learned) heavily quantitative department at Northwestern pending the completion of two semesters of calculus. *Calculus!* I had already discovered that geomorphology, in which I was interested as an undergraduate, would demand far more math than I was inclined to pursue. Charles R. Gildersleeve (1978), then an energetic and supportive young instructor at the Municipal University of Omaha (in whose urban course we virtually memorized Mayer and Kohn's (1959) landmark reader) who was himself a doctoral student at Lincoln, assured me (as did Nicholas Bariss (1967), Gordon Schilz (1949), and Phil Vogel (1956, 1960), my other much-admired Omaha professors) that Nebraska was a venerable department with a strong tradition of scholarship — and no calculus unless I wanted it. When Leslie Hewes offered a three-year National Defense Education Act fellowship, I eagerly accepted. It was unwittingly a felicitous choice because I underwent the "quantitative revolution" for myself (albeit belatedly) and experienced the tensions, emotions, resentments, angst, and excitement firsthand — even to the point of completing elective courses in calculus and matrix algebra in the math department.

steered students away from Visiting Professor Gwyn Rowley's quantitative courses.[20] In more dramatic fashion, cultural geographer Norm Stewart repeatedly pretended to dose off during the weekly general seminars and then allow his heavy field boots to drop suddenly with a resounding "boom" whenever a "numerologist" (as he called them) dared cast "statistical analysis" in a positive light. This was hard core academic theater that helped fuel lively discussions among the graduate students. Suffice it to say, partisan paradigmatic feelings ran very deep, well into the mid 1970s.[21]

Professor Stoddard, however, was never among the dogmatic advocates of novel techniques at other schools who ridiculed more traditional geographers for "their inability to understand the jargon of the fashionable algorithms of the day" (King 1979:127).[22] Without preaching a "new" geography *per se*, Bob slowly persuaded us through the reasonable light of logic, empirical demonstration, systematic method, and patient, lucid explications of our mistakes when we failed to solve quantitatively-framed exercises in his classes. Unlike some proponents of the "new" geography, Bob neither unthinkingly jettisoned the "old" simply for the sake of change, nor shunned earnest, hard-working regional geographers who still "got their boots muddy." Simultaneously pursuing his ever expanding interest in Asia, he created space for growth, dialogue, and cooperation between old and new geographers.

Exercising my editorial prerogative for an aside, allow me to say that Bob Stoddard is a modest man of unusual inner strength and personal integrity. When he agreed to hold an administrative position, it was only to serve, never to aggrandize. When he counseled students, it was always to assist, never to proselytize. When he

---

[20] Hewes generally assumed intellectual and administrative dominion over all new graduate students entering the department at that time. When I naively tried to register for Gwyn Rowley's urban geography course (Rowley was a decidedly quantitative geographer visiting from England), Hewes abruptly took a pencil and literally struck the course off my form, noting, "You will take urban from *our* Dr. Rugg when he returns [from sabbatical]." During the following summer, when Colbert Held assumed the reins of the Department, I took a delightful readings course with Professor Rowley.

[21] For myself, I was initially persuaded (some might justly say "enthralled") by the sheer elegance of many logical positivist arguments, especially in the early 70s, but I eventually adopted what I believe is a more discriminating — yet appreciative — critique of the limits of positivism in the social sciences (Hill 1977, 1981, 1984). Steve Kale related, "I was a student at UNL during the first half of the 1970s. These were turbulent times for society in general and for some of us in particular at the Department of Geography. From time to time, a few of us likely went way beyond where we should have, but I won't go into that here" (personal communication).

[22] Unlike Hewes, who was particularly self-confident, resilient, and thick-skinned, not all traditionally-trained geographers were immune to the barbed taunts from quantitative upstarts. At Nebraska, the late Dean S. Rugg struggled mightily to "re-tool," but to no avail — his heart was never in it.

writes, it is always to instruct, never to promote himself. He does not seek the public eye, but his views are nonetheless sought by local columnists.[23] If there were those among us, and there were a few, who wanted Bob to promote his professional work more aggressively and with greater entrepreneurial self-interest, it meant only that we failed to understand the true measure of the man.

During his long tenure at Nebraska, Bob offered a wide variety of courses, from the introductory World Geography and Geography of Asia courses for novice undergraduates to advanced courses in Field Methods and Quantitative Methods and a Seminar in Regionalization, the latter for graduate students only. He also offered individually-tailored Independent Study courses and gave endless hours of advice to thesis and dissertation writers. His principal courses at Nebraska included:[24]

World Geography. A survey of the principles of spatial relationships and their application to the regions of the world. Laboratory aids student insight into these principles through experience in scientific methodology.

Geography of Asia. The physical and climatic features of Asia in relation to the distribution of population, agriculture, industry, and trade. Special attention is given to India, China, and Japan.

Field Geography. For advanced undergraduate majors and graduate students. Study of techniques and practices used in making geographical observations in the field. Emphasis on study of natural and cultural landscape features in the field at selected localities.

Quantitative Methods in Geography. An Introduction to quantitative techniques utilized in geographic research. Fundamental statistical and mathematical techniques utilized in analyzing spatial relationships will be examined.

---

[23] See, for example, "Geography is More Why than Where, Professor Says," by Don Walton, *Lincoln Star* (May 11, 1992) and "Professor Says 'Society Finds Best Solutions,'" by Kevin Hanken, *The Journalist*, (November 1983). Like many academics, Bob is sometimes misquoted and misunderstood by newspaper correspondents, but he nonetheless remains courteous and open to reporters — a trait no doubt appreciated by his journalist daughter, Martha.

[24] Course descriptions from syllabi and various university *Bulletins*.

Geography of the Far East. For advanced students. Physical and cultural geography of far eastern countries, with emphasis upon Japan, China, and the Far East.

Seminar in Regionalization. Survey of recently developed quantitative techniques for objectively defining regions. Study of classification logics. Applied use of factor analysis and clustering procedures to generate regions.

Bob's courses were intellectually unique experiences, and no student's geographic training at Nebraska during Bob's tenure was considered complete without tuition in his extraordinary Saturday morning Field Geography course. All of Bob's courses were accompanied by detailed and copious handouts. In the Field Geography and Quantitative Methods courses particularly there were no available textbooks adequate to Bob's pedagogical aims. Thus, his handouts and miscellaneous assigned readings — together with our notes from his unusually lucid lectures — became our texts. His lectures were always current with the most recent professional literature. Furthermore, his course offerings were tailored, as no standardized cookie-cutter textbook could ever be, to the express needs and abilities of undergraduate and graduate students at the University of Nebraska. Two of these courses deserve special comment.

The Field Geography Course

I was privileged to be a member of Bob's first field methods course at Nebraska, taught during the 1968 spring semester.[25] It convened on Saturday mornings so that large blocks of time could be devoted to uninterrupted instruction and practical field exercises. Bob's geometric focus underlay the stated Objectives of the Course:

> This is in part determined by the nature of "geography." *Geography* is the discipline concerned with *where* any given phenomenon is located on the surface of the earth and with concern for the spatial relationships of phenomena located on the surface of the earth. One is thus less concerned with systematic questions of who, why, or

---

[25] The members of this class included: Anne Marie Aita, Charles F. Calkins, Jack Clair, Michael R. Hill, Emmertt McBroom, Nancy Rozman, Chet Staniulis, Sally Ann Webster, David J. Wishart, and Duane L. Younggren.

when, but with the question of *where*. One is also concerned with areal associations, or how things are related, and the analysis of the geometry of distributions.[26]

Typical class sessions opened with a concise lecture, replete with detailed handouts, followed by real world exercises. Bob's lecture notes were, in essence, the first draft of what became *Field Techniques and Research Methods in Geography* (Stoddard 1982). The course began in January (and the winter months in Nebraska are decidedly chilly), but by the third week our exercises took us out of doors, as did most of the subsequent exercises (including a then still exotic ride on the University's newly acquired Douglas DC-3 airplane — so that we could visually compare topographic maps with "bird's eye" views of the actual areal units and landforms represented on the maps).[27] The course covered the following topics:

I.   Introduction
II.   Sampling
III.   Interviewing
IV.   Remote Sensing
V.   Measuring the Cultural Landscape
VI.   Measuring Movement
VII.   Mapping Urban Land Use
VIII.   Observation along a Highway
IX.   Pacing and Compass Traverse
X.   Plane-Table Surveys and Determining Altitude
XI.   Model Building
XII.   Measurement of Soil
XIII.   Data from Topographic Maps

In addition to completing hands-on exercises, each student was also required to study recent literature, prepare abstracts, and report to the class on relevant professional writings. Bob required that our reviews of articles include:

---

[26] I find on inspection of my files that my notes for this course are not only typed but are surprisingly well organized, a direct consequence of Bob's requirement that each student submit a completed "field notebook" for evaluation at the end of the semester.

[27] Each major off campus field trip (of which there were three in the field course) involving travel in University-owned transportation, required, according to University regulations, each student to pay *exactly* 10 cents for insurance in case of injury. I can still picture Bob dutifully recording our payments as we lined up to plunk down our dimes before each scheduled departure.

22

I.   Name of article and complete bibliographical reference.
II.   Your name, and date of the assignment.
III. Kind of technique (title only, for example: interviewing, sampling, etc.).
IV.   Kind of data (brief description; list as "hypothetical" if it is a methodological article only.
V.   Description of technique (be brief).
VI.   Conclusion (list strengths, weaknesses, was it important enough to read again, etc.).
VII. Note: all of this should be on one typewritten page, any *necessary* diagrams or maps should be included in a supplement.

The triangulated techniques that found direct application in my doctoral research on the behavior of pedestrians (Hill 1982, 1984b, c): ethological observation, quadrat sampling,[28] land use mapping, interviewing, questionnaire survey, and measuring movement, were all thoroughly covered in Bob's remarkably comprehensive course. Indeed, most students found the course immensely useful.[29]

Applicable, yes, but that is not to say that every student necessarily enjoyed spending early weekend mornings in class quite as much as Bob apparently did. Steve Kale, who took the course a few years later, recalls, "Bob liked his Saturday morning classes considerably more than some of us did, especially after fun and games on Friday nights (and sometimes afternoons too)." But, all in all, we tried "our best to be dutifully attentive" when "Bob was demonstrating on the blackboard."[30] There was more to the course than demonstrations and exercises, however. There was also a formal, sit-down final examination.

Stoddard's final exam in the Field Geography course had several parts and required numerous essays, including critical analyses of pertinent quotations from Charles Davis' (1954) chapter on "Field Techniques" in *American Geography: Inventory & Prospect*; explications of several selected terms, and detailed reviews of

------

[28] I was subsequently amazed and delighted to learn that the "quadrat method" was, in fact, devised at Nebraska by Roscoe Pound and Frederick Clements (1898; Hill 1989b: 216-218).

[29] Some years later, when I stumbled across (and then edited the sesquicentennial edition) of Harriet Martineau's (1838/1989) *How To Observe Morals and Manners*, it was my grounding in Bob's field methods course that allowed me to fully appreciate the social scientific import of Martineau's profoundly original methodological treatise (Hill 1989a). So too, my analysis comparing the methodological strengths and weakness of Martineau versus Alexis de Tocqueville (Hill 2001) rests fundamentally on principles and insights taught in Bob's course. See also my ever increasing appreciation of Martineau's observational acumen (Hill (2004, 2017).

[30] Personal communication.

recent articles from the *Annals of the Association of American Geographers*. The core flavor of the course, however, is best represented in the applied problems that Bob set for us to solve:

1. Given an area approximately 20 miles by 30 miles in which a variety of crops are grown. Assume you are interested in knowing the percentage of land area devoted to crop X. Describe how this percentage value might be estimated by some sampling procedure. Then discuss the advantages and disadvantages of the sampling technique as compared with those of a complete land use survey.

2. The following question was sent to the residents of a Congressional district by their Congressman: "Do you favor expanding trade with Russia and other communist countries, even though they continue to supply our enemies in Vietnam? Yes ___, No ___, Undecided ___." Comment upon the validity of the returns received by the Congressman.

3. Given the "triangle of error" on a plane table as shown in Figure [1.6.1, below], locate the map position for resectioning.

4. Given the field notes for an elevation traverse as shown in Figure [1.6.2, below], draw a rough profile of the traverse. Indicate the maximum difference in elevation, and give the difference between the heights of position A and position G. (Note: the profile will be "rough" because no horizontal information is provided here).

5. Given the field notes for a closed compass traverse as shown in Figure [1.6.3, below], draw both the original and corrected map. Show your work. Use a ratio of 1 inch to 100 feet. Assume magnetic north coincides with geographic north.

These were, at base, classic geographic questions drawn from the cultural as well as the physical side of the discipline. I doubt seriously that any of us ever resorted to a plane table again, but having to learn — and execute — the *process* of rudimentary topographic mapping in the field[31] gave us a truly visceral and indelible understanding of maps as "constructions."

---

[31] Readers who know Lincoln will appreciate the fact that the plane table and mapping exercises were conducted in Pioneers Park, one of the few areas in Lincoln characterized by significant variations in relative relief.

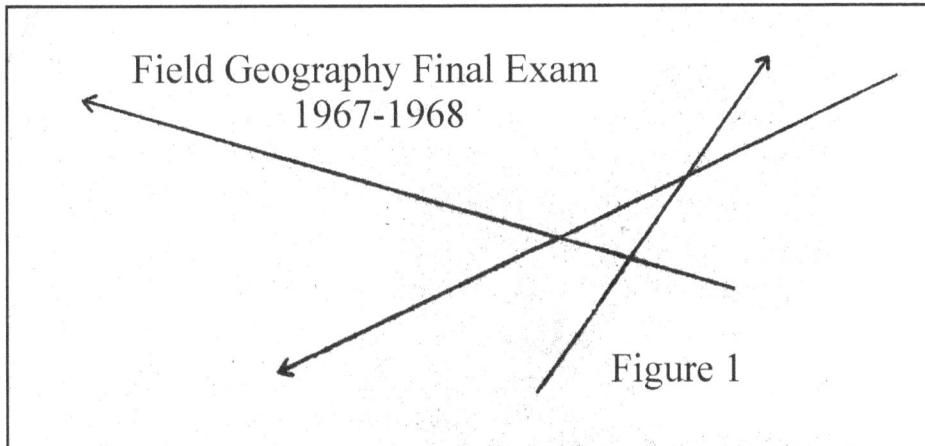

Field Geography Final Exam
1967-1968

Figure 1

Readings on Graduated Rod
(in Feet)

	1st Position		2nd Position
1st Pair:	A 12.4	←→	B 4.8
2nd Pair:	B 4.8	←→	C 6.6
3rd Pair:	C 10.8	←→	D 1.2
4th Pair:	D 11.2	←→	E 1.4
5th Pair:	E 12.2	←→	F 0.8
6th Pair:	F 1.0	←→	G 13.8

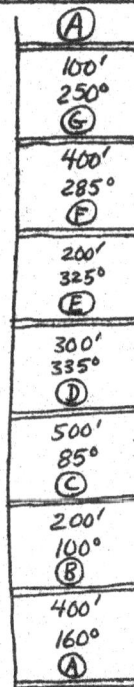

Figure 2

Ⓐ
100'
250°
Ⓖ
400'
285°
Ⓕ
200'
325°
Ⓔ
300'
335°
Ⓓ
500'
85°
Ⓒ
200'
100°
Ⓑ
400'
160°
Ⓐ

Figure 3

Figure 1.6. Figures 1-3, data to accompany final exam
questions 3, 4, & 5, above.

Regionalization Seminar

The regionalization seminar revealed a very different facet of Bob's teaching. Whereas the Field Geography course presented a fully worked out package of standard techniques, the 1973 seminar in regionalization was an exploration of methods then "under construction." Opening with a few weeks of readings and lectures (including an intensive short course in factor analysis and the intricacies of taxonomic logics), Bob brought us with him to the edge of the known methodological world.[32] We were thus given a clear view of Bob's mind at work on problems that by the time of his 1986 essay on regionalization in Sri Lanka (this volume, below) were for him routine.

As a group project, we constructed an atlas of multi-factor uniform regions in Omaha, Nebraska. The primary objective of this study was to experiment with the application of taxonomic classification principles as a method of objective regionalization. Factor scores on 72 socio-economic variables from the 1970 Census for 125 census tracts were computed. The factor scores were used to construct a matrix giving the taxonomic distance from each tract to every other tract. The tracts were grouped, adding in one tract at each step, on the basis of minimum taxonomic distance. The grouping was completed both with and without a contiguity constraint, the former being accomplished by the compilation of a contiguity matrix. Within-group variance at each step of the grouping, with and without contiguity constraint was graphed for comparison. The final result was a series of maps depicting the grouping or regionalization of census tracts based on their taxonomic similarity on several socio-economic variables.

It bears emphasizing that these were still "early days" for computer support at the University of Nebraska-Lincoln, with new equipment and various software upgrades flooding in at a fairly rapid pace. Bob reveled in it. He was on top of every new advance and quickly showed us how to adopt and adapt each new improvement to our goals and projects, how to think of new possibilities for using the University's ever more powerful computational facilities.[33] When Bob first introduced me to the IBM mainframe, it was located in Nebraska Hall in an unfinished warehouse setting

---

[32] The student members of the seminar included: Shail Agrawal, Robert Gaul, Michael Hill, and John Menary.

[33] My first adventure with "word processing" employed "cutting-edge" software that had been purchased and designed specifically to write and make emendations to legislative bills for the Nebraska State Legislature. A handful of new, state-of-the-art CRT terminals allowed access to a typing program that was cumbersome, quirky, and arcane, but you could make corrections to the draft of a paper *without retyping the whole thing.*

that had all the bombed out glamour of a post-World War III sci-fi movie set.[34] There were, I recall, three or four clunky key-punch machines, one card sorter, and possibly two card readers. *Symap* was the latest thing in computer cartography. Machine time was costly, processing was slow, and printouts were indeed primitive compared to today's desktop laser standards. But, it was nevertheless wondrous and amazing. It's *still* amazing to me.

Counselor

Throughout his many years of teaching, Bob's counsel was frequently sought by students (even in other disciplines). To this day, Bob is trusted and his advice is respected. When controversial issues were sometimes on the table, Bob could be relied upon for careful and impartial analyses offered with a view to helping students sort out the relevant facts for themselves.[35] Steve Kale (1978), who completed his dissertation under the supervision of Dick Lonsdale, recalled:

> Bob was the steady mentor, always fair and helpful even when he might not have been. He seemed to be "above the fray" much if not most of the time, at least as far as a lot of students were concerned. I greatly valued his comments on term papers, manuscripts submitted for publication, and especially the dissertation. Not to sound too self-centered but Bob was there when I needed him to be there, and for that I am thankful even now.[36]

As a professor, Bob was a determined watchdog for quality and competent performance, yet he was never unthinkingly dogmatic. Clear-sighted, analytical, and compassionate appreciations of each individual's needs, interests, and abilities remain hallmarks of his advising.

---

[34] Indeed, Nebraska Hall, the new quarters of the engineering school, was formerly a manufacturing plant.

[35] Bob's personal concern and genuinely helpful counsel, as I prepared to enter the U.S. military in 1968 during the Vietnam era, are treasured memories and models of compassion.

[36] Personal communication.

International Educator

Robert Stoddard's journey from Auburn to Lincoln, Nebraska, although short, as the crow flies, has nonetheless included several major adventures half way 'round the world. This is to be expected in the life of anyone who takes geography seriously. Bob's overseas travels began in earnest with a five-year stint as a teacher in the Woodstock High School in Mussoorie, India, from 1952 to 1957. There, Bob met Sally Salisbury, and they subsequently married (Figure 1.7).

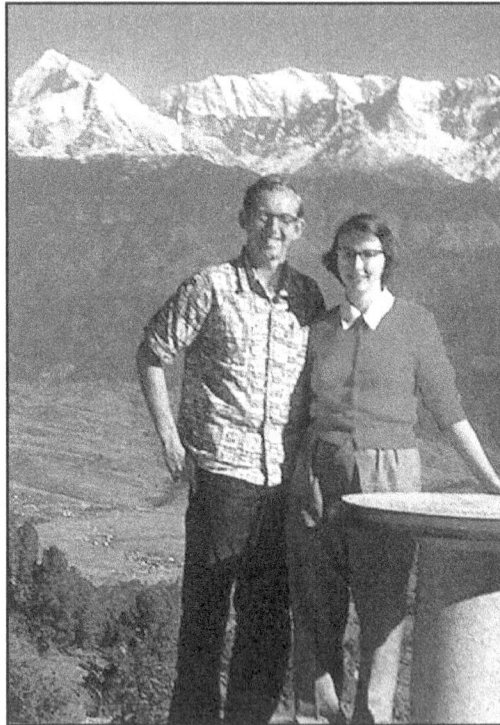

Figure 1.7. Bob and Sally in India.

As an educator, Bob was also Visiting Professor in the Department of Geography at Tribhuvan University in Kathmandu, Nepal, during 1975-76. His Nepalese sojourn was made possible by a Fulbright-Hays fellowship and resulted in a temporal as well as spatial break from Nebraska.[37] Bob wrote in August 1975:

---

[37] The Stoddard children who accompanied their parents to Asia, attracted no little notoriety in their own rights. See, for example, "Lincolnite Martha Stoddard Clearing Mt. Everest Debris," *Lincoln Evening Journal* (March 12, 1976, p. 7, col. 1) and "Hugh Didn't Know Much of India 'Till He Got There," by Patty Beutler, *Lincoln Star* (December 18, 1976, p. 1, col. 2, with photo).

Obviously the travel to another part of the world and the setting up a new home, etc., represented a major break in our lives. Soon after arriving here I began teaching at the Tribhuvan University, so "the year" had begun. Therefore, it is difficult to realize (or, "to feel") the fact that you folks are just emerging from a slack, or even vacation period. Likewise, you are about ready to begin a new academic year and the increase in fall activities. Here we are waiting until the monsoons end before thinking about a change in activities. This year the "break" near the end of September will be accentuated because classes for the new students are starting late (as a result of student strikes during the summer months that delayed the ending of the spring semester) . . . . I am interested in news from your end dealing with the Department, graduate students, and your own activities.[38]

Bob's continuing interest in student activities in Lincoln, despite his foreign location, was characteristic. This did not mean that Bob was always easy to contact, however, as testified by a package I sent to Bob in December 1975. It was subsequently marked "Unclaimed" and stamped "Return to Sender" replete with an astonishing set of cancellations and handwritten notations — to reappear in my mailbox crumpled, battle-worn and held together with coarse string to keep it from falling apart, a full *eighteen months* after Bob's return from Nepal. Bob and Sally traveled to China in mid-1986 (where she taught intensive English for a year and Bob taught part-time at Zhongshan University). In January 1986, Bob went on to the post of Visiting Professor in the Department of Geography at the University of Columbo in Sri Lanka. Bob and Sally then rejoined forces, visiting many Chinese cities. Throughout his career, Bob has made several shorter foreign trips to attend meetings and make professional presentations.

With so many inviting opportunities to reside and work elsewhere in the world, we are especially honored and thankful that this thoughtful and dedicated scholar has steadfastly made Nebraska his home base for all these many years. Bob has brought his international experiences directly to the Lincoln campus through public colloquia, his courses on Asia, and through his years of dedicated leadership and participation, since 1973, as an active member of the UNL Asian Studies Committee. This dual role, as a faculty member in the Department of Geography as well as in the Asian Studies Program, exemplifies his interdisciplinary outlook.

---

[38] Stoddard to Hill, 17 August 1975. Personal communication.

References

Anderson, Esther S. 1917. *Geography of the Beet Sugar Industry*. M.A. Thesis, Department of Geography, University of Nebraska.

_____. 1932. *The Sugar Beet Industry in the Inter-Montane and Great Plains Regions of the U.S.* Ph.D. dissertation, Clark University.

Bariss, Nicholas. 1967. *Geomorphological Characteristics of Loess Terrain: A Comparative Study of Five Sample Areas in the Midwestern United States*. Ph.D. dissertation, Clark University.

Blouet, Brian W. and Teresa L. Stitcher, eds. 1981. *The Origins of Academic Geography in the United States*. Hamden, CT: Archon Books.

Bowman, Robert G. 1942. *Soil Erosion in Puerto Rico*. Ph.D. dissertation, University of California-Berkeley.

_____. 1959. "The International Geophysical Year." (Past-Presidential Address, delivered April 18, 1958). *Proceedings* (Nebraska Academy of Sciences) 69: 24-30.

Burton, Ian. 1963. "The Quantitative Revolution in Geography." *Canadian Geographer* 7 (4): 151-62.

Carter, George F. 1950. "Isaiah Bowman, 1878-1950." *Annals of the Association of American Geographers* 40 (December): 335-350.

Case, Dale Edward. 1938. *Beaver Island: A Study of Insular Land Utilization*. S.M. thesis, Department of Geography, University of Chicago.

_____. 1955. *Oak Ridge, Tennessee: A Geographic Study*. Ph.D. dissertation, The University of Tennessee.

Davis, Charles M. 1954. "Field Techniques." Pp. 496-529 in *American Geography: Inventory & Prospect*, edited by Preston E. James and Clarence F. Jones. Syracuse University Press for the Association of American Geographers.

Doering, Thomas R. 1977. *Modeling Travel by Recreationists and Tourists in a Pass-through Region: The Case of Visits to Educational Attractions in Nebraska*. Ph.D. dissertation. Department of Geography, University of Nebraska-Lincoln.

Dundas, J.H. 1902. *Nemaha County*. Auburn, NE: J.H. Dundas and Son.

Gildersleeve, Charles E. 1978. *The International Border City: Urban Spatial Organization in a Context of Two Cultures along the United States-Mexico Boundary*. Ph.D. dissertation. Department of Geography, University of Nebraska-Lincoln.

Hill, Michael R. 1977. "Axiological Dialogue in Geography." *Antipode: The Journal of Radical Geography* 9 (2): 93-96.

_____. 1981. "Positivism: A 'Hidden' Philosophy in Geography." Pp. 38-60 in *Themes in Geographic Thought*, edited by Milton E. Harvey and Brian P. Holly. London (UK): Croom Helm.

_____. 1982. *Spatial Structure and Decision-Making Aspects of Pedestrian Route Selection through an Urban Environment.* Ph.D. dissertation. Department of Geography, University of Nebraska-Lincoln.

_____. 1984a. "Epistemology, Axiology, and Ideology in Sociology." *Mid-American Review of Sociology* 9 (2): 59-77.

_____. 1984b. "Stalking the Urban Pedestrian: A Comparison of Questionnaire and Tracking Methodologies for Behavioral Mapping in Large-Scale Environments." *Environment and Behavior* 16 (5): 539-550.

_____. 1984c. "Walking Straight Home from School: Pedestrian Route Choice by Young Children." *Transportation Research Record* 959: 51-55.

_____. 1989a. "Empiricism and Reason in Harriet Martineau's Sociology." Pp. xxii-lii in *How To Observe Morals and Manners*, by Harriet Martineau, with an introduction by Michael R. Hill. New Brunswick, NJ: Transaction Books.

_____. 1989b. *Roscoe Pound and American Sociology: A Study in Archival Frame Analysis, Sociobiography, and Sociological Jurisprudence.* Ph.D. dissertation. Department of Sociology, University of Nebraska-Lincoln.

_____. 1993. *Archival Strategies and Techniques.* (Qualitative Research Methods Series, Vol. 31). Newbury Park, CA: Sage Publications.

_____. 2001. "A Methodological Comparison of Harriet Martineau's *Society in America* (1837) and Alexis de Tocqueville's *Democracy in America* (1835-1840)." Pp. 59-74 in *Harriet Martineau: Theoretical and Methodological Perspectives*, edited by Michael R. Hill and Susan Hoecker-Drysdale. New York: Routledge."

_____. 2004. 2004. "An Introduction to Harriet Martineau's Lake District Writings." Pp. 25-54 in *An Independent Woman's Lake District Writings,* by Harriet Martineau, edited by Michael R. Hill. Amherst, NY: Humanity Books.

_____. 2017. "Harriet Martineau: The Founding and Re-Founding of Sociology." Pp. 69-83 in *Harriet Martineau and the Birth of Disciplines*, edited by Valerie Sanders and Gaby Weiner. London (UK): Routledge.

Hollingshead, August de Belmont. 1935. *Trends in Community Development: A Study of Ecological and Institutional Processes in Thirty-four Southeastern Communities, 1854-1934.* Ph.D. dissertation. Department of Sociology, University of Nebraska.

Kale, Steven R. 1978. *Labor Supplies for Rural Manufacturing Plants.* Ph.D. dissertation. Department of Geography, University of Nebraska-Lincoln.

Kennedy, Patrick. 2001. "Nemaha County's African American Community." *Nebraska History* 82 (Spring: 11-25).

King, Leslie J. 1979. "Areal Associations and Regressions." *Annals of the Association of American Geographers* 69 (March): 124-128.

Kohn, Clyde F. 1970. "The 1960's: A Decade of Progress in Geographical Research and Instruction." *Annals of the Association of American Geographers* 60 (June): 1211-219.

Martineau, Harriet. 1838. *How To Observe Morals and Manners.* Sesquicentennial edition, with a new introduction by Michael R. Hill. New Brunswick, NJ: Transaction Publishers, 1989.

Mayer, Harold M. and Clyde F. Kohn. 1959. *Readings in Urban Geography.* Chicago: University of Chicago Press.

McIntosh, Charles Barron. 1951. *Diurnal Amplitude of Temperature in Nebraska.* M.A. thesis, Department of Geography, University of Nebraska.

_____. 1955. *Weather and Coal-Mine Explosions.* Ph.D. dissertation, Department of Geography, University of Nebraska.

_____. 1996. *The Nebraska Sand Hills: The Human Landscape.* Lincoln: University of Nebraska Press.

McNee, Robert B. 1967. "A Proposal for a New Geography Course for Liberal Education: Introduction to Geographic Behavior." Pp. v-viii, 1-37 in *New Approaches in Introductory Geography Courses.* Commission on College Geography, Publication No. 4. Washington, DC: Association of American Geographers.

McNulty, Michael L. 1991. "In Memoriam: Clyde F. Kohn 1911-1989." *Annals of the Association of American Geographers* 81 (December): 697-700.

Pound, Roscoe and Frederick Clements. 1898. "A Method of Determining the Abundance of Secondary Species." *Minnesota Botanical Studies* 2 (June): 19-24.

Schilz, Gordon B. 1949. *Rural Population Trends of Iowa as Affected by Soils.* Ph.D. dissertation. Clark University.

Stoddard, Hugh P. and Mrs. Hugh P. Stoddard [c. 1967]. *An Informal History of Nemaha County, 1854-1967.* [N.p., n.p.].

Stoddard, Nainie Lenora Robertson (Mrs. Hugh P.). 1935. "The Biography of a Builder of Nebraska, Martha Jane Harshman Aldrich." (First Prize, Native Sons and Daughters of Nebraska, 1935 Contest). *Nebraska History Magazine* 16 (January-march): 2-13. Reprinted below, this volume, Chapter 3.

Stoddard, Robert H. 1960. *The Geography of Churches and Their Rural Congregations in Nemaha County, Nebraska.* MA thesis. Department of Geography, University of Nebraska-Lincoln.

_____. 1966. *Hindu Holy Sites in India.* Ph.D. dissertation. Department of Geography, University of Iowa.

_____. 1967. "The 'Iowa Approach' to Geography." General Seminar presentation, 5 October. Department of Geography, University of Nebraska-Lincoln. Mimeographed handout.

_____. 1982. *Field Techniques and Research Methods in Geography.* Dubuque, IA: Kendal/Hunt.

"Stoddard, Robert H." 1999. P. 4751 in *Who's Who in America: 2000.* Millennium edition, Vol. II. New Providence, NJ: Marquis Who's Who.

Stoddard, Sara E. (Sally). 1984. *Texture, Pattern, and Cohesion in Written Texts: A Study with a Graphic Perspective.* Ph.D. dissertation. Department of English, University of Nebraska-Lincoln

Van Royen, William. 1968. "Nels August Bengtson (1879-1963)." *Annals of the Association of American Geographers* 58 (September): 601-605.

Vogel, Philip E. 1956. *The Holland, Nebraska, Locality: A Comparative Study of Dutch and Non-Dutch Occupance.* M.A. thesis. Department of Geography, University of Nebraska.

_____. 1960. *A Geographic Study of Some of the Effects of Irrigation in the Nebraska Bostwick Irrigation Project.* Ph.D. dissertation. Department of Geography, University of Nebraska.

2

REMARKS ON FORM AND NUMBERS AS AUXILIARY IN REPRESENTING THE RELATIONS OF GEOGRAPHICAL SPACES [1]
[1828]

Carl Ritter

I shall venture to communicate now, in a desultory manner merely, a few remarks, the digested results of which would be more worthy of presentation here, if, at the present time at least, the means were not wanting for the attainment of such results. And, in truth, efforts made under very disadvantageous circumstances to lay out for one's self a scientific path through new and unexplored regions, demand of the judgment a measure of leniency, while the very effort is of some service in aiding the acquisition of means to lead us to valuable results.

In a former paper[2] it was my effort to reach the basis of the relations which spring from the position and the superficial divisions of the continents, and to develop those relations in reference to the entire surface of the earth. This could only be done in broad and rough lines, whether in reference to the collective forms and the more general subdivisions of the surface of the globe, or in reference to the course of history.

But should the application of these general relations lead us back to an instructive method of considering every special country, and of studying its people, and bring to clear view the share of every district in the collective circle of its influences, it would be necessary, it seems to me, in order to make these relations intelligible, that the auxiliaries of form and numbers should both be employed, and in a way hitherto but little used.

---

[1] Delivered January 17, 1828, to the Berlin Academy of Sciences. Edited from *Geographical Studies* by the late Professor Carl Ritter of Berlin. Translated from the original German by William Leonhard Gage. Boston: Gould and Lincoln, 1863: 209-238.

[2] "The Geographical Position and Horizontal Extension of the Continents." [1826]. Pp. 177-208 in Carl Ritter, *Geographical Studies*.

I

We call to our aid the auxiliary of form, in the use of well known geometrical figures, to bring into view before the mind, without the employment of measurements, the characteristic to which we would give prominence in the portion of the earth at any given time under our consideration. The right use of geometrical figures, and their intelligent application to the study of geographical forms, should be largely brought out in a scientific treatise, in order to conduct the student, in a very simple and direct manner, to well defined conceptions.[3] He may be securely led to new applications of these figures, and thus to a constant succession of new views, which shall exhibit in the distinctest manner whatever features of the earth's surface are capable of representation in geometrical forms.

This use of geometrical figures was a long time since introduced into botanical science with very great advantage, and, while it has imparted clearness to it, it has been not at all wanting in accuracy. But in geographical science this coadjutor has, with very few exceptions, and those mostly of a light and playful sort, not been brought into use, because people have hitherto been content with the old-fashioned descriptions, and

Figure 2.1. Carl Ritter

have made no attempt to reach scientific results, or even to grasp the central idea on which all special phenomena rest. In a method wide enough and consecutive enough to embrace the great system of countries that cover the globe, this use of geometrical figures, applied to superficial surfaces of very comprehensive or subordinate size, would lead to a clear view and definite comprehension of the earth's surface; provided only and always that these geometrical figures were not arbitrary and

---

[3] For a modern application of this prescription, see, R.H. Stoddard (1982).

36

imaginary, but plainly existing in nature, and expressing natural forms, as in a mathematical formula. How speedily would such a method lead geography to entirely new phases, and rid it, whether in its elementary or in its scientific forms, of the vast mass of mere undigested descriptions which only burden the mind with endless details. And it is just because these materials have not been brought into system, and still lie in this crude state, that geography is yet in its rudimentary condition, and that the scholastic works and the treatises for schools are all in their primitive form. The free and full application of geometrical progress to this science would lead, as may easily be seen, to a reconstruction of it, to greater breadth of scope, and to a thorough digestion into a systematic shape of facts now loose and burdensome.

In the preceding paper[4] the attempt was made to put to some use geometrical figures in the establishment of those general relations which spring from the grouping of the continents, their position on the earth, their respective length and breadth, their configuration, and brokenness or unbrokenness of outline.

This application of geometrical figures would lead to a clearer view, and therefore to a speedier and surer comparison of special countries, as well as to greater brevity and exactness in geographical terminology, because a geometrical outline conveys at a glance what it would take many sentences to describe. But in order to reach a more perfect conception of geographical forms, since geometrical figures are only partially exact, not strictly coinciding with the outlines of countries or continents, here falling short, here having an excess, we must designate the countries which overrun or do not come up to the limits of the figure taken as the basis by the + and - signs. This simple arrangement proves very convenient and serviceable.

In the application of geometrical forms in the manner just indicated, we should find that some countries were measured by the square, as Spain and the Peloponnesus; others by the rectangle, as Thessaly and Epirus; others by the circle, the ellipse, the triangle, the pentagon, and so forth: that these things meet the eye at a glance, and that this variety of contact with the surroundings gives immediate and perceptible occasion to direct results. Yet it is not easy, it must be confessed, to reach, in the generality of instances, the geometrical figure which best expresses geographical forms, because the number and size of the irregularities prevent the observer from imagining its base type in his mind, and reaching that pure outline on which depend, however, a great many important things, — the climate, the productions, the river systems; these all have much more intimate relation with the

---

[4] *Ibid.*

geometrical figure which is the type than with the + and - excesses or fallings off from it.

After the analogies had been carefully traced between different countries and geometrical figures, it would be time to advance to deviations from the base types, peculiar as they are in the case of every separate district. Even in the individuality of these deviations does every country show that it has a specially designated place for itself, and for its peculiar productions, surroundings, and relations. The two great triangulated countries of North and South America (to speak only of the largest), when brought into contact with the triangle of hither India and the south half of Africa, will offer, upon careful consideration, points of resemblance, and yet again points of difference; they will at the same time show many other features less studied, in respect to size far inferior, but in which everything dependent upon conformation is subjected, though in less degrees, to the same general laws and influences.

In this way there will result from the use of geometrical forms as the types of geographical configuration certain classes and classifications, which, in reference to the type and the deviations from it, allow of a sharp scientific statement of the relations and characteristics which spring from the entire class, from the subordinate divisions, and from individual members.

This making intelligible and bringing into subjection of the varied, unwieldy, and almost unmanageable mass of material, by the simple employment of the element of form, seems to be the great improvement of the age in geographical science, which has always remained in the rear of her sister sciences of natural history; and so continues today a vast helpless mass, of very little service in the instruction of schools, or for yet higher needs, and whose very ponderousness and shapelessness has prevented her being reduced to compact and useful forms.

These geometrical figures are not only applicable in this broad way to the different continents and their natural or arbitrary subdivisions, but they may equally well serve to clearly indicate other characteristics of the earth, such as tracts of water, mountain and plateau districts, plains, lowlands, wastes, fruitful spots, connected forests, regions watered by river systems, grain lands, mineral locations, and the like; and here, where there is not palpable regularity, but only an approximation to the coincidence of geographical configuration with geometrical form, the deviations may, as before, be designated by the + and - signs.

This second manner of applying geometrical figures to the other characteristics of a country besides mere extent, is, as may at once be seen, more difficult than the first, which merely embraces the relations of space and distance. The first would only presuppose a pure geometrical statement, to enable one to discern in the best existing maps and charts the simplest figures which would express the outline of any given countries. By applying a geometrical figure in this way, the maximum and minimum of deviation from it in the protrusion of peninsula formations would be instantly apparent. Thus Europe, to cite the most irregular of all the continents, the one which is the least congruent with a geometrical figure, and which is in this respect characteristically unlike the other grand divisions, would in a general view present itself as an immense right-angled triangle, with the shortest line from north to south, in the direction of the Ural as the basis, for a distance of about fourteen hundred miles. The right angle would fall at the Caucasian isthmus, not far from the mouth of the Volga. The next larger side would be that of the Mediterranean, from Astracan westward through all Europe, to Bayonne, more than twenty-three hundred miles; and the hypothenuse would pass from there northwards by the North Sea, the Baltic, and Archangel to the sources of the Ural, a distance of over twenty-eight hundred miles. The space embraced within this triangle would comprehend by far the greater part of the continental mass of Europe, about two-thirds of the whole, (two millions five hundred thousand square miles, the whole being three millions seven hundred sixty-seven thousand), and outside of it would lie the three peninsulas towards the south, Greece, Italy, Spain, and at the north, Scandinavia. Thus one-third of the whole would lie outside of the inscribed figure, and this third would be characterized by relations quite unlike those of the main body of the continent. In this case, while there would be much excess beyond the figure used as the norm, there would be few places where the measure would come noticeably short. The use of this figure is plainly valuable in helping to observe a large number of relations which are dependent upon the essential unity of the continental surfaces, in contradistinction to the contrasts produced by land and sea, or that which might be called the contrast between the body and members of the continent. In respect to the relations of temperature and the wind systems, in so far as they are dependent upon the configuration and position of the country, the name of the European climatic triangle properly pertains to it, and, in fact, has been recently applied by a French writer. What is true of temperature and wind systems, and their relation to the geometrical form of a country, will be found true of many other influencing agents. How instructive would it be always to have at easy command in this way a very simple and yet universally intelligible expression for action and reaction in comparative geography, and thus to indicate, in a word, the natural home of the various families of beasts and plants, of peoples, and whatever else might need expression. The bearings of this upon what may be technically called the qualitative relations, in distinction from quantitative relations (and by the term quantitative I mean all the conditions which result from extent, by the term qualitative all other conditions), can only be traced after a very careful preliminary acquaintance with the workings of nature; but after such an acquaintance it becomes at once apparent, as in an instructive and in every view masterly and comprehensive sketch of the outlines of South America, contained in the fifth part of Alexander von Humboldt's *Journey to the Equinoctial Regions of the New World*,[5] which has so greatly enriched geographical science. From the grouping of geometrical figures according to quantitative and qualitative relations, with all that is subordinated to this arrangement, the briefest expression would arise for the characterization of continents, countries, special tracts, provinces, districts; in short, a statement in brief, as a substitute for the general and unreliable descriptions which, in consequence of the constant repetition of the same principles, make geographical science diffuse and tedious, and thus inflict upon it serious injury. Nor does it need prolonged remarks to show what a ready means of characterizing arbitrary political divisions is also found in the same method, if they be regarded as readily determined sections of these geometrical figures.

II

From the employment of form for the more correct and profitable comparison of different countries, we pass to a large and important use of numbers, to aid in grasping another set of the relations of geographical districts to one another, and getting full and accurate knowledge of them. We shall not introduce, as is so often done in books of statistics and geography, that misuse of numbers which always creeps in where more stress is laid upon mere facts expressed in the numerical form than upon the relations which they indicate. We shall employ numbers solely and strictly for the determining of fixed and definite relations. As, in descriptive botany, figures and numbers indicate the different parts of a plant, as, for instance, stamens, pistils, glands, calyx, corolla, leaf-incisions, stem divisions, manner of flowering, and rootlets, and give a clear conception of all the qualities of the plant, and the relative place which it occupies in the vegetable creation, since all these things are but exponents of all the causes which condition it; so, in the formation of every natural division of the earth, there is a large number of physical relations capable of numerical expression, all of them essential to a true conception, none of them of indifferent worth and accidental position, like so many things thrown together at haphazard, but which are so regular and so needed that in them can be seen the

---

[5] Alexander von Humboldt, *Personal Narrative of Travels to the Equinoctial Regions of the New Continent, During the Years 1799-1804*. Translated by Helen Maria Williams. 2. Vols. London: Longman, Hurst, Rees, Orme, and Brown, 1814. N.B., there exists a large number of editions, condensations, re-issues, and translations of this work.

40

general principles which control the separation, connection, and grouping of similarly conditioned tracts, wherever they occur.

The numbers thus used will either indicate horizontal and vertical extents, and thus rest upon measurements in square miles, miles of length, and feet above and below the sea level, or they will be the statement in numerical form of matters directly kindred to these.

Measurements have already come into general use for the expression of certain relations, at least; commonly those of political divisions. And yet, for a true system of scientific geography, the statement of the area of political divisions does not suffice; that of the divisions marked out by nature itself, and expressed by geometrical figures, must be first ascertained in square miles, that such tracts may judged in their true relation to the entire globe. Hitherto no efforts have been made to ascertain any areas, excepting those of the continents, and of political states, — and these, indeed, are not without value, — but we ask in vain for the statistics of the size of natural divisions, as, for example, how large the right-angled triangle which is inscribed in Europe is, in proportion to the projections from that continent, and the seas, gulfs, straits, wholly or in part inclosed within it by means of these projections. And whence arises that varied share which these geographical forms, seas, gulfs, and straits have respectively had, and still have, in the powerful influences which they exert upon the entire continent? In what relative magnitude do the great and the small peninsulas stand to each other, to the islands which belong to them, and to the vast continental domains untouched by the sea? In what numerical relations can we estimate the area of the great and well-watered river basins; of the regions lying between them, poor in streams or wholly unwatered; of the coast lands, which are traversed by the short rivers characteristic of the shore, and which, therefore, are quite otherwise related to the sea than the central continental districts which are watered by important streams and their branches? We look in vain to find the area in square miles of fruitful plains, of great grain districts, of morasses, of peat bogs, of sand wastes, of heaths, of mountain regions; only here and there have natural features been subjected to measurement, and the relative areas ascertained of lakes, arable lands, forests, and meadows. Valuable as it is, for some statistical purposes, that we learn such facts as these, no less advantageous would it be for all historical and geographical ends that we ascertain such data as those alluded to a moment since, in order to be able to determine and compare, in tabular form, the varied influences of physical forms on countries and people. This would be a comparatively easy task, because such facts, having to do with inanimate and fixed forms, do not partake of that constantly changing character which marks the movements of men. After ascertaining the limits of the natural divisions of the earth, even if in an incomplete way, the various changes which past centuries have witnessed in the boundaries of states, the movements forward and backward of those boundaries in ancient aud modern times, the diffusion of nations and of languages, the progress of culture, and many other like things, could be established and indicated in a more precise way. A great mass of valuable historic relations could be indicated, for which language would otherwise have no fitting expression. Take, for example, the relation existing between the life and occupations of men, and the characteristics of the earth's surface where they live, and which supports them. Observe the people of the sea-coast, the people of the mountains, the dwellers on continental arable land, whether grain-producing or not, and see how great a share the nature of the soil on which they live has in determining their political states; see how mutual is the action and reaction, and what varied results flow from it in all the countries of Europe. Such topics as these, of wide and manifold relations, have been subjected to the severest investigations, and their principles, when ascertained, have been stated in those well known modern works, which have opened a new era in historical, geographical, and statistical sciences as connected. We will refer only to Malthus' *Essay on the Principles of Population*: London, 1803; Dupin's standard works on Great Britain and France (*Force maritime, militaire, commercielle et industrielle de la Grande Bretagne*, Vol. III., 1824; *Forces productives et commercielles de la France*, Vol. II., 1827); and on Italy the classical researches of Lullin de Chateauvieux, (*Lettres sur l'Italie*, Vol. I., where he treats of agriculture). Not unimportant would it be, in reference to every country of the world, be it great or small, to be able to speak in the same manner with which Humboldt commences his description of South America:

> "South America is one of those great triangular-shaped masses which constitute the three continental divisions of the southern hemisphere; of the area which it embraces, 6,560,000 square miles, the fourth part, 1,640,000 square miles, is covered with mountains which lie in ranges or groups; the other three-fourths are plains, of which four-fifths lie east of the Andes. The mountainous region, one quarter of the whole, is so divided, that somewhat over one-third forms the great chain of the Andes on the west. More than one-third of this chain, measuring by superficial area 577,400 square miles, lies above the snow-line; nearly two-thirds, 862,600 square miles, never reaches the snow-line, and lies mainly upon the east side of the Andes," etc.

The more simple the results from very intricate conditions as here, so much the more instructive. At once there are evolved from such clear exhibitions of relations the differences and contrasts of other regions in an entirely different way than from descriptions. The student is led on to further researches into their peculiarities, as, for example, the mutual relation of the three great mountain systems of the world, the Andes of America, the Himalayas of India, and the Alps of Europe, as ascertained from their areas and their most important dimensions. Through this method of study and criticism, he is led from these masses to see the nature of all elevations, to learn how countries are watered, to discover the constituents of soils, their mineral wealth, the extents of flora, of fauna, of nations, of political divisions and their resources, the number of roads over mountainous tracts, of passes through them, and of settlements upon them, and thus to bring them into a true and complete relation with all their surroundings and the whole earth. This method of treatment is almost unknown, even in our best descriptive works.

The final use which we make of measurements and of computations embraced in geometrical figures, and in the districts which can be considered as large or small, according as the point of view may demand, and according as they are regarded absolutely or relatively, — the final use of measurements is to sum up together a number of geometrical forms, i.e. to gain the aggregate of areas, in order to draw a general principle from them, to analyze them as a mass, to subdivide them and treat them historically, physically, or politically, in order to get at whatever may be peculiar to each, and thus to reach the minor characteristics of the parts which compose the great whole. Merely to indicate a few such will be for the present sufficient to show the diversity and the abundance of such analysis. We only name these: the varied configuration of coast, the effects of river systems, and the relations of medium heights to the loftiest mountains and the depressions which stand in direct contrast with them. Other examples we shall not need to cite.

Coastal Configuration

The relations induced by coast configuration depend upon the length of shoreline, upon the superficial contents of the area inclosed by the surrounding seas, roughly represented as it is by a geometrical figure, but more exactly expressed by the application of the + and - signs to those sides of the figure which overrun or fall short. There is for every assignable place a possible maximum or minimum of intricacy in the configuration of its outline, from the most simple outline of such continents as Australia and Africa, advancing to the favorable conformation of the shores of Asia and America, on to the intricate configuration of Europe, and its radical division into trunk, members, and isolated, dissevered fragments. There is met even such an extent of coast as to be a superabundance, where the word continent is a misnomer, where there is such a complete dismemberment by the intervention of the sea, that the combined periphery of the islands thus formed is equal to the coastline of a continent. This is the case with the Sunda group, which has a total shoreline nearly equal to Europe. To a less extent, the same principle holds good down to the smallest groups. The relation of the extent of coast to the area is a prime element in the establishment of a maritime character, whether in the largest or the smallest continents. We have, in previous parts of this work, showed, that although Europe is threefold less than Africa in area, yet it has a much greater extent of shore, 24,685 miles, — the distance around the world, — while Africa has but 17,300 miles of coast. Asia, with five times the territory of Europe, has but 32,000 miles of shoreline. These continents, thus widely unlike in respect to the extent of trunk, members, and isolated parts, or islands, correspond, briefly stated, to these numbers:

	Main body	Peninsulas	Islands
Africa	1	0	1/50
Asia	4	1	1/8
Europe	2	1	1/20

When one considers how dependent upon the coastline are the contact of the sea with the earth, and the whole vast variety of their mutual activity, influencing both animate and inanimate nature; when one thinks how the conformation even of countries has been conditioned by it, and how the various groups of elevations and depressions have received from it their boundary lines, their grades of ascent and of descent, and their absolute distance, whether upwards or downwards, and that all these results appear in the smallest peninsulas and islands, as well as in the largest continent; when one considers all this, it will be confessed to be a matter of the greatest geographical interest to judge the coastline always and everywhere in reference to the area to which it belongs, — to the land boundaries, to the country enclosed, and to every other feature; to grasp by numbers, computations, and measurements whatever relations they may disclose, and apply them as auxiliaries in every direction that may seem desirable. More than this; these numbers and computations ought to have a place in every delineation of the surface of the earth. Only then would appear every advantage possessed by countries by the sea, in their relative gain from winds and currents, in their configuration, in their ease and safeness of approach, and in their supply of harbors; and only then should we have all the data which we need to estimate rightly the relation of countries washed by seas and oceans, to the people who inhabit them.

44

River Systems

In like manner, by the application of measure and number, the form of territory watered by rivers can become very serviceable in the study of those districts which are usually the home of culture and the seat of organized political states, if the principle that underlies all relations comes clearly into view, and is made more conveniently available for scientific comparison than mere description allows. The various river systems of the earth have been entirely neglected thus far as to the marked peculiarity and individuality of form which appear in the plainest manner among the largest of them, and are capable of being seen in all. And yet this is a feature too prominent to allow us to forget on what foundation geographical science must stand that it may not suffer to lie unused one of the greatest means at our command for its enrichment.

In every description of a country the rivers are mentioned because they water it, and some scattered remarks are added; very rarely are details given regarding their rate of fall, the source as it is of movement in their current, or regarding their depth and navigableness, the source of their usefulness; and yet all such details might be exhibited in tabular form with great fulness. There do, indeed, exist treatises on the length of rivers from their source to their mouth, in which an attempt has been made to supply existing wants, and to ascertain the significance of streams, by presenting their length in tabular form, arranged in the order of relative magnitude. Among the most valuable of these are some measurements of Buache (1752), from which, however, he himself, as well as his followers, neglected to draw any useful inferences. *(Essai d'un Parallèle des Fleuves de l'Europe.)* But it was seen, notwithstanding, that here, as everywhere, there was in the phenomena of countries watered by rivers a close interior union, which would not be arbitrarily broken without being utterly lost. Very diverse features of the river systems had to be grouped in their mutual dependence at once, if the student would be led directly to a comparison of their characteristics, and to the true meaning of every detail in its connection with the economy of nature and the course of history. The relations of extent, which form the basis of all relations, and which, because essential to the highest wants of science, must, in the case of all leading streams, be first established, are more or less closely connected with the depression and elevation of the surface. The first one of these is the distance, in an air-line, from the source of a river to the mouth; the absolute fall is to be traced in the result of this measurement. The second is the maximum distance from source to mouth, following the bendings; in this is seen the tract of the intervale land which has gradually accumulated. The third is the area of the river basin, embracing all the valleys of tributary rivers; or, stated in other words, the area of the entire surface which is indebted to a river system for being

45

watered and enriched in manifold ways, and thus fitted for its place in influencing the human race. By being studied in reference to these three points, every river system assumes its true shape, allows all that is peculiar in itself to appear, and is itself formed by the combination of most diverse features. In following this method of research, it becomes possible, and at the same time greatly conducive to the furtherance of a scientific treatment in extended descriptions (needed in their proper place to complete our conception), to draw from a comprehensive view of relations such observations as can become a basis for all future teaching and investigation, but which, unless established by scales of magnitudes, would not become a part of true science. A few examples will suffice to exhibit this. The river Volga, measured from source to mouth, is at least two thousand miles in length; the Danube seventeen hundred,—about one-eighth shorter; while the Rhine is only eight hundred miles long, or about half the length of the Danube. Thus it may be seen that these European rivers, looked at in their relative length, do not vary widely from the proportions 3, 2, 1. But looked at in reference to the district which they water, the proportions change to 8, 4, 1; since the basin of the Volga, which is of nearly the same size as the Nile valley, embraces an area of about six hundred and forty thousand square miles; that of the Danube three hundred thousand, and that of the Rhine only seventy-five thousand six hundred. Looked at in reference to the fall of the rivers, as it is commonly called, together with the many phenomena which spring from this source, the proportions again materially change; for the sources of the Rhine lie eleven thousand feet, those of the Danube three thousand three hundred, those of the Volga one thousand two hundred feet, above the level of the sea. These proportions continue, not seriously changed, throughout the entire length of these rivers. Yet their general course is widely unlike, being southeast, east, and northwest; and, in consequence of their different situations in Europe, all the varieties of their attendant climate, seasons, high water, and productiveness are essentially modified. Simple as seem the lines on our maps that indicate the river courses, yet the greatest diversity appears in their influences, when first their relations are more carefully settled, and are grasped in a single conception. How much more complete is the result for the investigation of the whole, as well as of details, if the student take note in this manner of all the most important elements which manifest themselves.

The six most important streams of Europe which have a marked nearness in their course and in the place of their termination, are the Kuban, Don, Dnieper, Bug, Dniester, and Danube. Herodotus long ago wondered at the fact that the mouths of rivers so large and so long should lie in Southern Russia, in a land of not over four hundred miles in width, between the Kuban from Causasus and the Danube from Hungary. Among these six, the Danube is the most important; but next to the Danube is the Dnieper, whose whole valley is three times that of the Rhine and Elbe combined,—two hundred and thirteen thousand three hundred square miles. The entire length of the Dnieper, inclusive of curves, is nine hundred and seventy-eight miles; while its distance, as the bird flies, from source to mouth, is six hundred and twelve; the mere bendings adding about four hundred and fifty miles to its length. The result of this sinuous course is the enlargement of the relatively extraordinary extent of the district that it waters, the number of branches which run into it, and the great fruitfulness and variety of the surface where it leads its lingering way. Its neighbor on the west, the Dniester, pursuing a course also towards the southeast, and through a very similar tract of country, yet displays entirely different characteristics. It is, indeed, less in size, and yet it is not in this that the great reason lies which occasions so many different relations. The shortest distance from the source of the Dniester to the mouth is three hundred and eighty miles; its entire course, inclusive of all bendings, is only four hundred and forty miles; its sinuosities do not, therefore, prolong its course more than one-sixth of its length, as the bird flies. The district which it waters, considered relatively to its length, is very small; we might almost say, insignificant — thirty thousand square miles; about half that of the Rhine, and about equal to that of the Tagus. The low place which this river takes in the important hydrographical system of Eastern Europe appears not only when it is compared with its important neighbors, but also when compared with rivers not in themselves remarkable. From the fact that its course is so nearly straight arises the dependent fact that the area of territory watered is relatively to the length of the river the smallest known. Since it is so uniform in its course, and runs through a narrow strip of land extending from northwest to southeast, it lacks to a great extent the variety which tributary streams effect; hardly disturbed as yet even by the boats of explorers, it remains without interest, having little to confer upon geographical science, and having no history which it would be useful to unfold.

In striking contrast with this is the Vistula, the largest river that empties into the Baltic, constituting, with the Danube, the Elbe, and the Rhine, the four most important streams of Central Europe. In size, the Vistula stands in the general hydrographical system of the globe next to the Rhine,—between the Elbe and the Rhine. The direct distance of the mouth of the Vistula from its source is three hundred and twenty-nine miles; the length, including curves, five hundred and sixty-two miles; the windings themselves, therefore, occupy two hundred and thirty-three miles, or more than two-thirds of the entire length of the river. This accounts for the extent of the country that the Vistula waters. The shortest length of the Oder, that is, measured as the bird flies, is the same as the Vistula; but its winding is far less, only about ninety miles, and, therefore, it waters a tract far less in magnitude than the valley of its neighbor on the east. The Elbe is a much longer river, measured by the bird's course, than the Vistula, it being three hundred and eighty-four miles; but the

47

territory which it waters is relatively less. The Rhine in both of these respects surpasses the Vistula in absolute magnitude; the direct distance from source to mouth is about four hundred and fifty miles; its length, inclusive of windings, is about six hundred and seventy-two miles; but the sinuosities do not constitute two-thirds of the whole, and are, therefore, relatively inferior to the Vistula. This detracts a little from the greatness of the otherwise majestic Rhine, and the result of this circumstance is, that the territory watered by both is almost equal. The diversity, too, in the rate of descent in rivers introduces another new element, and demands attention in every hydrographical system; for this also gives rise to new contrasts, and occasions still other characteristic points of individuality to each river.

But we pass over an enlarged consideration of this, for our object is to show briefly how the application of form and numbers conducts us to the principle that underlies all geographical relations. Without this new employment of form and numbers, this grand principle would be unobserved; but with its use we reach a clear method of expressing what could hardly be expressed before, and attain that systematic statement which geographical science has so long needed, to enable its votaries to reduce into orderly arrangement the vast mass of confused materials.

Mountain Systems

To the third point referred to above, the relations of mountains of medium height to those of the loftiest altitude, we need only allude briefly in passing, because the very fruitful results of one eminent naturalist, who has carefully studied the structure of mountains and mountain chains, have been presented in his various treatises upon the ranges of India and in his journey to the equinoctial regions of the New World. That relation of mere height, which used to be exalted into a matter of prime importance in studying the characteristics of mountains, and which in the Pyrenees, Alps, Cordilleras, and Himalayas, is expressed in the series 1, 1½, 2, 2½, has withdrawn into the background, and now the ridge itself, taken in its average or rather its ordinary height, is thought to give a more complete and true idea of its characteristics, and, by being studied in a wider range of view, the height of the highest peaks is regarded as a single and subordinate element. This method is illustrated by the following brief category of relations, — relations which are just and real, and far more worthy of thought than those of isolated peaks. The general altitude of the Andes is the same as that of the highest mountains of the Pyrenees; the general altitude of the Himalayas is the same with that of the highest of the Alps; the range of the Alps is almost equal in its general altitude to that of the Pyrenees; they are slightly distinguished from each other by the superior height of individuals of the Alpine range. It will be easily seen that the study of the minimum elevation of great mountain chains reveals the available passes and places of transit; here is a fresh point to which a great number of facts join in new relations, and here is a germ whence results distribute themselves over entire continents; in its application to the making of charts, many vertical measurements of heights and depths become a rich and fruitful object of study.

These heights exhibited in tabular views from barometrical and other measurements, give a basis for generalizations and comparisons, which are convenient, and will ultimately be serviceable. We have introduced these remarks on the relations of vertical and other dimensions only as an index of the manner in which other relations should be viewed.

III

These remarks on the use of form and numbers, as tributary to the expression of many relations which otherwise would be difficult to make clear, may suffice, although the number might easily be extended, to show how much might and must be done in this direction, not only for the furtherance of geography as a science, but also to facilitate the communication of its results, before both scientific advance and the clear imparting of what science shall gain shall be promoted, as they should be, and shall take the high place that this new method will enable them ultimately to win.

As the ascertaining of these relations, although requiring no extraordinary exertions, would yet demand a patient survey of the best materials at hand, and a great number of observations made with this end in view, and as time and means for this are not at the command of every one, the question has recently been agitated, in consequence of the somewhat antiquated character of the maps published by the Academy of Berlin, whether the former progress in this department should not be still sustained, and the number of improved elementary auxiliaries be still enlarged. And it has seemed not unsuitable to undertake, in a manner easy of realization, and yet worthy of the Academy and of the needs of science, to assume anew this service, and to secure its accomplishment. With the materials now at command, there might be gradually formed a work which, while it should embrace all the relations that geography makes known, should also grasp the central principles of all *systems* of relations, reach the common ground on which they all, greater and smaller, rest, and present its results in mathematical expression. The clearest ascertainment of the weighty relations of the earth's surface to all departments of historical and physical, as well as natural and geographical, science, would be the first care, and the discharge of this ought to devolve upon a geometrician well acquainted with the entire body of details necessary for the successful preparation of maps. He should be supported by all the auxiliaries which could ensure success to the undertaking. The second care would be to display scientific results in the clearest manner, and so combined as to be applicable to all uses, meeting the needs alike of physics, natural history, geognosy, botany, history, and geography. To accomplish this, general charts, tables, and special maps should be employed, for these agencies serve best to display the relations with which the study of the earth's surface makes us acquainted. The third duty would be to follow this thorough scientific preparation by giving a better form to the textbooks of our schools, and thus to establish the real difference between the general chart or the reduced form, which, in consequence of its diminished size, has the appearance of a copy, and the special map or the real copy. Through these combined means, geographical science, as taught in our schools, would enter upon a new course, and, instead of being mere description, would become an organized system, marshalling its rich materials into orderly arrangement, and showing constant capacity of advancement.

3

THE BIOGRAPHY OF A BUILDER OF NEBRASKA:
MARTHA JANE HARSHMAN ALDRICH [1]

Nainie Lenora Robertson Stoddard
(Mrs. Hugh P. Stoddard)
Auburn, Nebraska

First Prize, Native Sons and Daughters of Nebraska,
1935 Contest [2]

A clipping from an old "Nemaha County Herald" contains the following paragraph, written by J. R. Huffman, formerly of Nemaha County, "Just as the morning sun drove the shadows of night away and the birds began their morning songs from the top of the great trees that had been planted almost half century ago by those young hands, Mrs. Aldrich closed her eyes to the beauties surrounding the place where the

---

[1] Reproduced, with permission of the Nebraska State Historical Society, from *Nebraska History Magazine* 16 (March 1935): 2-13. Nainie Lenora Robertson Stoddard (Mrs. Hugh P. Stoddard) was Robert H. Stoddard's mother. Martha Jane Harshman Aldrich, the subject of this sketch, was Robert H. Stoddard's great grandmother. The editor of *Nebraska History Magazine* was then Addison E. Sheldon, a Ph.D. sociologist trained by Franklin H. Giddings at Columbia, and the associate editor was Mari Sandoz, a gifted young writer who became Nebraska's premier sociological novelist.

[2] Miss Helen Tuttle chaired the Contest Committee. The 1935 judges were: Mrs. R.L. (Aileen Gantt) Cochran (wife of Nebraska Governor Robert Cochran); Dr. Elmer GuyCutshall (Chancellor of Nebraska Wesleyan University); and the Honorable Emil M. von Seggern (Nebraska state legislator and publisher of the West Point *Republican*). The prize was presented by Mrs. Marie Weekes during the joint annual dinner of the Nebraska State Historical Society and the Native Sons and Daughters of Nebraska at the University Club in Lincoln on Friday, October 4, 1935. According to the eyewitness account by Margaret E. Shelden (wife of Addison E. Sheldon), "Mrs. Weekes . . . called upon Mrs. Stoddard for [a] brief speech which was gracefully given" (Native Sons and Daughters of Nebraska, Minutes, MS 1119, Box 2, p. 92, Nebraska State Historical Society, Lincoln, Nebraska). The evening concluded with an address by Mari Sandoz "who spoke engagingly and crisply upon 'From the Sandhills of the Niobrara to the Hills of Boston' — giving her experiences during her recent trip to claim her *Atlantic* 1935 $5000, non-fiction prize for her ms 'Old Jules.' All agreed with Gov. Cochran that Miss Sanoz's literary efforts brought distinction to herself and to her native state as well" (N.S.D.N., Minutes, p. 98).

51

little barefooted children had played and where she had so carefully advised and guarded them while they passed from childhood to manhood and womanhood. To the casual observer the Aldrich farm is noted for its many trees, but to Mrs. Aldrich the great spreading elm near the house, the cool shady lane where the tall maple trees furnished shade in summer and protected the traveler from the beating winds of winter, and the small grassy plot south of the house surrounded by the mammoth evergreen trees, were just as much home to her as was the little white cottage where the meals were served and where the family gathered on holidays." [3]

Figure 3.1. Nainie Lenora Robertson Stoddard

Thus Mr. Huffman describes the passing, in August 1913, of one of the builders of Nebraska: Martha Jane Harshman Aldrich (born March 1, 1836, at Washington, Pennsylvania), who came to Nebraska from Wisconsin forty-eight years previous with her husband, Benton Aldrich,[4] and their three small children: Karl, nine; Nella, seven; and Mary, three.

Before starting for the new home in Nebraska, the Aldrich family visited relatives in Minnesota. It was here that Mr. Aldrich loaded the covered wagon and obtained the largest ox team he could find. Mrs. Aldrich had already prepared suitable clothing for the family that they might be comfortable as possible throughout the wearisome days of travel. Mr. Aldrich helped prepare a hard bread, or graham cracker, for food on the trip. This food kept well through-out the journey. In spite of

---

[3] See J.R. Huffman, "Noble Pioneer Woman Reached Journey's End," *Nemaha County Herald*, August 29, 1913: 1. See also, "The End Came," *The Granger* (Auburn, Nebraska), August 24, 1913: 1. The latter, on page 8, includes a photo of Mr. and Mrs. Aldrich.

[4] See the retrospective article by Dean Terrill, "Man Responsible for Thousands of Trees Little Known in State," *Lincoln Evening Journal*, April 21, 1966: 8.

all care taken to keep the family well, Mrs. Aldrich became ill on the trip and the family remained a week at a hotel in Iowa. The Aldrich family then came on, arriving at last in Nemaha County,[5] Nebraska, April 11, 1865, about six weeks from their time of starting.

They went first to the home of Mr. William Hawley,[6] who was living one mile north of the forty acres which was the Aldrich family's destination and which Benton Aldrich had previously purchased from the government for $1.25 an acre. Mr. Hawley, who was the first settler in the community which was called Clifton,[7] had helped Mr. Aldrich in selecting the forty shortly before the move to Nebraska was made, and the former now welcomed the new neighbors. With a queer look on his face he invited them in and led them to a bed where lay Mrs. Hawley. Turning back the covers a little, the Aldrich family beheld a new baby, Richard,[8] six days old. This was the first child born in Clifton.

A Frontier Nurse

Martha Jane Aldrich took charge, caring for the mother and babe as only she who was so gifted in such work, could. She had had plenty of experience already and strange as it might seem, her first confinement case had been the birth of her own first baby at which time she efficiently advised the neighbor women at her bedside. She knew what to do because she had obtained books and carefully studied them. But her wonderful ability in the care of the sick, her calming presence at beds of pain, and her tender solicitude in times of illness or death were outstanding characteristics of Mrs. Aldrich's life.

Mrs. Aldrich took up the task of nurse in the Hawley family for a few days. As she ministered thus to Mrs. Hawley she was destined to minister to scores of sick in southeastern Nebraska, for she became doctor, nurse, adviser, and helper to hundreds of neighbors and friends in this new community. To learn of the illness or

---

[5] Regarding the religious patterns of Nemaha County, see Robert H. Stoddard, "The Geography of Churches and Their Rural Congregations in Nemaha County, Nebraska." MA thesis. Department of Geography, University of Nebraska-Lincoln, 1960.

[6] William Henry Hawley came to Nebraska in 1863 "where he homesteaded one hundred and sixty acres on which he had his home" (Nemaha County Book Committee, 1987: 179).

[7] The Clifton community area was an informal designation. One authority puts it: "Clifton is not a city, was not a city, nor was it ever the abode of a townsite" (Dundas 1902: 21). Thus, Clifton does not appear in the standard compendium of Nebraska place names.

[8] Richard eventually married Anna Wayne, on August 10, 1887, and they had five children (Nemaha County Book Committee, 1987: 179).

death of a neighbor was but the signal for her to go at once to ease the pain and heartache of the loved ones at that home.

Mrs. Nerva Butterfield, who is now living on a farm joining the Aldrich farm, once wrote of Mrs. Aldrich, whose memory she treasures: "The blizzard of winter was never too boisterous nor the hot wind and sun of summer too intense for her to go both far and near where there was sickness or death. Many homes have been brightened at the darkest hour of night by her kind ministration of the sick. She knew just how to arrange the pillows. Her hands could smooth away the ache from the tired, nervous head. She could hold the hands of the sick and with her sweet and gentle voice calm to restful sleep the most stubborn case. Many persons owe their lives to her untiring care. Her very presence was like a benediction. Without money or without price she gave freely of the best years of her life, believing that: 'He worships best who loves and strives, whose prayers are acts of kindly deeds.'"

Her husband liked to tell that his wife had helped at the births of one hundred babies, with several sets of twins for good measure; and her daughter, Mrs. Nella Stoddard, recalls that of all those many cases, but one baby failed to live! What a wonderful record to have made! How often the sequence of incidences were repeated: the doctor far away, the need urgent, time short, and money scarce. The efficient Mrs. Aldrich always ready to go, afoot, horseback, or by lumber wagon to the scene and with her cheerful patience and tender administrations bring health, courage, and order back to the home.

Settlement

After a few days at the Hawley home, the Aldrich family drove on to its final destination: about eight and one-half miles northwest of the present town of Auburn, in Nemaha County, Nebraska.[9] Thus there came to Nebraska a woman who became a builder of that state. Although she and her husband had little money to bring to the new home, they had energy, good health, and a great ambition to build on this treeless prairie an attractive home where they and their children might live healthy, happy, useful lives.

So with eager hearts they began their new home which at first was in the wooden-covered wagon box which Mr. Aldrich lifted from the running gears and set on the ground. Side by side husband and wife set to work to build the house, digging out limestone near the surface of the ground for this purpose. Mr. Aldrich decided

---

[9] Alternatively, Dean Terrill (*op. cit.*) noted that the Adrich homestead, now beautifully wooded, was sited "three miles south of Brock and just east of Coryell Park."

to put the house, which was to measure about twelve by eighteen feet, half underground so that it would be warmer and also more protected from injury by the strong winds which blew with such intensity. Mrs. Aldrich helped with the larger stones, but most of the time she did the chinking: that is, putting the little stones between the larger ones, to make the wall tight and to make it look well. She aided in the shingling of the house and the making of the simple furniture from lumber hauled from Brownville, Nebraska. Later, Mr. Aldrich hauled dirt and banked up the north, south, and west walls to make the house warmer. The east end had a stone wall up about two and one-half feet, and the rest was of lumber. In this wall mere two windows and a door. There was a half window at the west end.

The children helped whenever possible and lived happy, out-of-door lives, exploring the new country. Karl, especially, made friends with the wild creatures, for he was a great lover of pets. On a hill about thirty rods south of the wagon, the prairie chickens congregated each morning during the mating season and the Aldrich family was interested in the booming and strutting of these wild fowls. Karl put out kernels of corn and finally coaxed one strutting male to come quite near the wagon for food.

It was an eventful day when the family moved into the new abode. It is true that there was only the ground as a floor, most of the few pieces of furniture mere homemade, the cookstove which had been purchased at Brownville, was quite small, but to the family it all meant a home. There was a homemade bedstead for the adults; for the children, wooden bunks three deep along one wall: Karl, the top one; Nella, the middle; while four-year-old Mary, the bottom one. The home contained one piece of furniture which came along with the family on its trip from Wisconsin — a wooden book cupboard. The Aldrich family were book-lovers and into this new community they brought all they could carry of these treasures of the printed page. A boot-box also came along on the trip when it was used as a food supply-box and as a seat. This box is still in good condition and is in use in the home of the eldest daughter, Mrs. Nella A. Stoddard, now living, at the age of seventy-eight years, on her farm one-half mile east of the old home.

As in the case of hundreds of pioneers, Mrs. Aldrich helped in the making of buildings, in breaking sod, planting garden, setting out trees, caring for stock, in doing all the tasks which go toward the making of a home in a new country. Odd incidents furnished material for interesting stories which were told as the years went on.

Frontier Incidents

One time the mother got lost. The oxen were worked during the day, and allowed to graze at night. Mrs. Aldrich took her turn at watching the oxen as they ate the prairie grass. One night when she was watching them she lost her bearings and so did not return at the time Mr. Aldrich thought she should. He could tell by the moon — for they had no timepiece — that she had been gone longer than usual, so he set out to find her. He called as he went and soon heard her answering call.

An amusing incident concerned the floor of the stone dugout. As the years passed the tramp of feet on the dirt caused hollows to appear but the children who romped in the cozy home were accustomed to the humps and hollows. But when, a few years later, a board floor was put in, the childish feet, unused to its even surface, stumbled and the children got many a fall.

Many, many years later when the youngest child, Alfred, was a man, he liked to tell his own children of the time when his mother and he had an unfortunate experience with an angry sow which had farrowed a long ways out in the tall prairie grass. Coyotes were numerous and many little pigs fell victims of their ravages. So it was necessary to bring the litters to the buildings. This time Mrs. Aldrich was attempting the task. She had Alfred, then a small boy, along with her. She placed him at what seemed a safe distance before approaching the sow. The latter grew belligerent and made a dash for the child. Mrs. Aldrich ran toward Alfred but the old sow won the race and knocked the little boy over. Mrs. Aldrich rescued him, but Alfred carried quite a scar as the result of this injury.

Tree Planting

From the first the family felt the great need of a windbreak to check the sweep of strong winds which blew across the unbroken spaces of the prairie. So Mr. Aldrich went to the sandbars of the Missouri River and pulled up many little cottonwood trees, and he and his wife set these out: he used the spade, she set the tree and spread out the roots by hand.

From along the Blue River Mr. Aldrich brought red cedar trees which furnished excellent windbreaks and which made a haven for birds. The latter paid for their homes by scattering the seeds which were found in the little blue berries which grew on the red cedars. The little trees that grew from these seeds were transplanted to the Aldrich garden where they received good care; and later were sold to other pioneers who desired windbreaks.

The fencing problem in this treeless country where lumber was scarce, high, and far away, and where barbed wire was yet a thing unknown, was solved largely by the planting of hedges. For this purpose no tree was so well adapted as the osage, which is very thorny. The little trees were set close together and after they had attained a diameter of three-quarters of an inch, their trunks were partly cut through and bent over at perhaps a forty-five degree angle. The interlacing of young branches made a barrier that stock seldom found their way through.

In later years, when the growth of the trees permitted, the hedges were cut for fence posts — unequaled by any other material. Many of the hedges thus set out in southeastern Nebraska in the early days came from the Aldrich nursery. The seed was purchased by the bushel, and then in order to break the hard, shell-like structure around the seeds, Mrs. Aldrich soaked them in warm water and worked them with her hands. Later she helped plant them in rows and when the little trees appeared she helped the children weed and hoe them.

Mr. Aldrich selected his original forty acres with the idea of having a good place to set out orchards and small fruit. Two acres of raspberry vines were set out, and a windbreak set to protect them. When the vines came into bearing, the fruit was picked, dried, put into sacks, and taken to Nebraska City, where it was sold to Robert Hawk, a store keeper, for a good price. Dried raspberries were considered quite a delicacy in those early days. Mrs. Aldrich had charge of the drying of this fruit which was spread out on muslin tacked tightly to wooden frames. These were set in the sun until the fruit was completely dried.

Many peach and apple trees were planted also on the Aldrich farm. The fruit of these trees was also dried and sold. Wooden racks were used for this purpose and the fruit dried over a slow fire, which was tended day and night until the work was done. Apple-picking time was a busy time for the Aldrich family. The whole family, as well as many hired hands were needed for the picking, the sorting, the selling. Mrs. Aldrich oversaw the sorting of the fruit.

A Nebraska Home

Of the four children born in Nebraska to Benton and Martha Jane Aldrich, two died at early ages; but Lina, who became Mrs. J. A. Butterfield of Pawnee City, and Alfred, who lived always on the original forty, grew to adulthood. Two additions to the original house were built, and more land was added to the farm. The parents planned and labored that each of their children might have a share of the farm for his home.

The family experienced all the inconveniences and privations incident to pioneer life, but the home with a mother like Mrs. Aldrich could not fail to be a happy one. Those who knew her spoke of her outstanding patience and successful handling of small children. A kind, intelligent guide to untutored minds, one to

57

encourage and help, one to be a companion to her children in each phase of their life. She was intensely interested in their education and taught her children in the home. Being one of a family of fourteen children, she had had but little schooling herself, but she embraced each and every opportunity to increase her own learning.

Before her marriage she had had a little experience in school teaching. Her sister, Margaret, had been elected to teach a term of school in Wisconsin, but when the time came she was unable because of sickness to fulfill her contract, so she persuaded Martha Jane to teach for her, for a short while. This school was composed partly of Indian and partly of white children. Martha Jane did so well at the job, and the children liked her so much, that the people persuaded her to finish the term, at the close of which she was given a teacher's certificate in recognition of her work.

Mrs. Aldrich attended school meetings in Nebraska and had the rare privilege of being a woman voter, because the Aldrich land was in her name. When a neighbor started a singing school, she walked through snow and cold, carrying her baby, that she might accompany her children to the school. With the exception of a few months of public school training which Karl had, none of the Aldrich children ever attended public schools in Nebraska, yet these young folk received splendid training and were carefully educated for practical life. Mrs. Aldrich saw that good textbooks were bought and studied. Books on botany, physical geography, and the like were very welcome in this home of nature lovers.

It was not long after the family settled in Nebraska that a neighborhood library was started. One corner of the Aldrich dwelling was fitted up, and with a half dozen neighbors who joined in the enterprise, the Clifton Public Library, the first public library in Nemaha County, was begun. Scientific, historical, biographical works, and books of fiction soon loaded down the shelves and the Aldrich children had access to many good books. This library soon grew so popular that parties from miles distant were regular readers.

The Clifton Post Office, established May 1868, was located in the Aldrich home, with Mr. Aldrich the Postmaster. This office brought a stream of callers and added responsibilities to the home.

These cares did not prevent Mrs. Aldrich from going to the homes of neighbors to help in the times of sickness, death, or distress. One former neighbor, who is living today, often tells how her own life was saved by Mrs. Aldrich.

It was after the birth of her first baby and the new mother lay dangerously ill. Kind neighbors flocked to the home with good intentions and many congratulations for the parents of a new baby. The ensuing excitement was proving too much for the patient, when Mrs. Aldrich appeared.

"Do you not know?" she said, " that in this house lies a woman dangerously sick who must not hear one bit of noise?"

In a firm yet kindly way she quickly dispersed the visitors and cleared the house of unnecessary people. Then, entering the sickroom where the young mother lay tossing restlessly, she calmed and soothed her and soon the patient dropped off to refreshing sleep.

This same neighbor tells also of an incident which happened when she was but a child in her parents home. A little sister lay dying and the household was wrapped in sorrow. Hearts were heavy. A terrible storm of blizzard-like intensity was raging. But neither the bitter wind nor the deep snow prevented Mrs. Aldrich from visiting that home.

"We felt as though an angel straight from heaven entered when she came," relates this neighbor.

These acts of kindness and calls of love were part of Mrs. Aldrich's very life. She did not think of herself when she saw the need of a friend or neighbor. Yet she took time to train her children carefully, to entertain the many callers at the home, and to take active part in the affairs of the community, outstanding among which was the Farmers' Institute — later known as Johnson Farmers' Institute—which held its first meeting in Brock, Nebraska (1882). She, like her husband and many others, was interested in the problems of the farmer and farm life.

In 1896 Mrs. Aldrich delivered an address, a duty of her office as Lady President to which she had been elected. At one time she gave an interesting talk on "Gardening," and 1892 "Care for the Sick" — a subject about which she was well-versed from varied experiences.

She entered into the discussions which were such a helpful part of these meetings, offered prizes for best piece of knitting and darning done; and met and associated with the outsiders who came as speakers at the institute.

Among the latter were many professors from the State University of Nebraska. Some of these men became friends of the family, visiting at the Aldrich home. Dr. Charles E. Bessey, Prof. Lawrence Bruner, and Prof. S. R. Thompson found the Aldrich farm a welcome place of delightful associations.[10]

---

[10] Charles Edwin Bessey (1845-1915) was a leading American botanist who served the University of Nebraska starting in 1884; Lawrence Bruner (1856-1937) was an entomologist who taught at the University of Nebraska from 1888 onward; and Samuel Rankin Thompson (1833-1896) was the first Professor of Agriculture (1871) and the first Dean of the College of Agriculture (1872-1875) at the University of Nebraska. In what appears to be a list of contacts for 1884, Thompson included the name of "B. Aldrich – Brock" (Samuel R. Thompson Papers, Notes and Memorabilia, RG 8/8/11, University Archives, University of Nebraska-Lincoln).

J. R. Huffman, who was one of a group of hired men on the Aldrich farm about 1883, wrote later in the "Nebraska Farmer"[11] of Mrs. Aldrich's influence:

> "One thousand farmers in southeastern Nebraska can testify to words of wisdom and encouragement from her lips in farmers' institute. Her motherly advice, her helping hand in sickness, her soothing words to the dying, her sympathy for the poor, and respect for all the laws of nature, made her one of the sweetest and best-loved old ladies that has ever contributed to the greatness of Nebraska."

During her own childhood Mrs. Aldrich's father had had the care of a great many sheep, and her mother had taught the girls of the family to knit stockings, mittens, and other wearing apparel. Knitting therefore, had been throughout her life one of Mrs. Aldrich's favorite pastimes, and she enjoyed in later years knitting for her grandchildren. She also liked to teach her grandchildren reading, spelling, and arithmetic before they started to public school.

The last two years of Mrs. Aldrich's life passed pleasantly in a more up-to-date house, built (1911) quite close to the original house, which was torn down and removed from the dooryard. This new structure became the home of Alfred Aldrich and family who remodeled it a few years ago. It is now the home of Mrs. Cremora Aldrich,[12] widow of Alfred,[13] who passed away October 17, 1933, on this farm where he was born and where he lived his life amid the trees and shrubs which his parents had set out and which he cared for as a sacred memory.

The old elm, referred to by Mr. Huffman, grew, in 1866, out of the dirt banked against the walls of the stone house. It was allowed to remain, and spread as a canopy over the old home. Still a thrifty tree, it stands, beautiful and wide-spreading, in the present dooryard and furnishes much shelter with its spread of over ninety feet.

---

[11] Reference here is to comments in J.R. Huffman's column from Nemaha County, "Farm Glimpses," which appeared regularly in the *Nebraska Farmer* and, in this instance, on September 3, 1913: 858-859.

[12] Cremora Aldrich died at age 78 on December 26, 1955, while visiting a daughter in New Jersey. See the obituary, "Brock Lady Died In New Jersey City," *Nemaha County Herald*, December 30, 1955: 1.

[13] See the obituary, "Alfred Aldrich Summoned Hence," *Nemaha County Herald, October 19, 1933:5. He was born December 23, 1874.*

It was among the people she loved and served and amid the surroundings she enjoyed that Mrs. Aldrich passed at the age of seventy-seven years, five months, and twenty-two days. Mr. Huffman's tribute is quoted:

"Hundreds of neighbors and friends were there (at the funeral) with bowed heads to pay respects to the fine old lady who had perhaps traveled more miles to nurse the sick, to help the poor, and to console the dying than any other woman who has ever lived in Nemaha County. Mrs. Aldrich did not break into the ranks of the idle. When she could not further add to the comforts of her own family she looked about her for others whom she could help. Her body was laid away in the pretty cemetery at Johnson. Flowers will bloom over her grave next spring. Her husband, children, grand-children, and her hundreds of friends will miss her, but this thought is consoling to us all — the county and the state are richer as a result of her industry and influence."

———————————

4

A MODEL FOR ESTIMATING THE TOTAL NUMBER OF HOTEL/MOTEL AND BED & BREAKFAST UNITS IN NEBRASKA COMMUNITIES [1]

Tom Doering

Introduction

This report presents the results of a study of the major variables affecting the distribution of hotel, motel, and bed & breakfast units, or lodging rooms, in Nebraska. The study gathered data from published resources and from a survey of lodging establishments in the state. It then applied correlation and multiple regression analysis to the data gathered.

The primary result of this study is an equation for estimating the expected total number of hotel/motel and bed & breakfast units in communities in Nebraska on the basis of local population, highway traffic counts, and distance to the nearest larger city. The equation results identify communities where possible shortages of hotel/motel and bed & breakfast units exist and therefore where investment in commercial lodging might profitably be made.

The study area is all cities and towns in Nebraska where at least one hotel/motel or bed & breakfast establishment operates. There are 166 such communities in the state.

Data on Hotel/Motel and Bed & Breakfast Units

Preliminary data on existing hotel/motel and bed & breakfast units were obtained from local convention and visitors bureaus, chambers of commerce, telephone listings, and community contacts. Final figures were acquired through a direct mailing of questionnaires to each known hotel/motel and bed & breakfast establishment in the state, inquiring about the number of units. The survey responses plus the earlier contacts yielded data on units available per establishment that could then be summed to produce, for each community, the total number of units.

---

[1] Revision of a study originally completed in 1994.

Other Variables

Data were also gathered for three other variables: highway traffic counts, population, and distance to the nearest larger city. These variables were all believed to be associated with the number of hotel/motel and bed & breakfast units in communities.

The source of data on highway traffic was the "1993 State of Nebraska Traffic Flow Map," produced by the Nebraska Department of Roads. Taken from the map were annual average daily traffic counts for all major Interstate highways and Nebraska primary highways at approximately a ten-mile distance from each community with a hotel/motel or bed & breakfast establishment. The choice of the ten-mile distance was to minimize as much as possible the effects of local resident traffic. Summing the figures for the monitored highways around a community produced a total annual average daily traffic count. Proceeding from the assumption that the need for commercial lodging and other highway services grows as the highway traffic grows, it is believed that a strong positive relationship exists between highway traffic and the number of hotel/motel and bed & breakfast units in a community.

Data on community population were taken from *1992 Local Population Estimates*, produced by the U.S. Bureau of the Census. Population should be expected to have a high positive correlation with the number of hotel/motel and bed & breakfast units in a community, since larger communities are more apt to be centers for business, conventions, entertainment, recreation, and family and social gatherings — all of which stimulate commercial lodging use.

Figures on distance to the nearest larger city along major highways were found on the "1992 Official Nebraska Highway Map," produced by the Nebraska Department of Roads. A high positive correlation is believed to exist between the number of lodging units and this distance measurement, since a town located within a few miles of a larger community seemingly experiences less traveler demand for (and therefore fewer) lodging units than a more isolated community of similar size. Put another way, the more isolated community is believed to have more lodging units because there are fewer alternative nearby communities of its size or larger in which a traveler can stay overnight.

Correlation and Multiple Regression Analysis

The correlations between the number of hotel/motel and bed & breakfast units and each of the other variables are in Figure 4.1. As expected, all three independent variables have high positive correlations with the number of lodging units, with the population variable producing the highest correlation.

Based on the correlation results, a multiple regression equation was produced to predict the number of hotel/motel and bed & breakfast units in communities. The order in which each independent variable appears in the equation is according to how much it contributes to explaining the dependent variable (number of units).

The standard error for the equation is 98. Consequently, in approximately 68 percent of the communities the number of hotel/motel and bed & breakfast units predicted by the equation will be within 98 rooms of the actual number of units. In 95 percent of the communities, the predicted number will be within 197 units (or within two standard errors).

A very high 98.4 percent of the variation in the number of lodging units among the communities is explained by the joint linear influences of the independent variables. The equation is as follows:

$$Total\ hotel/motel\ and\ bed\ \&\ breakfast\ units =$$
$$.015(Population)+.007(Traffic)+3.996(Distance)-85.658$$

This equation may be used to predict the number of hotel/motel and bed & breakfast units in individual Nebraska communities. For example, to find the predicted number of lodging units (Y) in Ainsworth (the first community listed in Table 4.1), enter into the equation the actual values of Ainsworth's total highway traffic, population, and distance to the nearest larger city. Therefore:

$$Y=.015(1,810)+.007(1,200)+3.996(45)-85.658$$
$$Y=130$$

The equation predicts that Ainsworth, because of highway traffic, population, and distance to the nearest larger city, should have 130 lodging units. The actual number is 95, thereby producing a difference of 35. In other words, for Ainsworth, the equation overpredicts (compared to the actual number) by 35 units.

The multiple regression equation was used to estimate the number of hotel/motel and bed & breakfast units in each of the 166 cities and towns studied. Actual values, predicted values, and the differences are in Table 4.1.

Analysis of the Residuals

The predictions for eight communities lie beyond two standard errors, or 197 units, of the actual number of units (see Table 4.1). This prompts discussion of the particular characteristics of these communities that might have influenced this over- or under-estimation. The eight communities are Alliance (-198), Fremont (-203), Kearney (+405), Lincoln (-391), North Platte (+603), Ogallala (+377), Sidney (+203), and South Sioux City (+304).

Among the communities having larger differences, or residuals, from the predicted number of hotel/motel and bed & breakfast units, the equation underestimates for four cities along Interstate 80 in central and western Nebraska (Kearney, North Platte, Ogallala, and Sidney). This may be explained by variations in traveler origins in the traffic counts dominated by Interstate 80 versus other highways. Travelers on Interstate 80 are more likely to be from outside Nebraska and traveling greater distances than travelers using non-Interstate routes. That intensifies the influence of Interstate 80 even beyond its comparatively high total traffic, leading to greater concentrations of commercial lodging than predicted by the equation.

Another community where the actual number of lodging units is greatly underestimated by the equation is South Sioux City. This may be explained by the equation's failure to account for South Sioux City's presence in the Sioux City, Iowa metropolitan area, the nearness of local gaming facilities, and the close proximity of Interstate 29 in Iowa.

For three cities — Alliance, Fremont, and Lincoln — the equation strongly overestimates the number of hotel/motel and bed & breakfast units. Here, the closeness of Fremont and Lincoln to a much larger community, Omaha, appears to have an effect not fully measured by the equation. Alliance might be overestimated due to the equation's not fully measuring the influence of Alliance's distance to the nearest larger city (Scottsbluff).

Of course, some additional variables may be included in the equation to help refine it. The variables could measure economies of scale or agglomeration (effects of a "motel row"), the influence of Interstate versus non-Interstate highway location, and quality differences among lodging establishments. However, there is often more subjectivity to these variables than the ones chosen, making them more difficult to measure. Because the equation produced in this study provides a reasonably "good fit" for the data, it could already be taking into account the two or three most important variables determining commercial lodging distribution. These variables have the added advantage of being reasonably straightforward to measure. So, in general, the equation could be useful in providing an initial look at the adequacy of the size of a Nebraska community's commercial lodging industry.

_____

FIGURE 4.1

CORRELATION

	Units	Population	Traffic	Distance
Units	1			
Population	0.973186	1		
Traffic	0.714898	0.676604096	1	
Distance	0.707066	0.619588147	0.468629	1

SUMMARY OUTPUT FOR HOTEL/MOTEL AND BED & BREAKFAST

Regression Statistics	
Multiple R	0.9843643
R Square	0.9689732
Adjusted R Square	0.9683986
Standard Error	98.34072
Observations	166

ANOVA

	df	SS	MS	F	Significance F
Regression	3	48927827	16309276	1686.4284	6.8028E-122
Residual	162	1566685.339	9670.8972		
Total	165	50494512.34			

	Coefficients	Standard Error	t Stat	P-value	Lower 95%	Upper 95%
Intercept	-85.65757	12.92456625	-6.6275	4.822E-10	-111.1799355	-60.135198
Population	0.0146653	0.000383193	38.271404	4.718E-83	0.01390864	0.015422
Traffic	0.0073191	0.001545335	4.7362504	4.727E-06	0.004267494	0.0103707
Distance	3.9955063	0.437029913	9.1424092	2.455E-16	3.132495625	4.858517

TABLE 4.1

Nebraska Hotel/Motel Units and Bed & Breakfast Units by Community and Predicted Units Based on Population, Highway Traffic Counts, and the Distance to the Nearest Larger City

City	Population (7/1/92)	Highway Traffic Counts	Distance to Nearest Larger city	Actual Hotel/Motel Units	Actual B & B Units	Actual Total Units	Predicted Total Units	Predicted Minus Actual Units
Ainsworth	1,810	1,200	45	91	4	95	129	34
Albion	1,838	-	41	40	-	40	105	65
Alliance	9,536	2,230	64	128	-	128	326	198
Alma	1,195	2,515	23	59	-	59	42	-17
Ansley	562	740	14	8	-	8	-16	-24
Arapahoe	985	2,940	15	31	-	31	10	-21
Arnold	659	-	35	4	-	4	64	60
Atkinson	1,319	1,695	18	15	-	15	18	3
Auburn	3,364	3,700	20	83	-	83	71	-12
Aurora	3,818	16,740	20	81	-	81	173	92
Bassett	733	1,850	17	56	-	56	7	-49
Bayard	1,144	2,140	15	10	-	10	7	-3
Beatrice	12,299	4,750	40	195	6	201	289	88
Beaver City	706	-	15	9	-	9	-15	-24
Beemer	653	3,905	8	15	-	15	-16	-31
Bellevue	30,994	4,700	10	398	-	398	443	45
Benkelman	1,133	660	21	15	-	15	20	5
Big Springs	479	10,110	20	62	6	68	75	7
Blair	6,974	6,525	25	50	6	56	164	108
Bloomfield	1,171	-	20	21	-	21	11	-10
Blue Hill	764	1,690	18	15	-	15	10	-5
Brewster	14	-	15	-	4	4	-26	-30
Bridgeport	1,587	3,420	36	33	-	33	106	73
Broken Bow	3,846	1,600	46	137	3	140	166	26
Brownville	144	2,360	5	-	5	5	-46	-51
Burwell	1,245	-	16	39	-	39	-3	-42
Butte	418	-	9	9	-	9	-44	-53
Callaway	520	-	26	4	5	9	26	17

TABLE 4.1

City	Population (7/1/92)	Highway Traffic Counts	Distance to Nearest Larger city	Actual Hotel/Motel Units	Actual B & B Units	Actual Total Units	Predicted Total Units	Predicted Minus Actual Units
Cambridge	1,099	1,790	25	11	5	16	43	27
Cedar Rapids	398	-	16	-	3	3	-16	-19
Central City	2,927	2,300	18	29		29	46	17
Chadron	5,488	2,645	57	199	10	209	242	33
Chappell	990	5,965	16	16	6	22	36	14
Chester	340	2,400	9	13	-	13	-27	-40
Clay Center	843	-	9	8	-	8	-37	-45
Columbus	19,818	4,435	47	483	3	486	425	-61
Cozad	3,935	13,890	14	65	-	65	130	65
Crawford	1,098	1,120	23	38	4	42	31	-11
Creighton	1,164	-	13	8	-	8	-17	-25
Crete	4,934	3,370	29	40	2	42	127	85
Crofton	773	-	15	8	-	8	-14	-22
Crookston	109	590	11	-	4	4	-36	-40
Curtis	770	-	37	6	-	6	73	67
Dannebrog	334	-	10	-	7	7	-41	-48
David City	2,538	-	17	18	-	18	19	1
Dixon	86	-	3	-	4	4	-72	-76
Edgar	609	-	15	10	-	10	-17	-27
Elgin	688	-	11	-	6	6	-32	-38
Elm Creek	877	14,335	16	67	-	67	96	29
Elwood	713	1,050	13	20	-	20	-16	-36
Ericson	115	-	14	12	-	12	-28	-40
Ewing	455	1,305	21	6	-	6	14	8
Fairbury	4,238	2,140	27	51	8	59	100	41
Falls City	4,692	2,110	55	108	-	108	218	110
Fremont	23,606	11,150	36	279	4	283	486	203
Fullerton	1,448	-	18	5	-	5	7	2
Geneva	2,272	3,285	24	26	-	26	68	42
Genoa	1,057	-	16	5	-	5	-6	-11
Gering	7,942	2,150	3	69	-	69	59	-10
Gibbon	1,512	16,040	13	19	-	19	106	87

TABLE 4.1

City	Population (7/1/92)	Highway Traffic Counts	Distance to Nearest Larger city	Actual Hotel/Motel Units	Actual B & B Units	Actual Total Units	Predicted Total Units	Predicted Minus Actual Units
Gordon	1,761	710	46	67	4	71	129	58
Gothenburg	3,325	12,660	10	58	-	58	96	38
Grand Island	40,036	24,410	92	1,237	5	1,242	1048	-194
Grant	1,174	-	19	-	4	4	7	3
Greeley	560	890	21	-	2	2	13	11
Greenwood	556	27,050	6	63	-	63	144	81
Gretna	2,395	2,590	8	-	4	4	0	-4
Halsey	104	670	10	11	-	11	-39	-50
Harrison	262	530	27	10	2	12	30	18
Hartington	1,556	-	24	16	-	16	33	17
Hastings	22,740	3,515	26	348	5	353	377	24
Hayes Center	243	-	14	4	-	4	-26	-30
Hebron	1,753	3,340	22	63	-	63	52	-11
Hemingford	956	680	18	-	4	4	5	1
Henderson	986	15,900	17	34	-	34	113	79
Holdrege	5,703	3,160	30	71	3	74	141	67
Howells	599	1,400	6	-	2	2	-43	-45
Humphrey	704	-	10	13	-	13	-35	-48
Hyannis	215	500	38	11	-	11	73	62
Imperial	1,984	500	48	24	-	24	139	115
Kearney	24,889	14,840	42	957	4	961	556	-405
Kimball	2,542	8,330	37	172	-	172	160	-12
Laurel	936	1,290	14	19	3	22	-7	-29
Lemoyne	-	-	17	52	-	52	-18	-70
Lexington	7,986	14,550	35	206	5	211	278	67
Lincoln	197,488	35,930	58	2,901	13	2,914	3305	391
Lodgepole	343	6,370	10	6	-	6	6	0
Long Pine	404	2,350	9	16	7	23	-27	-50
Loup City	1,126	-	27	34	3	37	39	2
Lyons	1,088	2,240	27	6	-	6	55	49
Madrid	251	-	10	-	3	3	-42	-45
Marquette	225	-	9	50	-	50	-46	-96

TABLE 4.1

City	Population (7/1/92)	Highway Traffic Counts	Distance to Nearest Larger city	Actual Hotel/Motel Units	Actual B & B Units	Actual Total Units	Predicted Total Units	Predicted Minus Actual Units
McCook	7,936	4,865	68	243	3	246	338	92
Merriman	141	710	24	8	-	8	17	9
Milford	1,876	18,800	13	31	-	31	131	100
Minatare	766	3,370	10	18	-	18	-10	-28
Minden	2,666	1,980	23	87	3	90	60	-30
Mullen	499	650	70	12	-	12	206	194
Murdock	293	-	6	-	2	2	-57	-59
Nebraska City	6,591	7,910	27	233	5	238	177	-61
Neligh	1,710	1,755	33	24	3	27	84	57
Nelson	596	-	13	7	-	7	-25	-32
Niobrara	358	-	11	15	-	15	-36	-51
Norfolk	21,792	6,965	77	492	-	492	593	101
North Platte	23,262	15,450	100	1,371	-	1,371	768	-603
Oakland	1,288	2,030	14	16	3	19	4	-15
Ogallala	5,000	12,530	52	664	-	664	287	-377
Omaha	339,671	47,520	187	6,157	9	6,166	5991	-175
O'Neill	3,814	3,095	76	189	-	189	297	108
Orchard	428	535	11	9	-	9	-32	-41
Ord	2,429	-	49	63	-	63	146	83
Orleans	462	-	7	25	-	25	-51	-76
Osceola	825	995	8	10	-	10	-34	-44
Oskosh	922	1,550	29	25	-	25	55	30
Osmond	739	1,050	10	-	4	4	-27	-31
Oxford	941	605	19	13	-	13	8	-5
Papillion	10,840	-	8	40	-	40	105	65
Pawnee City	930	-	14	10	2	12	-16	-28
Paxton	541	11,940	12	-	5	5	58	53
Pender	1,181	-	18	10	-	10	4	-6
Plainview	1,327	1,320	12	28	3	31	-9	-40
Ponca	869	-	26	16	-	16	31	15
Randolph	966	1,095	23	16	-	16	28	12
Ravenna	1,404	1,035	29	-	4	4	58	54

TABLE 4.1

City	Population (7/1/92)	Highway Traffic Counts	Distance to Nearest Larger city	Actual Hotel/Motel Units	Actual B & B Units	Actual Total Units	Predicted Total Units	Predicted Minus Actual Units
Red Cloud	1,182	1,200	29	18	4	22	56	34
Republican City	192	640	8	22	-	22	-46	-68
Rushville	1,113	1,690	14	33	-	33	-1	-34
Sargent	682	600	21	13	-	13	13	0
Schuyler	4,281	4,220	19	51	-	51	84	33
Scottsbluff	14,051	6,560	112	487	-	487	616	129
Scribner	932	4,005	12	-	4	4	5	1
Seward	5,682	20,160	25	56	-	56	245	189
Sidney	5,961	8,300	41	425	4	429	226	-203
South Sioux City	9,886	7,995	2	430	-	430	126	-304
Spalding	574	-	20	-	5	5	3	-2
Spencer	521	735	31	-	15	15	51	36
Springview	273	500	32	12	-	12	50	38
St. Libory	-	2,780	10	-	2	2	-25	-27
St. Paul	2,041	1,400	21	35	-	35	38	3
Steinauer	92	-	7	-	5	5	-56	-61
Stratton	405	820	12	8	-	8	-26	-34
Superior	2,346	-	38	25	-	25	101	76
Sutherland	1,021	12,810	20	16	-	16	103	87
Sutton	1,363	1,030	22	6	4	10	30	20
Syracuse	1,639	5,020	17	10	-	10	43	33
Table Rock	287	-	7	-	3	3	-53	-56
Taylor	188	280	9	6	-	6	-45	-51
Tecumseh	1,657	900	21	15	-	15	29	14
Tekamah	1,791	885	17	8	-	8	15	7
Thedford	220	1,420	26	24	-	24	32	8
Tilden	883	2,690	14	6	-	6	3	-3
Trenton	595	990	22	12	2	14	18	4
Uehling	284	2,025	6	5	-	5	-43	-48
Valentine	2,824	1,605	76	187	16	203	271	68
Wahoo	3,754	5,220	24	17	3	20	103	83
Wallace	310	-	24	3	-	3	15	12

74

TABLE 4.1

City	Population (7/1/92)	Highway Traffic Counts	Distance to Nearest Larger city	Actual Hotel/Motel Units	Actual B & B Units	Actual Total Units	Predicted Total Units	Predicted Minus Actual Units
Waterloo	497	6,615	3	-	3	3	-18	-21
Wauneta	616	1,120	19	4	-	4	7	3
Wausa	579	-	13	5	-	5	-25	-30
Wayne	5,180	-	31	98	3	101	114	13
West Point	3,121	3,905	34	27	3	30	125	95
Wilber	1,484	-	10	-	10	10	-24	-34
Wisner	1,218	3,710	17	7	-	7	27	20
Wood River	1,170	16,300	14	18	-	18	107	89
Wymore	1,608	1,180	13	8	-	8	-1	-9
York	7,987	21,280	44	474	-	474	363	-111

5

GEOGRAPHERS AT WORK IN A STATE TRANSPORTATION AGENCY

Steve Kale

The Oregon Department of Transportation (ODOT) employs about 4,100 persons, of whom no fewer than 25 have or are working toward degrees in geography. About half of those with degrees in geography work in field offices of the five ODOT regions; another 30 percent work for ODOT's Transportation Development Branch in Salem. Most of the remainder work in the Technical Services Branch in Salem, primarily in the Project Support Services Section. Twelve employees have the words "planner" or "planning" in their job titles, nine employees are managers or supervisors, and five work in environmental or project management/coordination.

The majority of ODOT's geographers were educated in Oregon's colleges and universities. Schools most represented are Oregon State University (7 employees) and the University of Oregon (6 employees). The remainder have degrees from Portland State University, Western Oregon State College, or out-of-state schools. Several geographers also have degrees in business administration, economics, geology, public policy, and urban and regional planning. Highest degrees obtained in geography are Ph.D. (2), Masters (13), and Bachelors (9).

ODOT's planners are responsible for coordinating state, regional, and local transportation planning. Project and program managers work mostly with transportation planning or environmental analysis and documentation. Specific duties include arranging and leading public meetings; writing memos, letters, reports, and other documents; interpreting laws and regulations and assuring their compliance; writing contracts and interagency agreements; preparing requests for consultant proposals and managing consultant contracts; and working with data and other information.

Skills required include: writing concisely in non-technical terms, speaking coherently at meetings, working in a team environment, understanding maps and how they are used to show transportation and other features, working independently with few guidelines and little supervision, and completing projects on time and on budget.

Geographers at ODOT are heavily involved in corridor and modal planning. Corridor plans deal with 31 major transportation corridors in Oregon. Modal plans address movements of people and goods via autos, trucks, trains, buses, and other modes. Corridor and modal planning are multi-year efforts to improve decisions about transportation investments.

As transportation investment needs outpace funding levels, state governments are exploring a variety of alternatives for improving efficiency and stretching available dollars. At ODOT, this has included contracting with universities. Two work efforts illustrate arrangements with Oregon's colleges and universities.

ODOT's Inventory and Mapping Unit has worked closely with the University or Oregon's Department of Geography to prepare the biennial State Highway Map. For the most recent map the department's Cartography Laboratory did the edit checking of map features. The department also is helping ODOT update about 240 city maps on the lab's Intergraph Computer Aided Drafting system.

To identify existing and allowed land uses in the state's 36 counties and nearly 175 cities along major transportation corridors, ODOT contracted with five universities. About 40 geography students conducted windshield surveys and inventoried local comprehensive plans, zoning ordinances, and amount of developable land. Three contracts were with geography departments at Eastern Oregon State College, Oregon State University, and Southern Oregon State College. The Planning, Public Policy, and Management School at the University or Oregon and the Center for Urban Studies at Portland State University held the other contracts.

Planning and environmental documentation and analysis will continue to have an important role at ODOT. This assertion is supported by ODOT's emphasis on planning and environmental analysis in efforts to improve the project selection and development process, state requirements for integrating transportation and land use planning, and the U.S. Department of Transportation's emphasis on better planning through the provisions of the Intermodal Surface Transportation Efficiency Act of 1991.

It is unclear whether Departments of Geography at colleges and universities will continue to provide the types of education and training relevant to ODOT's mission and activities. About half of ODOT's geographers are involved in transportation planning and land use planning. Training in these two areas typically is provided through courses in economic, urban, and resource geography, subjects which seem to be receiving less emphasis in Oregon's colleges and universities.

While planning-related fields are receiving less emphasis in geography departments, they are receiving more emphasis at two of Oregon's universities with programs in planning and public policy. These programs may play an increasingly important role in the training of students in subjects relevant to ODOT's future needs.

On the positive side, Geographic Information Systems technology is becoming more important at ODOT. Thus far, however, only three geographers at ODOT are employed in mapping/GIS positions. This is in part because mapping position descriptions in the past have been written to favor existing staff following an career path in engineering specializations. In recent years GIS and mapping job announcements have been written more broadly to allow job-seekers in many fields, including geography, to qualify.

Shifts in politics often play a role directly or indirectly in the role of geographers at state transportation agencies. Planning and environmental analysis are sometimes adversely perceived by those supporting a *laissez faire* approach to meeting societal needs and desires. Such perceptions may lead to reductions in budgets for activities considered unnecessary or overemphasized. Over the long term, political shifts may be as important as any other factor when assessing job prospects for geographers in transportation or other governmental agencies.

6

ROSCOE POUND AND THE SAND HILLS
BOTANICAL EXPEDITION OF 1892 [1]

Michael R. Hill

Roscoe Pound's 1892 botanical expedition through the Sand Hills region of western Nebraska was a defining event in the origin and history of the American school of plant ecology. It was a propitious beginning. In 1892, Pound was still a young man, only twenty-two years of age. During his lifetime (1870-1964), Pound became an accomplished interdisciplinary scholar who made foundational contributions in three major intellectual disciplines: botany, sociology, *and* law.[2] It is, perhaps, Pound's extraordinary stature and later reputation as a jurist that in part dulls the collective memory of his earlier and no less important work in botany and sociology.[3] My task here is to illuminate one of the pivotal events in Pound's botanical career. Further, the 1892 expedition was not an isolated or exceptional event, but provided a conceptual and methodological template for several of Pound's major contributions in other fields, especially his later work on the Survey of Criminal Justice in Cleveland, the National Commission on Law Observance and Enforcement, and his field study of criminal justice in China (Hill 1989).

It is comparatively recently that Pound's early botanical work, after a long hiatus, is receiving due scholarly attention. Most notably, David Wigdor (1974) opened this re-examination in a chapter in what remains today the best overall Pound biography. Ronald Tobey (1981) furthered the examination in his study of academic botany at the University of Nebraska, *Saving the Prairies: The Life Cycle of the Founding School of American Plant Ecology, 1895-1955*. I am pleased to contribute to this lengthening line of inquiry (Hill 1988, 1989, 1993, 2011), and offer my comments in that light.

---

[1] Revision of a paper presented to the interdisciplinary symposium on *Exploring the Great Plains* sponsored by the Center for Great Plains Studies, University of Nebraska-Lincoln, April 1992.

[2] This assertion is advanced elsewhere in greater detail (Hill 1989). For direct bibliographic evidence of Pound's extraordinary interdisciplinary grasp, examine the detailed bibliography of his published works in Setaro (1942).

[3] The perverse and often punishing barriers to interdisciplinary communication constructed by department-based academic disciplines in American universities also contribute to this outcome.

Pound was an extraordinary young man whose undergraduate career at the University of Nebraska was marked with enthusiastic *joie de vivre,* high academic honors, organizational elan, and a bachelor's degree in 1888. He was the playful yet serious instigator of the Sem. Bot. (or *Seminarium Botanicum*), the student scientific club that transformed the course of botany in the United States. The history of the Sem. Bot. is documented elsewhere (Wigdor, 1974, Tobey 1981; Hill 1988, 1989).[4] What is important here is that the Sem. Bot. was the organizational umbrella under which the botanically most significant of Pound's corporate inventions emerged in 1892, specifically: the Botanical Survey of Nebraska.

The formation of the Botanical Survey, with Pound as its Director, evolved in tandem with Pound's transformation from a novice graduate student into a mature scientist. Pound earned a masters degree in botany in 1889 at the University of Nebraska[5] and then went to Harvard intending to study in Asa Gray's prestigious department. Gray died, however, and Pound decided alternatively on a year of courses in the Harvard Law School. He returned to Lincoln a year later, in 1890, his funds depleted, and pursued parallel intellectual tracks, studying law in his father's legal firm and initiating doctoral studies in botany at the University of Nebraska.

Figure 6.1. Roscoe Pound

Pound's 1898 doctoral dissertation, *The Phytogeography of Nebraska,* co-authored with Frederic Clements (Pound and Clements 1898a, 1900), changed the course of plant ecology in the United States (Tobey 1981).[6] As Raymond Pool, a later Nebraska botanist and faculty member, once wrote:

---

[4] See also The *Book of the Sem. Bot.* (a 29-page historical pamphlet written, probably by Pound, sometime after 1906) and "The Records of the Sem. Bot" (the handwritten journal of the club's activities). Both are found in Department of Botany, Records of the Botanical Seminar, 1886-1970, University Archives, University of Nebraska-Lincoln.

[5] The specifics of Pound's master's degree work are found in Hill (1988).

[6] See also Pound and Clements (1989b, 1898c) for additional innovations.

80

This was the first noteworthy and truly scientific treatise on the subject of plant geography in America and at once it attracted the attention of botanists throughout the world . . . . It was a *masterpiece* and it served to establish Nebraska as an internationally known leader in that field . . . . [7]

And, Clements surmised:

It is perhaps not too much to say that out of the latter [*The Phytogeography of Nebraska*] developed a synthesis of the new field of dynamic ecology, which has since spread over the globe . . . . [8]

Methodologically, *The Phytogeography* centrally depended upon the cooperative, state-wide specimen collecting efforts of Pound, Clements, and their student colleagues in the Sem. Bot. and the Botanical Survey of Nebraska.

When Pound began his doctoral project, the collection of plant specimens in Nebraska was often haphazard and serendipitous.[9] A large number of Nebraska plants had been collected by students in the Sem. Bot., by university professors (notably Charles Bessey), and by amateur enthusiasts, all of which were catalogued by Herbert Webber (1890, 1892), a member of the Sem. Bot. But in presenting the "Plan and Scope" of the Botanical Survey, the members wrote (in a voice that reflects Pound's dominant influence):

To continue to add to Mr. Webber's catalogue in a haphazard way will needlessly and indefinitely postpone the complete presentation of our flora which is desirable. Systematic botanical exploration of the state will bring such a catalogue much sooner, make it afar better

---

[7] Pool to Sayre, 13 July 1946, Paul Sayre Collection, University Archives, University of Iowa, Iowa City.

[8] Unpublished reminiscence by Clements enclosed with letter, Clements to Sayre, 17 January 1945, Box 125, Dr. Edith S. Clements and Dr. Frederic Clements Collection, Division of Rare Books and Special Collections, The Library, University of Wyoming (hereafter, Clements reminiscence).

[9] Indeed, some of the botanical reports may have been fraudulent. Pound and Clements (1900: 19) noted, "The pretentious catalogue, enumerating some 2,000 species, put forth by Professor Aughey in 1875, and his lists given in other writings, might lead one to suppose that the flora of the State was well known when he severed his connection with the University. The facts are otherwise."

one, and cannot fail to develop many things of practical as well as scientific importance.[10]

The significant point here is that Pound's 1892 Sand Hills expedition was the inaugural collecting effort reported under the auspices of the Botanical Survey of Nebraska.[11]

The 1892 expedition was not the earliest example of plant collecting in and about the Sand Hills region,[12] but, importantly, it was the first to be conceptualized as part of a larger, coordinated, and specifically scientific effort. Pound's role as the organizational and intellectual leader of this larger project was crucial. As Frederic Clements later reminisced:

> Although the Seminar owed much to Dr. Bessey indirectly, its actual origin and the brilliance of its performance through two decades were due to Pound's insight and perspective, as well as to his scientific cast of mind. This is attested by its course after he left the University, when it gradually lost momentum and finally ceased to exist.[13]

Throughout the formative period of American plant ecology, the Botanical Survey of Nebraska published its investigations (often with Pound's personal subvention), and Pound presented accounts of the Survey's work to the Nebraska Academy of Sciences. In his first formal report to the Academy on the work of the Survey, Pound (1894a: 7) began in part:

> Since the organization of the Survey, the following collections have been made: In 1892, Mr. Smith and Mr. Pound traversed the sand-hill region and the lake region of Cherry county. They also collected between Johnstown and O'Neill, and between O'Neill and Lincoln.

---

[10] Botanical Survey of Nebraska (1892), I: 6. The "Plan and Scope" statement was unsigned but Pound was likely the principal author.

[11] Cf., Botanical Survey of Nebraska (1893), II: Report on Collections Made in 1892.

[12] For lists of relevant collecting trips in Nebraska, see Clements (1894), Pound and Clements (1900: 17-22), and McKelvey (1955). For a bibliography of relevant scientific studies of the time, see Pound (1894b).

[13] Clements reminiscence.

Such was the bare description of Pound's 450-mile trek across Nebraska during July and August, 1892.[14] For a map of the route, see Figure 6.1, below.

The preceding introduction places the 1892 Sand Hills expedition in a far more systematic and scientifically significant context than one would glean initially from a local newspaper account at the time. The arrival of Pound and his companion, Jared Smith, at the western starting point of their trip made sufficient stir to warrant the following notice:

> J.G. Smith and Roscoe Pound, two young gentlemen from Lincoln, arrived in Alliance Wednesday to undertake a novel expedition. The boys are out on a botanizing excursion for the State Board of Agriculture and will work across the country from here to O'Neill, making the journey afoot and expecting to consume thirty days tinle in the hills between the two places. Their caravan, consisting of a small pony drawing a road cart, upon which was loaded their trappings and provisions, attracted considerable attention as the boys marched out of town on their long tramp.[15]

Although subsequently reported as the first expedition of the Botanical Survey per se, it appears that Pound did travel under the banner of the State Board of Agriculture after having secured funds, via Bessey, from the Board in the amount of $50.00.[16]

---

[14] Cf., Pound gave progress reports to the Nebraska Academy of Sciences in 1893 (published in abstract (Pound 1894a)); 1894 (not published, but listed in the "Program of the Fifth Annual Meeting," *Publications of the Nebraska Academy of Sciences,* V, Proceedings, 1894:1895, p. 6); and 1897 (not published, but listed in the "Minutes of the Annual Meetings" for 1897, *Publications of the Nebraska Academy of Sciences,* VII, Proceedings, 1897-1900, p. 5). In 1898, Pound presented a paper to the Academy on "The Phytogeographical Features of the Sand-Hill Region" ("Minutes of the Annual Meetings," *Publications of the Nebraska Academy of Sciences,* VII, Proceedings, 1897-1900, p. 6). Pound's final report to the Academy was offered in December 1900 and published in abstract (Pound 1901). Pound (as well as Bessey) was a charter member of the Nebraska Academy of Sciences, and Pound was elected to the Board of Directors for the year 1898.

[15] The *Alliance* [Nebraska] *Times,* Friday, July 8, 1892, Vol. 6, No.4, p. 1, col. 2.

[16] The expedition was financed, at least in part, by the State of Nebraska via Charles Bessey's position on the Nebraska State Board of Agriculture as "State Botanist." Pound noted on June 29, 1892, "I drew my warrant for expenses today and am in for it" (Pound to Hershey, 29 June 1892, Paul Sayre Collection, University Archives, University of Iowa, Iowa City). The funding mechanism appears to be a warrant drawn against the State Board of Agriculture by Bessey on June 23,1892, for a "Botany appropriation," in the amount of $50.00 (cf., Warrant No.88, June 23, to C.E. Bessey, "List of Warrants," *Nebraska State Board of Agriculture, Annual Report,* 1892, p.26).

The question of external funding for scientific research was a matter of no little gravity for the young botanists in the Survey. They announced with a flourish that:

> the Survey will be entirely under the control of the Seminar .The Seminar selects the members and assigns the work, and its members will bear the entire expense of the Survey . . . . [17]

And there was a considered rationale for assuming the cost themselves:

> In entering upon the Survey, the Seminar is fully aware of the difficulties which must necessarily beset such an undertaking when conducted by private means and enterprise. But if there are difficulties attending the conduct of the Survey by private enterprise, there are also undoubted advantages. The members need never fear to do purely scientific work, they need not spend their time in strengthening their official rather than their scientific position, and they need not be distracted from more important matters by the burden of continually demonstrating to doubting Thomases the practical nature of their undertaking. [18]

Given that Pound accepted funds from the Nebraska State Board of Agriculture, it requires some mental gymnastics to reconcile the Survey's official claim to be funded at the start entirely from private sources in as much as the 1892 Sand Hills expedition was the first collecting trip officially associated with the Botanical Survey of Nebraska. The official date of organization for the Survey, however, is reported as August 24, 1892, some *two weeks after* Pound and Smith returned to Lincoln. The verbal sleight of hand published by the Survey states that:

> although the general plan of the Survey was agreed upon in June of this year, ... no little collecting [was] done in accordance with it in July and August. [19]

---

[17] Botanical Survey of Nebraska (1892), I: 5. Emphasis added.

[18] Botanical Survey of Nebraska (1892), I: 5.

[19] This refers specifically to the 1892 summer trip made by Pound and Smith. Botanical Survey of Nebraska (1892), I: 5.

By setting the official date of organization in August, several days *after* Smith and Pound returned to Lincoln, the Seminar's prospectus could state "honestly" that it was a wholly private enterprise.[20]

I infer that Pound chafed at pressure to demonstrate the "practical" dimensions of what he intended to be a primarily scientific undertaking. The official account of the 1892 expedition was published by the Botanical Survey (Smith and Pound 1893), not the State Board of Agriculture. In Bessey's annual report as State Botanist for the State Board of Agriculture there is, interestingly, no mention of Pound's name in referring to the expedition, and there is a definite emphasis upon its *practical* potential:

> During the year an investigation was made of the region in northern Nebraska known as the Sand Hill country, in order to ascertain what native plants grow naturally upon the hills, and in the valleys, with especial reference to their value in supplying forage to domestic animals. The results of this examination prove to be of unusual interest, showing us that in the Sand Hills we have a region quite unlike the remainder of the State in many of its physical features. The report made by Mr. J.G. Smith at once suggests the possibility of turning these hills and valleys to some better use than they now serve, and the probability that with some effort they might be covered with a profitable forest growth (Bessey 1893:199).

The report by Smith (1893) that Bessey referenced above was published as part of Bessey's annual report as State Botanist, and dealt only with grasses (about 1/10th of the nearly 300 specimens collected by Pound and Smith).

It is significant that Pound did not join Smith in reporting to the State Board of Agriculture whereas Pound promptly communicated to the Nebraska Academy of Sciences, presenting a paper titled, "The Flora of the Sand Hills" (together with Smith who read a companion piece on "General Features of the Sand Hills").[21]

---

[20] The collective memory on this point was sometimes fluid, some accounts place the organization of the Survey during the early summer of 1892. In *The Phytogeography,* Pound and Clements (1900: 20) explain it this way, "The members of the Seminar have carried on the work of this survey almost entirely with their private means, but at times have been assisted somewhat by the State Board of Agriculture and the United States Department of Agriculture." It was the USDA that funded Per Rydberg's (1895) more southerly transit of the Sand Hills a year later in 1893.

[21] Cf., "Minutes of Third Annual Meeting, 1892," *Publications of the Nebraska Academy of Sciences,* III, 1893, p. 9.

(Parenthetically, the division of labor announced in these two papers for the Academy clarifies individual responsibility for the work reported in their joint article (Smith and Pound 1893) for the Survey). Pound apparently resisted coercion, even from the likes of his mentor Bessey, into a subservient position vis a vis the distorting political demands of state-funded research—a position that today's grant-getting entrepreneurs should consider emulating.[22]

The expedition was a long trek in summer heat, starting on July 6, 1892, and ending 32 days later on August 6th. The entire trip was made on foot, the distance from Alliance to O'Neill accounts for at least 245 miles, with an unanticipated foot journey from O'Neill to Lincoln (occasioned when they could not sell their horse, Moses, at a fair price) adding at least another 200 miles, making a grand total in the vicinity of 450 miles. That the actual mileage was somewhat greater is reflected in Pound's observation that in going north to south any route in the Sand Hills has to "zigzag about 150" miles to cover 60 miles as the crow flies;[23] in their once having to backtrack several miles to catch their runaway horse; and, later, in their getting lost on the leg back to Lincoln. Many plant specimens were collected although the number of specimens collected varied from day to day, with an average of about 10 samples per day (see Table 6.1.).

The day-to-day details of the trip are engagingly related in a series of letters from Pound to Omer F. Hershey, a friend he made at Harvard during his year at the law school in Cambridge. The text of these letters appears below in the Appendix, but a few excerpts are worth emphasizing here. Importantly, Pound's letters document that it was he, and not Smith, who selected and prepared the plant specimens while Smith attended to a host of necessary domestic chores required to

---

[22] Years later, when sociologists were under pressure from certain "young turks" to become "more scientific" (i.e., to ape the methods of the so-called "value free" natural sciences), Pound warned, "I might say to you that I have no desire to make over the social sciences in the images of physics or biology. Having had a considerable experience in botany, I know that things are quite as much at large there as in the social sciences, and quite as much infected with practical problems. But the practical problems are not of such immediate and obvious social importance as to lead to general public appreciation of the situation. In other words, the biological sciences are not much more out of Egypt than we are but can get by where we cannot" (Pound to Maurice Parmelee, 1 October 1931, Box 5, Folder 4, Roscoe Pound Papers, Harvard Law School Library).

[23] Pound to Omer F. Hershey, 7 August 1892, Paul Sayre Collection. Due to the extreme difficulty of north-south travel, Pound and Smith stuck largely to the long, east-west valleys of the Sand Hills region.

keep the two-man expedition fed, watered, and sheltered. The letters also document that the expedition was very hard work:[24]

August 7; 1892

There are a great many things about the expedition that will amuse you. ...Now I will only say that it was hard work, the hardest I ever did from sunrise til 9-10 P .M. *every day,* that it has been of considerable scientific value and that I got home dirty greasy *ragged* and in the very best of health. The last three days we were at it from 4 A.M. till midnight and got only about 3 hours sleep a day. I have to make up for a day or two yet. ...

August 9, 1892

Here let me describe a days labor. Up at 4:00 (sunrise there). Smith got breakfast—makes bread, coffee, cooked game if any, if not bacon. I oil cart, pack tent etc. Breakfast about 5:30. Continue packing and start about 7:00. He drove and I collected, carrying case knife etc. If he saw game, I held horse if in the neighborhood, or he unchecked horse and let him eat and went after it. Thus we went on, going by sun or our compasses—for there are no roads except close to ranches where the rule is two cowpaths make a road—till about 2 or 3 P .M. Then or as soon after 2 as we reached [illegible copy] . . . . to dig for it, we lamiated Moses, unpacked, set up tent. I put plants in press, changed other press and dried sheets taken out day before. By hard work I could generally do this in 4-5 hours. Smith would meanwhile rustle up water and fuel (a good 2 hours job) and get supper. After dark I would help him and by 8 or 9 P.M. we would have supper. After supper we could spread the canvas over the presses, put up a rubber coat for a fly and between 9 and 10 turn in. If the mosquitos were bad, we would take turns—one keeping awake and feeding the flames with manure (called by the cow boys "chips"—hold fire a long time and make a great deal of smoke) to

---

[24] The expedition also provided an exemplar of Pound's well-known capacity for remembering details, as Pound lost his field notes and had to recall the location where each specimen was collected entirely from memory (see the Appendix, especially the last paragraph of the letter dated August 14, 1892).

keep up a smoke while the other slept. This was our every day program with little variation. Two meals a day was the invariable rule.

August 15, 1892

I haven't told the half of what happened though. My sitting down on a rattlesnake, and some experiences with prairie dog towns were not bad—I should like to tell you some of them—writing don't pay.

Pound's letters include a detailed itinerary of their Sand Hills route, and the late Professor C. Barron McIntosh of the UNL Department of Geography mapped much of their course in its more minute particulars.[25] Persons interested in retracing portions of the route (an endeavor which, from personal experience, I highly recommend) will find that a particularly scenic section traverses the publicly accessible Valentine National Wildlife Refuge in the heart of the Cherry County lake district.[26]

It its centennial year, the empirical results of the 1892 Sand Hills expedition are still with us today in a very physical sense. Several (if not all) of the specimens brought back by Pound and Smith are preserved in the herbarium in the University of Nebraska Museum where they are available to botanical researchers.[27] Nebraska's young botanists were clearly aware that the ecology of Nebraska was undergoing change. The 1892 prospectus for the Botanical Survey noted:

The changes which are taking place in the flora of the state have already been noted . . . . The rapid settlement of the western portions of the state is undoubtedly accelerating these changes, and requires that those regions be examined at once, while the native flora is intact.[28]

---

[25] The late C. Barron McIntosh excitedly showed me the topo sheets on which he had mapped the route based on my transcription of Pound's letters. MacIntosh's (1974, 1975, 1976, 1981, 1988, 1996) studies of the Sand Hills are examples of historical geography at its best. Figure 6.2, below, is based on his preliminary mapping of the route.

[26] For more information about access, contact the Refuge Manager, Fort Niobrara-Valentine National Wildlife Refuge Complex, Hidden Timber Rt., HC 14 Box 67, Valentine, Nebraska 69201.

[27] The herbarium is located in Nebraska Hall. I thank Dr. Margaret Bolick, Curator of Botany, who helped me locate several specimens for inspection.

[28] Botanical Survey of Nebraska (1892), I: 5.

One hundred years ago, Pound and his youthful colleagues understood that, ecological pioneers though they might be, they were nonetheless engaged in a salvage operation to document the original plant geography of the Sand Hills before it was irretrievably lost. That is the living legacy that Pound gives to us, and for which the 1892 Sand Hills expedition is an enduring symbol. Intellectually and organizationally, the 1892 expedition marked the start of Pound's mature botanical scholarship and served as part of the empirical support for his subsequent transformation of American ecology with Clements in *The Phytogeography*. In addition, the 1892 expedition is a paradigm exemplar of scientific research against which to compare Pound's later field investigations in sociology and law, a project which lies well beyond the assignment of the present paper.

———————————

Table 6.1.

Number of Specimens Collected by Date

Date	County	No. Specimens	Date	County	No. Specimens
06 July	Box Butte	18	21 July	Cherry	10
07 July	Box Butte	32	22 July	Cherry	09
08 July	Sheridan	01	23 July	Cherry	11
09 July	Sheridan	21	24 July	Cherry	06
10 July	Sheridan	05	25 July	Cherry	02
11 July	Sheridan	11	26 July	Cherry	22
12 July	Sheridan	23	27 July	Cherry	13
13 July	Sheridan	08	28 July	Brown	06
14 July	Cherry	06	29 July	Brown	17
15 July	Cherry	14	30 July	Rock	02
16 July		—	31 July	Rock/Holt	02
17 July	Cherry	02	01 August	Antelope	01
18 July	Cherry	03	02 August	Antelope	05
19 July	Cherry	22			
20 July	Cherry	14			

Total 286 [29]

[29] For a grand total of 298 (including 12 specimens for which no collection date was specified). On average, slightly more than 10 specimens were collected per day. For original data, see Smith and Pound (1893).

The Route of the 1892 Botanical Expedition,
Alliance to O'Neill, Nebraska

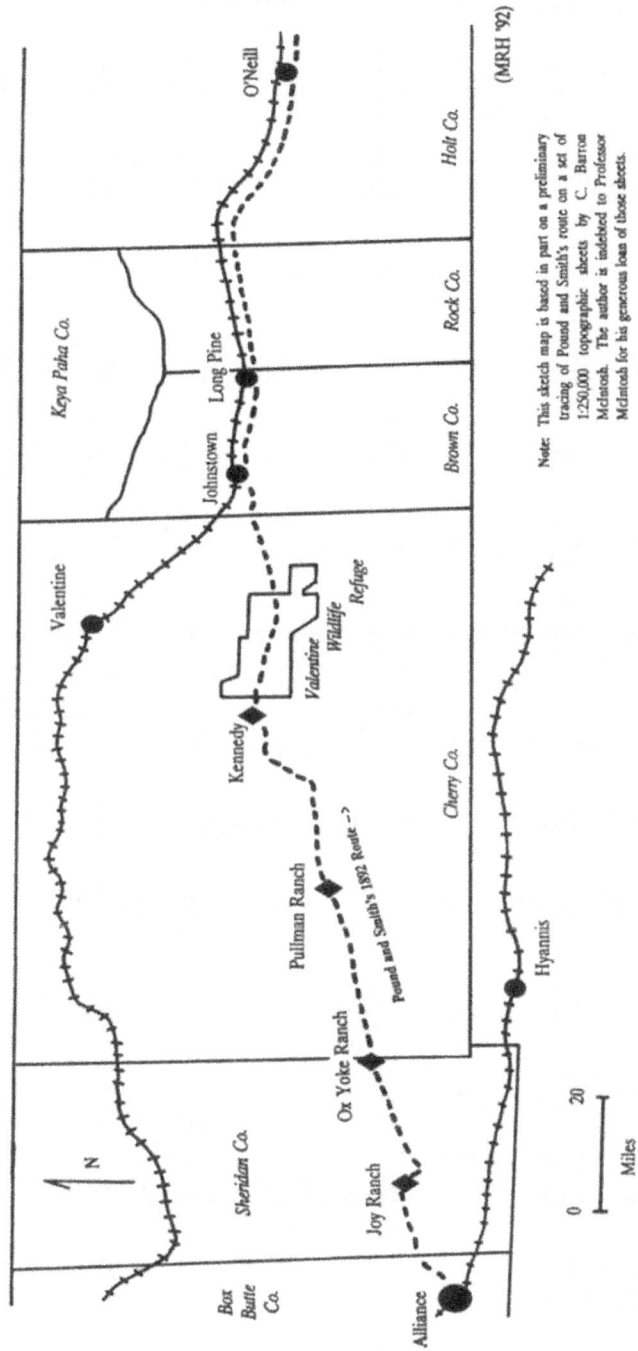

Figure 6.2. Pound's Sand Hills Route

91

References

Bessey, Charles E. 1893. "Seventh Annual Report of the Botanist." Pp. 199-293 in *Report of the Nebraska State Board of Agriculture, 1892*. Lincoln, Nebraska.

Botanical Seminar. 1892. *Botanical Survey of Nebraska, Part I: Preliminary: The Plan and Scope of the Survey*. Lincoln: The Seminar.

Botanical Seminar. 1893. *Botanical Survey of Nebraska, Part II: Report on Collections Made in 1892*. Lincoln: The Seminar.

Clements, Frederick E. 1894. "A Preliminary List of the Botanical Expeditions in Nebraska, 1803-1893." Pp. 39-42 in *Botanical Survey of Nebraska, III: Report for 1893*. Lincoln: The Seminar.

Hill, Michael R. 1988. "Roscoe Pound and the *Seminarium Botanicum* at the University of Nebraska, 1888-1889." *Transactions of the Nebraska Academy of Sciences* 16: 185-190.

Hill, Michael R. 1989. *Roscoe Pound and American Sociology: A Study in Archival Frame Analysis, Sociobiography, and Sociological Jurisprudence*. Ph.D. dissertation, Department of Sociology, University of Nebraska-Lincoln.

Hill, Michael R. 1993. "Mentoring, Paradigmatic Change, and Institutional Structure: Charles E. Bessey and the Origins of the *Seminarium Botanicum* at the University of Nebraska." Paper presented to the Charles E. Bessey Symposium, Historical Section, Botanical Society of America, Iowa State University, Ames, Iowa, 1993.

Hill, Michael R. 2011. "Botany, Sociology, and the Nebraska Sand Hills: Unraveling the Origins of the Chicago School of Human Ecology. Colloquium presentation, Department of Sociology, University of Nebraska-Lincoln.

McIntosh, C. Barron. 1974. "Forest Lieu Sections in the Sand Hills of Nebraska." *Annals of the American Association of Geographers* 64 (March): 87-99.

McIntosh, C. Barron. 1975. "Use and Abuse of the Timber Culture Act." *Annals of the American Association of Geographers* 65 (September): 346-362.

McIntosh, C. Barron. 1976. "Patterns from Land Alienation Maps." *Annals of the American Association of Geographers* 66 (December): 570-582.

McIntosh, C. Barron. 1981. "One Man's Sequential Land Alienation on the Great Plains." *Geographical Review* 71 (October): 427-445.

McIntosh, C. Barron. 1988. "The Route of a Sand Hills Bone Hunt: The Yale College Expedition of 1870." *Nebraska History* 69 (2): 84-94.

McIntosh, C. Barron. 1996. *The Nebraska Sand Hills: The Human Landscape*. Lincoln: University of Nebraska Press.

McKelvey, Susan Delano. 1955. *Botanical Exploration of the Trans-Mississippi West 1790-1850*. Jamaica Plain, MA: Arnold Arboretum of Harvard University.

Pound, Roscoe. 1894a. "The Progress of the Botanical Survey of Nebraska." Pp. 7-8 in *Publications of the Nebraska Academy of Sciences, IV, Proceedings, 1893*. Lincoln, Nebraska.

Pound, Roscoe. 1894b. "Bibliography of the Flora of Nebraska." Pp. 43-48 in *Botanical Survey of Nebraska, III: Report for 1893*. Lincoln: The Seminar.

Pound, Roscoe and Frederic E. Clements.1898a. *The Phytogeography of Nebraska*. Lincoln: Jacob North & Company.

Pound, Roscoe and Frederic E. Clements. 1898b. "A Method of Determining the Abundance of Secondary Species." *Minnesota Botanical Studies* 2 (June): 19-24.

Pound, Roscoe and Frederic E. Clements. 1898c. "The Vegetation Regions of the Prairie Province." *Botanical Gazette* 25(6): 381-394.

Pound, Roscoe and Frederic E. Clements. 1900. *The Phytogeography of Nebraska*. 2nd edition. Lincoln: University of Nebraska, Botanical Seminar.

Rydberg, Per Axel. 1895. *Flora of the Sand Hills of Nebraska.* (Contributions from the U.S. National Herbarium, Vol. 3, No.8). Washington: U.S. Government Printing Office.

Setaro, Franklyn C. 1942. *A Bibliography of the Writings of Roscoe Pound*. Cambridge: Harvard University Press.

Smith, Jared G. 1893. "The Grasses in the Sand Hills of Northern Nebraska." Pp. 280-291 in *Nebraska State Board of Agriculture, Annual Report, 1892*. Lincoln, Nebraska.

Smith, Jared G. and Roscoe Pound. 1893. "Flora of the Sand Hills Region of Sheridan and Cherry Counties, and List of Plants Collected on a Journey through the Sand Hills in July and August, 1892." Pp. 1-30 in *Botanical Survey of Nebraska, II: Report of Collections Made in 1892*. Lincoln: The Seminar.

Tobey, Ronald C. 1981. *Saving the Prairies: The Life Cycle of the Founding School of American Plant Ecology, 1895-1955*. Berkeley: University of California Press.

Webber, Herbert J. 1890. "Catalogue of the Flora of Nebraska." Pp. 175-302 in *Report of the Nebraska State Board of Agriculture, 1889*. Lincoln: State Journal Company.

Webber, Herbert J. 1892. "Appendix to Catalogue of the Flora of Nebraska." In *Transactions of the Academy of Science of St. Louis* 6 (No. 1). St. Louis: Academy of Science of St. Louis.

Wigdor, David. 1974. *Roscoe Pound: Philosopher of Law*. Westport: Greenwood
    Press.

———————————

Appendix:

Transcripts of Pound's Letters of Omer Hershey [30]

June 29th [1892]
[Wednesday]

My dear Hershey:

As there is no such thing as a tree in the Sand Hills, your remark about the good you would do me by insisting on my camping under everyone I met is amusing . . . . your "ignorance of our institooshuns is astonishin . . . ."

There aren't more than two or three post offices in our road in the Sand Hills. There are none in our road. but we shall try to digress and take them in (they are 50,000 miles apart) to send home material and lighten our baggage. I think I shall be able to send in my weekly remarks. I am confident that it will do me a pile of good. Anyway I drew my warrant for expenses today and am in for it. Start probably the 7th of July. Go to Alliance and walk over 200 miles to O'Niell. Visit the lakes(?) in Cherry Co. If you have a map you can get an idea of the thing. But enough of this. It will be a taste of roughing it which I think will do me good. I am not entirely new to the business—have done similar things on smaller scale before . . . .

July 3rd [1892]
[Sunday]

I shall start two days sooner than announced . . . . I have made all needful preparation—revolvers, ammunition, knife (of formidable proportions) leather leggings etc. and in heavy marching order look quite dangerous . . . .

---

[30] These edited transcripts omit material unrelated to Pound's expedition. The original letters reside in the Paul Sayre Collection at the University of Iowa in Iowa City, Iowa.

Pullman, Neb.
July 19 [1892]
[Tuesday]

Here we are at a P.O. first time since we started. Here is a sod house . . . .,
a P.O. Store etc. We are having a bully time just lots of hard work. Absolutely *no
population* for miles. Hot as-------.

We are behind time four days—lost two by rain and two by horse running
away, but have made up half today . . . .

———————

Johnstown, Nebraska
July 28, 1892
[Thursday]

Here we are at civilization at last and with only about 80 miles left—plain
going and the *luxury of a road* (such as it is, you wouldn't call it one).

Am sitting in a chair for the first time these many days. All well and have
had good luck. As quick as I reach Lincoln will write fully and explain all . . . . The
region is worse than I had an idea of—this is the second accessible P.O. and out of
the work originally planned.

———————

August 7 [1892]
[Sunday]

. . . I only got home yesterday at 1 p.m. and this (except last night, when I
was too sleepy to stay up) is the first chance I have had to write anything of any
length since we left Lincoln. When we reached O'Neill last Monday we found that
it was utterly impossible to sell our horse cart and harness as everybody knew we
wanted to. To stay two or three days at O'Neill would be very expensive so we
decided to ship our goods to Lincoln and drive across country to Lincoln. Packing
took a good deal of time and as time was very valuable from then on we started off
without informing our friends—I wrote just a line to Father—had no cards left or
would have informed you. Bad roads in Antelope Country and misdirection near
Valparaiso lost us about half a day. We should have reached Lincoln Friday night
. . . .

After taking a bath and a square meal yesterday I was very glad to find a large number of letters from you awaiting me. I am very sorry I kept you in such suspense. It was really unavoidable. You will notice several post offices in our path on the maps. They are sod houses along the north and south stage road from one R.R. to the other. In going 60 miles the country is such that the road has to zigzag about 150. These sod houses (some ranches) are (when not deserted) P.O.s. The stage goes through once a month. At Pullman (so named from owner of ranch) we were told that the stage was due in three days. Evidently the p.m. had lost count, as our letters do not seem to have started for three weeks after we were there . . . .

There are a great many things about the expedition that will amuse you, and I think I shall give you an account of it all as soon as I can get to it. Now I will only say that it was hard work, the hardest I ever did from sunrise till from 9-10 p.m. *every day*, that it has been of considerable scientific value and that I got home dirty greasy ragged and in the very best of health. The last three days we were at it from 4 a.m. till midnight and got only about 3 hours sleep a day. I have to make up for a day or two yet.

My head is still in too chaotic a condition to write—I have been eating and sleeping all day. I will write not singly but in battalions from now on till I catch up.

Regard this as only a note to tell of my arrival—I will get to letter writing presently. I hope this is the last time I ever have to go a month without hearing from you or keep you a month in ignorance of my whereabouts. I had really no idea of the country I was going into or of what a rough time I would have . . . .

———————

August 9 [1892]
[Tuesday]

I have a little leisure now which I may as well devote to enquiring "where was I at?" and going on where I left off. I am still eating and sleeping for the most part. Have only just begun to get matters straightened out here. Last night I was obliged to show myself to the public (I am still a curiosity to look at, though about fifteen shades lighter than when I landed) and got no time to write. I hope to be left to myself tonight. As there is not likely to be anything in particular to do now (5 p.m.) till dinner time, I may as well devote my reading time (Lord knows where or what I was reading!) to an account of myself and what I have been doing for the last month.

July 5 at 12:20 p.m. left for Alliance and got there at 2 a.m. We sent our cart up some days in advance. A classmate (Smith and I are '88 men) was on the train and got off at Alliance with us. We had to wait in the depot till 7 a.m. and mount guard over our baggage. At 7 a.m. we got a place to put it got breakfast and were ready for the fray. We got our cart and when ready to set it up found that the bolts had all been left behind. We procured the services of a blacksmith and about noon the cart was up. Meanwhile we examined critically all the horses in Alliance and about noon agreed to take one for $40.00—just ten dollars more I learned later than its owner paid for it the day before. Meanwhile also we had laid in a spade hatchet frying pan etc. After dinner we paid our money and all Alliance looked on and held its breath while I drew a bill of sale which was duly signed witnessed and delivered. Smith had brought a harness and we unpacked our stuff, Smith put an addition on the cart and by 4:00 all was ready and we started Smith walking behind and driving, I walking everywhere collecting. We had on the cart two presses of 200 sheets each, one half press for dried plants, one for wet sheets, a shelter tent with no fly, stakes, two poles, a canvas sheet to cover all in case of rain, a huge satchel which we called the telescope, three grain bags containing (1) grub, to-wit 50 lbs flour, (2) 15 lbs beans, 2 bacons, coffee, sugar, etc. also frying pan, 2 tin plates, 2 knives forks and spoons. This we called the bean bag. (3) Clothing ammunition etc. called from nature of its contents the "free for all." Besides we had roll of 2 blankets and one quilt and two rubber coats. Spade, 2 pails, hatchet and jug.

We went about 6 miles and camped. I went in a sod house for water. Next day we were up at 4:00 but pressing kept us busy till 9. when we started crossing Box Butte Co. and stopping on the edge of Sherridan Co. at 6 on account of threatened rain. We camped on shore of a fine lake—fine to look upon but water was alkaline. Just after supper it began to rain. We had little fuel and only by accident found that tumble weeds and the manure of the range herds are the native fuel. From this time on, we depended on that and sand cherry roots entirely. It rained all night and all the next day, keeping us inside in very narrow quarters as tent was only 42 inches high. Smith did get out and shoot a duck or two—we had duck or snipe or curlew or prairie chicken or all of them about every night. We passed 23 deserted houses up to this time and perhaps 4 or 5 inhabited.

Next morning it was clear and we were off, passing through the magnificent lake valley with fine lakes and into the Sand Hills. Throughout the western end of the region wet valleys run east and west connected by short divides of very bad Sand Hills or by long dry valleys. The wind is always S.E. during the day. At night it shifts and clouds come up and it may rain a little. It drys in a flash. The sand holds no water. For several days we went on camping by lakes and using lake water. One day we waded through a long marsh to Joy's ranch where we saw human beings once more. We were [illegible copy].

The horse flies are thick all over the hills. Some times I would have to fight them off Moses (the horse) while Smith drove. They bite right through ones clothing, the blood flows, clots and rubs against your clothing and makes a bad sore. The flies bothered us so that like fools we went on beyond the ranch and lake and into a dry valley. It was so long that we had to stop and camp in the middle of it and dig for water. Jerry got very good water about 4 feet down. Next morning we filled our jug from it and then used the well as a bath tub. The flies finally drove us wild here. They were not so bad for some days after. Here let me describe a days labor. Up at 4:00 (sunrise there). Smith got breakfast—makes bread, coffee, cooked game if any, if not bacon. I oil cart, pack tent etc. Breakfast about 5:30. Continue packing and start about 7:00. He drove and I collected, carrying case knife etc. If he saw game, I held horse if in the neighborhood, or he unchecked horse and let him eat and went after it. Thus we went on, going by sun or our compasses—for there are no roads except close to ranches where the rule is two cowpaths make a road—till about 2 or 3 p.m. Then or as soon after 2 as we reached [illegible copy] to dig for it, we [lamiated] Moses, unpacked, set up tent. I put plants in press, changed other press and dried sheets taken out day before. By hard work I could generally do this in 4-5 hours. Smith would meanwhile rustle up water and fuel (a good 2 hours job) and get supper. After dark I could help him and by 8 or 9 p.m. we would have supper. After supper we would spread the canvas over the presses, put up a rubber coat for a fly and between 9 and 10 turn in. If the mosquitos were bad, we would take turns—one keeping awake and feeding the flames with manure (called by the cow boys "chips"—hold fire a long time and make a great deal of smoke) to keep up a smoke while the other slept. This was our every day program with little variation. Two meals a day was the invariable rule.

———————

August 14 [1892]
[Sunday]

... "Where was I at" anyway? My recollection is that I had just left Joy's Ranch—on that assumption I will begin. From our camp beyond Joy's we had to go south as the hills east were impassible. The hills south were bad enough but we were told to go S.E. to Wilson's ranch and that from there on we could go N.E. (our direction). The trail (cowpath i.e.) lay over the most abominable stretch of Sand

Hills I had dreamed of. (We struck several worse afterwards). For 6 miles we had to push on the wheels most of the way up hill and down. The formation of the whole region is peculiar. It is crossed by E. and W. lakes long and narrow or by dry valleys. The lakes are at the east of wet valleys. Between the valleys are divides of low sand hills. The sides of the valleys are steep and high sand hills—often 300 feet—or more, with huge blowouts. A blowout is a great crater blown out of a hill by the wind. Well we went over this divide for 6 miles or so and came out in a magnificent valley running N.E. with a fine lake. The valley was not as large as many we saw later and the lake smaller and ranch smaller, but the hills were so high and steep, and the shape and lay of the valley such as to make it the finest sight we saw. The trail ended here and we went on across country over a long divide. This divide was dry and we had a hot time of it. The heat was intense—the hottest day we had—and we drank all the water out of our jug and couldn't find more. About 3 we fastened Moses to a sand cherry root (sand cherry grows about 6 in. high) and I went east and Smith north after water—both exhausted. We didn't find any and nearly got lost. One hill is so like another that one cannot find his way back half a mile unless he is very careful. Finally, Smith found a suitable place to dig and while he dug I unpacked and put up the tent. While he was digging 100 yards off (we camped on high ground to avoid mosquitos and horse flies) a rain came up unexpectedly and made me hustle as I ever did to get the presses inside. Just as I got through and Smith came up, it stopped and in 15 minutes was so dry that I got out the sheets used the day before and dried them and changed the presses. Meanwhile Jerry's well had filled with water which on inspection proved to be indubitably alkaline. We were both about ready to drop, but he managed to dig another only about 3 ft deep about 100 yards off which gave good (enough) water. So we used well no. 1 for a bath tub. Next day we were all day on the dry divide or in a dry valley, but a well gave good water. The day after we came to the Ox Yoke ranch on the Elkhorn Valley Lake 2 miles from the Cherry Co. Line. The lake is 5 or 6 miles long by 1/2 to 1 mile wide. We went on into Cherry Co. and camped on the east end of the lake where we had to sit up alternately by the fire and keep up a smoke on account of mosquitos. We learned that there was a trail S.E. to the [B&N] road at Hyannis 35 miles—this becomes relevant hereafter. We went on N.E. through a wet valley full of small ponds (1 day) past another and into a long dry valley. We found a small springy pond here and camped. Next day (July 16 memorable) we went on still in the same dry valley. We found afterwards that it was about 45 miles long. (The county is 96 miles long).

Now our beast Moses was so named for his intense meekness. He was to all appearances as innocent and meek as could be—and we had come to believe and trust him considerably. Smith (who has handled horses a great deal) had been in the habit of letting Moses stand unchecked and unfastened (what could he be fastened to anyway?) and letting him nibble at the grass while he hunted wherever game was in sight and I not in reach. The man we bought him off told us he would stand all right this way. On this eventful day about 10:30 I was in a blowout about 300 yards off and Smith seeing a small pond full of ducks halted Moses and unchecked him and proceeded about 100 feet to the pond. He shot two ducks and waded in for them. By this time I came down and joined him—I gathering algae in the pond while he put on his shoes leggings etc. When we came up to the knoll on the other side of which Moses had been stationed he was no where to be found. We dropped our stuff and Smith went west and I east beating up the low hills and valleys thinking he had started on for better grass. After wasting half an hour or more this way and fifteen minutes to half an hour finding our way back, we struck his trail—marks in the sand—where he had turned around and started back over our trail coming. We could see our tracks coming and to the left his going in the sand. Everything that we had was on that cart speeding for Alliance. I had with me a pocket flask of whisky, my collecting case, note book, knife, compass, pocket book, and revolver. Jerry had his gun, collecting case and knife. His pocket book and money were on the cart. He had no ammunition. He also had two ducks. We both had on light overalls—our trousers were in the cart—but fortunately had our coats on. We started back following the two trails as fast as we could walk. At ponds along the trail we could see where he had stopped to drink. To our satisfaction we found nothing spilled from the cart. We went on from a little after 11 a.m. til about 7:30 p.m. when it began to get too dark to follow the tracks and we had to look for water—being extremely thirsty as we had walked between 25 and 30 miles on a hot day with very little water. We strayed off from the trail over an old fire guard till we struck a nice lake in a small wet valley. We got a drink and as a rain seemed to be coming struck for a blowout and by good luck finding an inexhaustible supply of sand cherry roots built a fire. We had had nothing to eat since 5:30 (about) that morning and were infernally hungry. Smith dressed one of the two ducks (he had kept fairly well in the case) and cooked him on the end of a sand-cherry-root-spit. This was all we got for supper. Fortunately it did not rain, but there was a howling cold N.E. wind and a heavy mist which wet us considerably. We slept a little by the fire shivering most of the time. At 4:30 we held a council of war. It was misting badly and threatened rain. We had wandered far to the north of our trail in search of water and had grave doubts of our ability to find it. We had no notion where we were. We thought we would try to find the Ox Yoke ranch and there Smith could get a horse (I could hire it and he ride it) and strike out in pursuit. But this didn't seem very feasible as our goods were likely to be scattered to the winds. Besides we had small hopes of ever reaching the ranch—as it is largely a matter of chance—the valleys running parallel—if one strikes the right lake. Our plan was to go straight south trusting to luck and knowing that the R.R. and civilization were about 45-50 miles south. We thought we could keep up till we struck the R.R. and then go home. The night was the roughest toughest and most abominable I ever passed. You can't imagine the thing. No blankets—overalls cold as the devil, mist, hungry as could be and tired. But we were mighty game just the same and took it remarkably cool, if I do say it. We cooked the other duck as before and called it breakfast. We then struck south at about 5 a.m. The walking was bad as there were hard sand hills to climb and it was dark and misty. About 6:00 we were pleased to find a cowpath. Cowpaths are always welcome for they lead to water every time or else to a ranch—generally from one to the other. Following it we came about 6:30 to the Elkhorn Valley Lake! We were mighty pleased at this and soon after found unmistakable signs that Moses had passed, for near the site of our camp of 3 days before we found our canvas sheet used to cover the presses. As we went on tent poles, parts of presses etc. Well at last we got to the ranch and there found Moses—stopped by cow boy the night before about the time we stopped for darkness. They gave us a good breakfast at the ranch and at 9:30 we hitched up and tied on our things—most of them still in the cart and went back. We found (I abridge here because I am quite sure I went over it to you before—but not perfectly so because I have had to supply the loss of my note book from memory and can't remember what I wrote hurriedly in the office) everything but one tin cup, and my spectacle case blue glasses and tooth brush. We went on beyond our days journey of three days before and going at our best rate too. It had turned hot and clear about noon and we dried things out and rested our limbs. Next day was uneventful. Day after we got to end of the dry valley and into a wet one where we found a lake, ranch, and fine spring and there a P.O. was 6 miles off. We went on through abominable hills to Brush Lake the head of the north fork of the Loup to Pullman—to wit one sod house with say 15 more in a radius of 10-12 miles (liberal estimate). Here we wrote cards to our parents and friends—I put yours in an envelope and Jerry did the same for a certain young lady. The Mosquitos (I give them a capital) raised the unmentionable that night. Next day we were directed to a short cut to "the falls" reputed 12 miles off where there was a trail to "Kennedy!" We went over the worst lot of sand hills we saw on the trip. Absolutely barren and abominable generally. Camped on banks of pond near the Loup. As usual every night it threatened rain but only misted—but I had to hustle with the presses. Next day we crossed the Loup—magnificent cold clear water—and went along for some distance over fair country. A Swede about 1 p.m. who has a tolerable farm in the valley (sod house of course) told us to cross back and go on 5 miles and we could find the falls and the trail to Kennedy. We went on 15 or more and found no trail. There were small falls all along the river but no crossing place. Finally we stopped for fear of rain and camped. A slight rain and wind did nothing worse than make me hustle to cover the presses during the night. Next day we made a portage of the Loup near the camp and Jerry got a huge dose of poison ivy. I am not susceptible fortunately and got off easy. We thought we would take a day off, but after pitching the tent, the state of the presses (I had botanized a good deal that morning and pressed nothing for two days before) kept me at work till supper time! Next day we went over a very difficult divide between Loup and the Gordon—very hard work. Sunday we reached the Gordon and as it was unfordable went on south side abandoning the trail (which we had only found a short time before) and came to the P.O. of Kennedy—only we were on the other side. Kennedy is a sod house of course, but nearby is another sod house with a cross on it—a mission where a preacher comes from Valentine once a month. There are 12-15 people about the valley to whom he preaches (I suppose). We tried to beat our way east toward Ainsworth, but the conformation of the country was such that we did not succeed. I was taken sick the first day out and when we struck a trail about 5 (I guess) rode a mile or so till at last we struck a small pond containing stonewort, a sure sign of good water. We were very glad to get to this, as I was weak and Jerry tired and it was outrageously hot. Next day we tried to go east but failed and going N.E. came to Dad's Lake—a valley full of water—a magnificent sheet of water and the largest lake in the State probably. We were now in the lake region. Pelican Lake and [Marsh] Lake (among others) we passed. From a hill near Pelican Lake 24 good sized lakes are visible. Here we saw a large number of "free claims." We went over to Hanna's Lake—three lakes end to end in a wet valley—29 miles from Johnstown. Camped near the first lake some miles from the ranch. There are two ranches owned by brothers—one at each end of the valley. Johnston is 24 miles from east end. We had to stand guard all night to fight off droves of horses. (Escaped and wild. They get off before they can be branded and run wild—belonging to nobody.) In the morning I went into the lake after water plants and while coming out a cold north wind came up suddenly. It was cold as ice and as a result I got a frightful cold. It rained just as we got started and for about an hour thereafter we went on making tracks for Johnstown—with the tarpaulin over the cart and rubber coats on. About 4 o'clock Alliance time—5 Johnstown—time changes somewhere here rain came up—hard this time. We were in a bad fix. Fortunately we came to a house that was not deserted—we had passed any number that were—and got permission to put our presses in the barn—and finally in the house. In a hard rain we pitched the tent and got our stuff inside and built a fire. (I had by good luck put on a lot of boards from a deserted house on the way.) We got supper and went shivering to bed—for it was cold. Next morning we dried out—hot clear day—and were delighted to hear a R.R. whistle. Johnstown was 5-6 miles off. We got there at noon over hilly road, and got

103

dinner at the hotel (?!). Here we ate enough for 20 men (bacon beans and bread) to the astonishment of the damsel who waited on us. She would go outside and look in the window—pretending all the time not to be looking—till she saw we had cleaned everything up, when she would come in and fill everything up again. We shipped all the plants we could to Lincoln, wrote cards to our parents and friends. At 5 p.m. we started on. Three not very eventful days of hard work brought us to O'Neill—the end of our journey we supposed.

The rest I have told—how and why we drove home across country. One thing I ought to mention. The day we drove from Neligh to St. Edwards we stopped at Albion to get some grub as we knew we would be going till late and were hungry. Jerry bought some beef steak off a butcher there and when about 9 p.m. hungry as blazes we got ready to cook it, lo and behold it was everlastingly and hopelessly spoiled. The scoundrel saw we were two jays passing through and put off his old spoiled dog meat on us. We had mighty little to eat that night.

We were truly a spectacle when we reached Lincoln. Our clothes were in the last stages of raggedness, we were tanned almost black, dirty greasy and armed to the teeth. A week at home has made me 15 degrees—25 degrees lighter. I got lighter in three or four days. I still have an enormous appetite—am sleepy lazy and stupid.

One thing I should like to know is how much of the above itinerary is repetition. I lost my book in Antelope Co. and have been labeling plants from memory so that I don't know whether it is from that or writing it to you once before that I hear everything so clear in my head. I remember everything very well. Smith's book only has dates—so my memory has to serve for plant localities etc. It is OK there but to my surprise and disgust fails me when I try to remember how far I got in the office the other night. There are myriads of things I could tell—trouble had with one cuss about wheat must—with another because we wouldn't join a grand wolf hunt in which all able bodied men for 50-60 miles were engaged, etc. etc., but there must be some end to this . . . .

———————

August 15th [1892]
[Monday]

I seem to have been stupid and rattled last night and spun out my tale of woe about the Sand Hills to some length. I have got to write a report from memory which may account for my glibness and repetition—I haven't told the half of what happened though. My sitting down on a rattlesnake, and some experiences with

104

prairie dog towns were not bad—I should like to tell you some of them—writing don't pay . . . .

Yours,
Roscoe Pound

7

The Materiality of Identity in the Indian Diaspora: Hindu Temples in Trinidad and Malaysia

Carolyn V. Prorok

Abstract

Religious structures are common forms of material culture in landscapes of most parts of the world. As such, they can be analyzed as conscious, collective, public expressions of a people's cultural identity; particularly if the group in question is a minority. In this study, the building and rebuilding of Hindu temples in Trinidad and Malaysia are analyzed in terms of the conditions of migration, the colonial social environment and postcolonial political environment for each group. Trinidadian Hindus have chosen localized transformation in architectural styles with a contemporary flowering of the Hindu presence in Trinidad, while Malaysian Hindus have chosen traditionalism with a contemporary focus on rebuilding existing temples according to classical prescription.

Introduction

Expressing one's ethnic identity as a minority community in a plural society is achieved in a multitude of ways. Much of the academic literature on the subject focuses upon political, social, economic and cultural contexts and behaviors. Some of these behaviors result in concrete expressions, such as foodways, musical systems and art, while most others are less tangible in form such as political behavior and religious beliefs. A less common form of research in this area is the analysis of religious material culture in the landscape as a means of assessing the collective identity of a minority community.

Sullivan (in P. Lewis 1994) notes that people and the buildings they create express each other within and without, and that buildings can be used as an index to a community's identity. In addition, Pierce Lewis (1994) goes on to explain that people's houses, like culture itself, springs from the past. Thus, migrants are likely to carry their ideas about proper house types with them to their new home, and one can trace the persistence of their culture through time and space by observing continuity or discontinuity in the kinds of houses people build.

In this paper, I propose that Hindu temples, like houses, reveal much about the communities that build them in Trinidad and Malaysia. As public, material expressions of religiosity in the landscape, temples are imbued with issues of collective intention regarding identity and community cohesion. For the Hindus of Trinidad and Malaysia, temples are laden with social, political and religious meanings that reflect generations of tension and negotiation within the community in counterpoint to the dominant social and political milieux in which they live. In this project I formulate a typology of temple forms in Trinidad and Malaysia, and I track the history of building and rebuilding in order to illustrate the synergistic relationship between people, their identity and their landscape.

Method of Study

My primary objective is to investigate the evolution of spatial changes in the form and function of temples in diasporic Hindu communities.[1] Ancillary objectives included the following questions: how are the temples used; what do the temples mean to those who use them?; and finally, how did the temples take on their current physical characteristics.

Fieldwork in the form of a structure survey was the primary means of collecting data for this study. Work in Trinidad (eastern Caribbean) began in 1984 with a preliminary study, and a full survey of temples on the island in 1985. Since then I have returned to Trinidad in 1988/89, 1993/94 and again in 2003 for follow-up studies. Work in Malaysia (southeastern Asia) began in 1993 with a feasibility study, and a full survey of temples in the state of Pulau Pinang (know to the British as Penang - northwestern, peninsular Malaysia) in 1994. Given the large size of Malaysia, the state of Pulau Pinang (which includes the island of the same name and Seberang Perai or Province Wellesley — to the British — on the mainland) was selected for study because it is one of the oldest areas of settlement by Hindus since British contact in the region, and it is representative of the Hindu community at large. Finally, visits to villages in the central part of the Bhojpuri Hindi speaking region (between Varanasi and Patna) and Tamil Nadu (from Madras to Madurai) in India during the summer of 1988 and again in 1995 completed the fieldwork. They

---

[1] My focus is on the mainstream Hindu traditions (folk and Sanskritized) that the earliest Hindu migrants carried with them from 19th century India, and which persist to this day. I do not consider sectarian movements such as Arya Samaj (Forbes 1984) and the more recent phenomena of Satya Sai Baba worship (Klass 1991; Mearns 1995).

represent the dominant regions of origin for Trinidad's and Malaysia's Hindus respectively.

Both surveys generated a mass of architectural, demographic, historical and site/situation data on 186 extant temples in Trinidad and 140 extant temples in Malaysia. In both cases, topographic maps (1:25,000) were used and every road was systematically driven to identify temples. When a temple was located, informants were easily found and interviewed about the history, usage and meaning of the temple. In addition, I observed and noted structural and site/situation features. Finally, supporting data and documentation was acquired in local libraries and government offices.

Building Temples

People invest spiritual, emotional, social and physical resources into their places of worship. For Hindus, this entails the karmic benefits of helping to create and maintain a place of worship, as well as the personal relationship they may evolve with a particular deity. Social organization provides the network of human resources available for creating and sustaining a place of worship, thereby establishing grounds for the collective negotiation of a temple's spiritual integrity (even if worship events are individual experiences). Finally, the availability of physical resources and the culturally traditional selection of certain resources for the building of temples temporally grounds the spiritual, emotional and social realities of a worship event.

Establishing a temple at a specific site necessarily demands a particular resource base, notions about how and where to build, and the meeting of the spiritual needs of the local community. Thus, one would expect to see temples that resembled those in the homeland erected within a reasonable amount of time from the onset of migration. Over the years the needs of the Hindu community and the level of tolerance of the dominant culture would preclude the expansion of temple sites and the manner of building temples. Rebuilding or renovating temples, often by replacing a structure with a new one, becomes a viable option as communities re-invest in their socio-religious infrastructure and their collective identity. Trinidad's Hindus have chosen transformation, while Malaysia's Hindus continue to choose traditionalism as a guiding principle in the temple building and re-building experience.

Hindu Temples in Trinidad [2]

Hindus represent approximately 25% of Trinidad's population, and they have several kinds of places for worshipping deities. These include *puja* (ritual offering) rooms in their homes, shrines and temples. Some shrines are associated with local supernatural beliefs, but in most cases Sanskritized[3] deities are the focus of worship at all types of ritual centers. Temple building in Trinidad emerges through several stages in form and material. Changes in material parallel closely those for homes and other types of structures among both Asian Indians and Creoles on the island; i.e. from thatch roofed, wattle and daub structures to wooden structures to concrete ones today (J. N. Lewis 1983). Changes in temple form and function reveal changes specifically associated with Trinidad's Hindu population.

According to Collens (1888), Hindu migrants depended on holy books, plants and small statues of the deities (*murtis*) that they brought with them. Since folk deities are generally propitiated under trees throughout India, it is safe to assume that Hindus in Trinidad continued this practice from the earliest time. Eventually, home shrines gave way to specially constructed traditional-style temples of northern Indian vernacular styles in the house yard or garden. The earliest known temples in Trinidad were erected by the 1860s and were mainly of bamboo or wattle and daub construction with a thatch roof, which I designate as *simple traditional* temples (Photo 7.1). By the 1880s more substantial structures were established in "clay brick" and stone, which I designate as *traditional* temples (Photo 7.2). Traditional

---

[2] All material presented on Trinidad in the paper is based upon previous work that I have published, and a tremendous number of primary and secondary sources. I include a number of them here as a general citation, with specific notations in a limited number of places. Besson 1985; Biswas 1980; Brereton 1979; Census of Trinidad (all available years); Clarke 1986; Collens 1888; Crooke 1926; Jha 1974; Kingsley 1871; Klass 1961; Lewis 1983; Prorok 1988; Singh 1974.

[3] Hinduism's range of myths, doctrines and ritual practices are categorized by Marriott (1955:191193) as 1) the great tradition, where, "that tradition is understood to be the literate religious tradition, embodied in or derived from Sanskrit works which have a universal spread in all parts of India," and those of 2) the little tradition, which is that body of ritual behavior associated with the village and surrounding area and not explained by Sanskritic tradition nor understood by villagers in Sanskritic terms. Ritual institutions in India are classified as great or little traditions and they can be analyzed in terms of the process of the little tradition becoming absorbed into the great tradition, whereby local festivals, deities and ritual acts slowly take on Sanskritic rationales. Marriott (1955:194) indicates some ritual institutions have several layers of "explanations" and devotees are not necessarily concerned with a 'right' Sanskritic origin. More important is identification with the Sanskritic tradition. Srinivas (1956) describes the process of transforming little tradition by great tradition explanations and ritual institutions as "Sanskritization."

temples are relatively small, square and always have a *sikhara*, or dome that enshrines the deities.

During the 1920s a new temple type was introduced called the *koutia*. In India, the word and architectural form are multi-faceted in significance. According to Rana Singh,[4] the term derives from the Sanskrit, *kuti*, which means a hermitage of a great sage in Vedic times. It is also a vernacular (Bhojpuri) term that refers to a temple compound (more commonly called *matha*) or to the structure that houses the person (*pujari*) who takes care of the temple. In Trinidad, the koutia took on the function of an assembly hall, when it was added to a traditional temple (see photo 7.2 again) during the visits of itinerant Hindu holy men from India. Eventually it became a temple in and of itself, though it is difficult to determine exactly when and where this took place. Koutias are rectangular, rather than square, and have a flat, shed roof or low-angle gable roof (Photo 7.3). They rarely have domes, except in some cases where one was added to the front porch.

The koutia temple evolved into the Trinidadian temple by the 1950s. The addition of a dome in the back of the structure where the deities were enshrined successfully merged the traditional form with the koutia (Photo 7.4). Thus, the Trinidadian form is rectangular also, with a raised platform and dome at one end and the rest of the structure extending away from it with space to seat several hundred people in the larger versions. Trinidadian temples always have a dome and an assembly hall attached to the domed area. Thus, a congregational style of worship emerged parallel to the traditional pattern of individual and family worship, and in conjunction with a transformed sacred space.

Hindu Temples in Malaysia [5]

In Malaysia, Hindus constitute approximately eight percent of the population. As in Trinidad, Malaysia's Hindus have puja rooms in their homes, shrines and temples. Unlike Trinidad, temples in Malaysia continue to be primarily traditional in form and function. Thus, the typology presented here is based on a combination of the characteristics of form and function from the original, southern Indian folk

---

[4] Rana P.B. Singh is a cultural geographer and scholar of Hinduism at Banaras Hindu University. Personal communication in 1995.

[5] This material is based upon a standing structure survey and consultation with K. Ramanathan at the Universiti Sains Malaysia. I also used his unpublished paper, "Hindu Temples in Malaysia: Problems and Prospects," presented at the annual meeting of the Association of American Geographers in San Francisco in 1994 to identify particular features of Malaysia's Hindu temples as well as his PhD dissertation (1995).

styles and *dravida* styles transplanted by migrants, rather than one reflecting evolutionary changes in form and function.

From the earliest known migration of Hindus to Malaysia in the modern era (1790) to the present (1994), temples were established in a similar fashion, and they fall into two basic categories. *Agamic* temples are those built according to the Sanskritic *agamas*. They tend to be substantial structures, though this is not always the case. Second are folk temples, which are often simpler in form.

Several features are consistently present in an agamic temple; 1) a *vimana*, which is literally the temple itself as the house and body of God. This is understood to be the main, domed structure that enshrines the deity. 2) a *mandapa*, which is a pillared hallway extending away from the vimana. 3) at least one *gopura*, or towered gateway that rises anywhere from 20-50 feet and often dominates the entire sacred space (Photo 7.5). It is also notable for the plethora of carved and colorfully painted figures that reflect Hindu mythology. Agamic temples are expensive to build, require skilled artisans, and are dependent on a wealthy patron or the wealth of donations from a substantial number of devotees.

Folk temples in Malaysia are generally small in size, made of local timber with pitched roofs of corrugated iron and they can be viewed in two ways. The first are those established at sites with a natural feature that is often imbued with sacred significance. This can be along a river bank or waterfall, at a cave (as with the Batu Caves outside of Kuala Lumpur), under special trees such as the pipal (*Ficus Religiosa*) or neem (*Azaderachta indica A. Juss*), and particular termite mounds (*Odontotermes obesus*) (Photo 7.6) which are called *kalayan* in Tamil and believed to house cobras.

People believe that local spirits manifest themselves at such places, and if an extraordinary experience occurs in conjunction with such a site then often a simple structure is erected in association with, or around, the natural feature. The second type of folk temple was usually established on the estates or along the railroad where many Hindus labored. They were also of simple construction, but may or may not have been built in association with a special natural feature (Photo 7.7). Remembered village deities, caste deities and some Sanskritized deities were often enshrined.

Establishing and Rebuilding Temples in Trinidad and Malaysia

Because the act of building or renovating a temple entails such a significant investment on the part of a family or community it becomes a useful gauge for assessing group activities at a large scale. In addition, the relative permanence of temples in the landscape provides a visible record of past choices made by a community. Thus, the following data on establishing and rebuilding temples illustrates past and present patterns of Hindu interaction with the dominant cultures of Trinidad and Malaysia. For the purposes of this study, the terms renovating and rebuilding are used interchangeably, and though not synonymous, they refer to major architectural additions which often include a rebuilding of the original structure.

Trinidad — Based upon the 1985 field survey, 186 temples have been established in Trinidad at their present sites. In 2003, a reconnaissance of the island indicates that at least another 50 temples have been added to this list. Certainly, there would have been temples established and possibly abandoned over the last 150 years, however, their numbers should not be great and would unlikely detract from the pattern illustrated in Figure 7.1. During the period of indentureship (1845-1917) nearly 20 temples are known to have been established. All of them were simple traditional or traditional temples that survived in some form to this day. In the late nineteenth century many Hindus would have worshipped at small shrines in their gardens or fields.

Building temples during the indenture period was fraught with difficulty for Trinidad's Hindus. But, with the Hindu community well established and freely settled by the end of the first quarter of the twentieth century, the stage was set for expansion of temple sites. Reaction to the pressure of Christian proselytization, and the catalytic effect of charismatic religious leaders such as Jamini galvanized many Hindu communities who built temples as a part of their new found sense of community cohesion and identity (Samaroo 1981; Singh 1974). Nearly four times as many temples were built from 1925-1934 as in the previous decade, and it is during this time that the innovation of using the koutia as a temple occurred. Expansion of the Hindu population and the politicization of the Hindu community in the wake of universal enfranchisement in 1945-6 produced an environment of frenetic temple building when compared to previous decades. It had taken 100 years to establish the first 50 temples, and then from 1945 to 1964, during which independence had been achieved and Hindu political aspirations were in their incipient, yet heady stage (1962), 66 temples were built; this represents one third of all extant temples. During the period from independence to 1985 another 69 temples were established, though the total number for each decade seems to be in decline. Follow-up studies in 1988/89, 1993/94, and 2003 though not comprehensive, indicate that new temples continue to be established.

Figure 7.2 indicates the pattern of rebuilding temples in Trinidad. The earliest renovations in the late 1920s and 1930s mainly entailed the addition of a koutia to an already standing traditional temple. Thereafter, most renovations replaced earlier temple forms with a newer form. For example, Shiva Mandir in El

Dorado (between Tunapuna and Arima) began as a simple traditional temple in 1926. It was rebuilt as a traditional temple in 1950, had a koutia attached in 1956 and was rebuilt (with the original traditional temple incorporated into the structure) as a Trinidadian temple in 1983. In this case one can see that renovation and rebuilding are as significant as the original establishment of the temple in terms of spiritual, social, and economic investment. During the economic boom period of the late seventies and early 1980s, renovations outnumbered the building of new temples for the first time, indicating first and foremost the sense of political and social transition many Hindu communities felt, and secondly that they had the financial means to act upon this sensibility (Vertovec 1990 and 1993).

Both the establishment of temples and their renovations have grown in number during the independence period, and they follow a provocative pattern in that there are significant upsurges of building activity during election years (Prorok 1988). This points to the central role of the temple as an organizing principal around which political leaders have been able to effect power and influence. Given the minority position of the Hindu Indian population and their substantial numbers in several districts in western Triniadad (sugar cane areas), they have constituted the oppostion party most of the time though they have posed a real challenge to the power base of the party in power (PNM-People's National Movement which is mainly Creole). Until 1996, when they were successful in electing Trinidad's first Hindu Prime Minister (Basdeo Panday), minority politicians would organized political rallies at temples and often make a "donation" towards its upkeep. The infusion of new cash resulted in the renovation of existing structures and the desire of some communities to have their own temples (for both spiritual and political reasons). Mr. Panday remained Prime Minister until 2001 when he was replaced by the PNM. During his tenure, he increased public monies available to all religious organizations and Hindus, for the first time, felt they were receiving their fair share of public resources. Not surprisingly there has been a major building and rebuilding boom throughout the 1990s. They are able to build temples anywhere they own land. In Trinidad, Hindus have arrived!

Malaysia [6] — Based upon the 1994 survey of Penang, Malaysia 140 temples were established at their present sites. As in Trinidad, this survey represents only extant temples and does not include any temples that may have been built and then

---

[6] As with the Trinidad material, some of my work (Prorok 1998) as well as many primary and secondary resources were brought to bear in this section. Abraham 1986; Ackerman & Lee 1988; Andaya and Andaya 1982; Arasaratnam 1970 ; Hua 1983; Hussain 1990; Kua 1987; Lee and Rajoo 1987; Sandhu 1969; Tinker 1990.

114

disappeared for various reasons. Figure 3 shows the pattern of building from 1790 to 1994.

Contact between Indians and Malayans probably dates to the pre-Christian era, and Hindu culture certainly has dramatically influenced various regions of southeastern Asia since then. In the modern state of Malaysia no extant temples and few archaeological sites remain from that era. The temples of Penang (Pulau Pinang) date only since the time of British hegemony in the region, which began in 1786.

In the early years Hindu migrants were merchants, domestic servants or laborers. By 1870, Indians — of whom at least 80% were Hindu, replaced the Chinese as the principal laborers in an expanding sugar industry in Penang and Seberang Perai or Province Wellesley (the mainland section of the state of Pulau Pinang). Until the 1890s, when rubber estates were commercially established, Indian migrants formed a small, but significant, population in Malaysia. Thus, the period from 1790-1890 reveals a slow, but inexorable establishment of temples to serve the Hindu community.

The period from 1890-1909 shows a remarkable surge in the building of temples. This is primarily due to the influx of substantial numbers of Indians systematically (*kangani* recruitment) brought in by the British to labor on rubber estates. Establishing temples drops dramatically in the next decade and recovers at a moderate level until the period of Malaysian independence.

A number of reasons occur for this pattern. First, Penang (Pulau Pinang) and Province Wellesley (Seberang Perai) were the earliest locales in the establishment of rubber estates. Experimentation with trees began in the late 1880s and the first estates created in the mid-1890s. Second, rubber takes six to eight years to mature before harvesting can begin. Trees planted in the mid-1890s would be ready for harvest only at the turn of the century when labor needs would be greater. The first rubber boom came in 1905, at which point rubber became the dominant crop of Province Wellesley. Prices stabilized and then another boom came from 1908-12, whereupon rubber estates expanded rapidly. This expansion mainly occurred in other states, as Penang (Pulau Pinang) and Province Wellesley (Seberang Perai) were nearly saturated with estates on available land. Finally, the Hindus who were recruited to labor on the estates would often find a temple already established near their housing unit. Unlike Trinidad, estate owners (both British and Chinese) would help the incipient Hindu community to establish a temple and a toddy shop (a fermented palm drink) right away with the assistance of the *kangani* recruiter. One reason given for this practice was that plantation owners believed that workers were more productive if these two institutions were immediately at hand. Another reason given for establishing the temples is that it helped in the recruitment process of Tamilian Hindus. There is an old Tamil adage attributed to the Sage Auvaiyar, and which is repeated by many to this day; "kovil illa uril kudi irrukka vendam" or "do not live in a place where there is no temple."[7] Thus, recruiters often assured prospective migrants that temples already existed on estates. Once laborers arrived, they often expanded the number of temple sites on the plantation or in the surrounding area.

The pattern of establishing temples as revealed in Figure 3 reflects the early and rapid growth of rubber estates in Penang and Province Wellesley, as well as their stabilization by the 1910s. Temple building recovered as the larger Hindu population established second and third temples on some estates, migrated to create their own communities in rural areas, or went in search of work in local towns. The dramatic drop in establishing new temples from 1980 onwards reflects the difficulty of Hindus to get permission to build new structures in the independence period (Ramanathan 1995:249).

Figure 7.4 indicates that renovation of temples in Malaysia is primarily a recent phenomena with more than three quarters of them occurring in the last 25 years. Also notable is that there have been more renovations (152) in this time frame than the total number of temples in existence. This results from some temples having been renovated more than once. In addition, several temples have been physically removed to different locations due to pressure from development schemes and government intervention (Ramanathan 1995:250).

A politically complex scenario emerged in the late 1960s and early 1970s that dramatically impacted the Hindu community (as with other religious and ethnic groups) in Malaysia. First, the federal elections of 1969 were fraught with racialized/ethnic polemic, and two ethnically based opposition parties (Gerakan and DAP)[8] won seats at the expense of the Malay controlled Alliance party. Public celebrations in the streets by supporters of the opposition parties, and a counter-rally by Alliance supporters degenerated into violence, whereupon it took four days to restore order to the city.

A state of emergency was called. Within several months of the riots the government established a Department of National Unity to formulate a national ideology in order to prevent another recurrence of ethnic animosity. In 1970, on Independence Day (August 31), the new ideology — *Rukunegara* — was proclaimed (Andaya & Andaya 1982:281):

---

[7] This expression was repeated by many informants during my fieldwork, and older informants on many plantations indicated that the plantation owner funded the building of the original temple.

[8] Gerakan refers to the "Gerakan Rakyat Malaysia" or Malaysian People's Movement and DAP refers to the Democratic Action Party.

116

Our nation, Malaysia, being dedicated to achieving a greater unity of
all her peoples; to maintaining a democratic way of life; to creating
a just society in which the wealth of the nation shall be equitably
shared; to ensuring a liberal approach to her rich and diverse cultural
traditions; ...

The government continued to establish committees whose task was to provide
positive and practical guidelines for inter-racial co-operation, and laws were enacted
that restricted public speech and behavior that could lead to communal violence. In
keeping with its anti-communalism campaign, the government announced in 1971
a new "National Cultural Policy" or NCP. Its three basic premises are as follows
(Kua 1987:14):

1. The National Culture must be based on the indigenous culture of this
   region.
2. Suitable elements from the other cultures can be accepted as part of the
   National Culture.
3. Islam is an important component in the moulding of the National Culture.

There is not much in this policy that would surprise anyone knowledgeable about
Malaysia's postcolonial politics. Assertion of a politicized Malay identity during
decolonization was central to the creation of the modern Malaysian state. Also, the
Malaysian Constitution identifies Islam as the state religion, while granting the right
of every religious group to maintain its religious institutions. The Malay dominated
committee that produced this policy in large part were reaffirming what was already
fait accompli as far as the politico-cultural environment was concerned. British
authorities had assured Malay Sultans that the position of Islam was inviolable when
they signed agreements in 1874 that imposed British rule on the peninsula.
Subsequent agreements (1948) made Islam the official religion (Ramanathan 1994,
1995).

So then, why does the NCP play such a pivotal role in inter-ethnic relations
when its position was already a public reality? First, new civil regulations that
governed public cultural events were based upon the policy. The regulations cover
many issues, such as permits for public processions, school cultural programs, public
performances of dance and theater, access to radio/television airtime and the
establishment of new cemeteries and places of worship. Since these regulations were
primarily made by Malays, the interpretation of what was "suitable" from non-Malay
cultures was often applied in a limiting and restrictive manner as Malay nationalism
continued to intersect with more rigorous notions of what constituted the 'proper'

117

practice of Islam. In addition, such interpretations were inconsistent from one region of Malaysia to another. Secondly, the NCP was produced from a commission whose task was to promote ethnic harmony. Much to the dismay of Malay political leaders, Chinese and Indian communities criticized the policy as assimilative and unfair. From the Chinese and Indian point of view, the policy did nothing but promote the status quo. While Malays saw the NCP as a means to actively promote *Rukunegara*, Chinese and Indian leaders saw the NCP as contradictory to it.

To cap the series of events that led from the riots to the NCP, a new political party — the National Front — emerged between 1971 and 1973 that formed a coalition among ten Malay, Chinese and Indian parties. Parliamentary procedure was re-established in 1971, although it became a seditious act to discuss Malay special privileges, Bahasa Malay as the national language and the status of Islam as the official religion. In the 1974 elections the National Front swept the polls with guaranteed positions for Chinese and Indian political leaders in the system.

For Indians in Malaysia, particularly non-Muslim Indians, negotiating the mine field that is Malaysia's postcolonial cultural politics is difficult in the least. They are guaranteed government representation, but not a free expansion of worship sites. Given the central role of the temple in Hindu spiritual, cultural and social life, it is not an understatement to recognize the renovations of temples as a paramount resistance, yet a fairly safe resistance, to the current political climate.[9]

Today, renovating temples usually entails the complete rebuilding of small, vernacular temples as substantial Agamic temples, a process that is also promoting the Sanskritization of many of Penang's temples (Lee & Rajoo 1987). Communities with limited resources will generally focus on building up the *vimana* dome, or creating a *gopura* for a temple that only has the *vimana* and *mandapa*. It is extremely difficult to get a permit to establish a new temple, but it is often possible to receive public funds to renovate an existing temple. This is the hall of mirrors that is the NCP and the regulations that derive from it.

Conclusions

Building and rebuilding temples in Trinidad and Malaysia clearly reveals complex social and political interactions between a religious minority such as the

---

[9] Ramanathan (1995:252) interprets the revitalization and focus on agamic renovations of temples as incorporative of the revitalization of Islam among Malays with their respective focus on the 'right' way to practice Islam (as understood in its Arab origins). That is, the revitalization of Islam among Malays has positively influenced Indian Hindus to take a similarly intense interest in Hinduism.

Hindus and the dominant milieux of colonial/post colonial Christian and Islamic cultures. Thus, temples make explicit the association of the differential maintenance of ethnic identity among people and the religious material culture that they create in the landscape.

Trinidad's Hindus chose transformation of their material culture, while Malaysia's Hindus chose a conservative traditionalism. Both choices serve to maintain a special, public identity for their respective communities. The dramatic difference in how each community does this rests mainly in the socio-political conditions in which each community lived and worked, and to a lesser degree in the differences in their original cultural origins per se.

A number of circumstances can be elucidated in regard to each situation. These include; (1) method of labor recruitment and manner of relocation, (2) socio-political conditions during colonial times, and (3) socio-political conditions in the post-colonial period.

The method of labor recruitment for rubber estates in Malaysia was much different than that for Trinidad's sugar estates. In Trinidad, labor was recruited mainly in northern India and based upon indentured contracts for specified periods of time. Co-workers on the sugar estates may or may not have derived from the same village or even have spoken the same language. Bhojpuri Hindi became the lingua franca among Indians since this group dominated demographically. Significant social and economic relationships formed between those that travelled together on the same boat, or labored together on the same estate, thus a shifting of alliances that devalued traditional ascriptive characteristics, such as caste and village of origin, emerged (though did not eliminate them) (Haraksingh 1981). Resulting from this social environment where new alliances were formed was a situation whereby localized religious practices from India often gave way to more universally recognized practices that were mainly Sanskritized in form (Jayawardena 1966). Also, partly due to the significant distance between India and Trinidad, programs were established to give laborers parcels of land in return for their passage. The number of returnees declined and contact with India became difficult, although infusions of new laborers until 1917 continued to refresh Hindu traditions. Also essential to understanding the Trinidad experience was the fact that Indian laborers moved off of the estates and established their own villages relatively early, while Indian laborers in Malaysia remained on the plantations if they stayed in Malaysia. This encouraged a certain degree of autonomy and contact with non-Indians for Trinidad, and a certain degree of dependancy and isolation from non-Indians in Malaysia.

In Malaysia, the *kangani* system prevailed. The term derives from a Tamil word that refers to a labor foreman, a laborer of standing and eventually a labor recruiter. In the 1860s coffee planters in Malaysia experimented with this system, which originally served the tea and coffee plantations of Ceylon (now Sri Lanka). A kangani employee of an estate would return to his home village (mainly in Tamil Nadu) and recruit labor for the estate. Because they were "free" laborers, these workers were not subject to as much government regulation and fluctuations in the labor needs of the planters were more easily controlled (with laborers repatriated and re-recruited as needed). Thus, the newly emerging rubber estate owners chose the *kangani* system over the indentureship system which prevailed in other British colonies. Since each estate was likely to have a large number of workers from the same village or district in India, traditional caste ascriptions and interpersonal relationships were more easily reconstituted and vernacular religious traditions, such as worship of a particular village deity, where transplanted more readily. Also, a combination of the *kangani* style of recruitment and the short distance between southeastern India and Malaysia meant that there was a high rate of return and contact with home villages.

The second, and probably more significant, circumstance that affected each community was the dominant socio-political environment during colonial times. Hindus arrived in mid-nineteenth century Trinidad to find a predominantly Christian, multi-racial society where Victorian era values infused public behavior (especially among the planter class). Their movement was restricted during the indentureship period, and they lived under conditions where establishing a place of worship was difficult at best. Both Europeans and Christianized Africans found Hindu religious practices alien, and even intolerable in some cases. Some traditions, such as firewalking (usually practiced by Trinidad's small south Indian population), were actively discouraged by the planter class (and even the Hindu elite) and eventually disappeared (Besson 1985). By the late 1860s an intensive program of Christian proselytization by the Canadian Presbyterian mission began. It was supported by the plantocracy and effectively helped to place Hindu practices on the margins of acceptability. Thus, Trinidad's Hindus were constantly, and consistently, placed in a position of defending who they were. Creating new social and economic alliances among Hindu brethren was a necessary strategy.

In Malaysia, on the other hand, a different situation occurred. First, Hindus arrived to find an established indigenous culture that had received significant infusions of Hindu culture (particularly in the Sanskritizing of Malay court language) over the centuries. Also, at the time, Islam in Malay villages was predominantly syncretized with pre-Islamic Malay practices (known as *adat*), which included animistic beliefs (Endicott 1991). Thus, Hindu practices (both vernacular and Agamic) generally were not perceived as 'alien' by Malays. Secondly, both the British and Chinese rubber planters assisted (usually financially) the earliest laborers

120

in establishing a temple on estate grounds. But more importantly, the British planters in Malaysia were basically indifferent to Hindu practices, and if not indifferent, they did not actively support an organized proselytization effort. The Chinese, particularly Chinese laborers, were as likely to worship at Hindu shrines or temples as they were at their own places of worship. To this day, most Hindu temples in Penang can count large numbers of Chinese devotees among worshippers. Thus, the establishment of traditional Hindu practices and sites for worship had an assumed and taken for granted quality without any sense of being challenged by non-Hindus.

The third contributing factor to the circumstances with which Hindus had to face was the decolonization process and the post-colonial political environment. In Trinidad, decolonization brought Hindus into the political limelight as their numbers were too significant to ignore; a position that many resisted at first because they felt an independent Trinidad would be even less accommodating to Hindu culture than the colonial one (Lowenthal 1961). Yet, as Hindu political leaders played a newly significant role in the West Indian Federation government, a fresher and more open environment emerged for Hindu organizational efforts. One might even speculate that universal enfranchisement and decolonization set the stage for an astonishingly revitalized Hindu presence. Hindu schools were opened, Hindu marriage rites recognized, and cremation became legal. Despite the racialized political environment, Hindus were able to express their religious culture more openly and with even greater exuberance. In this environment, the Trinidadian style temple emerged, and over the next thirty years the type of temple that a community erected, in part, depicted how they saw themselves as an ethnic group in independent Trinidad (Prorok 1988). From the early 1960s to 1985, fully one third of all temple building events resulted in a Trinidadian style temple.

With a more open and freshly assumed presence tension within the community can rise to the surface more readily. Sometimes identity differences within villages erupted in local conflicts. A case in point is a village in north central Trinidad. A traditional temple served the community for many years. In the early 1980s some villagers began raising money to replace the 'old' temple with a 'new' Trinidadian style structure. At first, there seemed to be much support for this process as the new temple took form. Part of the older temple had already been dismantled, but then conflict within the temple committee resulted in a halting of the project.[10] It took over a decade to finally raise enough money to make the

---

[10] There are many layers of interaction in this conflict (including but not limited to personality conflict, residual caste conflict and disagreement over the involvement of local politicians in the temple building process) which cannot be dealt with here.

Trinidadian temple usable, though it still does not have its sikhara (thus, it looks more like a koutia temple now). A substantial number of people had decided that they did not want the 'old' temple dismantled. Some people worship at the traditional temple without ever attending services in the new temple and visa versa, although these two temples literally adjoin one another now.

In Malaysia, the process of decolonization worked differently for Hindus. Due to their small numbers, and their relative isolation on estates, they did not play as significant a role in decolonization as Trinidad's Hindus did. Primarily, political tension existed between the Malay and Chinese communities, and Hindus had to struggle to even have a voice in the situation. Decolonization gave rise to a fervent Malay-Muslim nationalism that continues to dominate post-colonial politics. As described above, this political environment has dramatically curtailed the ability of Hindus to publically express themselves. In areas where Hindus can be found in large numbers, such as Penang, religious processions are relatively common as they have a long (and entrenched) history. However, even in these areas procession permits are known to have been denied. More importantly, it is difficult for Hindus to establish new temples.

Under these circumstances, conflict within the Hindu community and with the larger society emerges.[11] On the one hand, some Muslim youths (from particularly conservative communities) have been known to vandalize and destroy Hindu shrines and temples since the late 1970s, with several dying at the hands of Hindu 'temple guards' in one case (Ramanathan 1995:240-243). This experience, despite government intervention, served to galvanize the Hindu community into greater organizational efforts. On the other hand, a case of intra-community conflict can be found in north central Seberang Perai (Province Wellesley). In 1970 a small temple was built at a site where some people say that an image of the god Vinayagar (or Ganesha — the elephant-headed god that is the son of Shiva) emerged from the earth. As the politics of the NCP blossomed over the next two years, the local government challenged the existence of the temple. A local Hindu leader (my primary informant) was consulted about the veracity of the story. He said that he could not lie, and could not vouch for the authenticity of the story.[12] Soldiers from a nearby base were sent to destroy the temple because they did not have the proper

---

[11] Mearn (1995) describes the centrality of the temple and temple rites in Hindu identity in Malacca (Melaka), as well as the class, caste and ethnic conflict that emerges as different groups contest control over temples.

[12] Few people were willing to discuss this event with me. My informant insisted that his response was based solely on his personal ethics of telling the truth, which placed him at odds with many members of his community. At the very least, this conflict may have deeper roots from the perspective of the community.

permit, but my informant convinced them to only remove the roof and exterior walls as it would be highly improper for them to do anything to the *murti* (God's image). As a substantial number of Malays still recognize the efficacy of Hindu sacred places, the soldiers did not destroy the altar. Through negotiation with local Malay leaders, and the donation of a parcel of land by a wealthy Hindu family, the temple was moved to a new site. In 1987, the temple was rebuilt as an Agamic temple with the support of public funds. This temple is one of only a few to be established in the state of Penang since 1970.

What is clear is that the juxtaposition of working conditions and the socio-political environment created by the dominant culture serves to contextualize temple building efforts made by Hindus in Trinidad and Malaysia. While Trinidad's experience was characterized by an early restrictiveness and contemporary flowering of Hindu expression, the Malaysian one was the inverse. Thus, these two Hindu communities faced similar circumstances at different times in their migration and settlement history, which resulted in making divergent choices about how to preserve the integrity of their collective identity.

Closure

Based on the material presented in this paper, one can surmise that temples symbolize a fundamental dialectic of human experience: conflict and unity — within the Hindu community and between Hindus and other ethnic groups, and identity and identity crisis — being Indian and being *Trinidadian or Malaysian* (not Malay). Resolution of the dialectic is presented to the public at large through the symbology of the temple. That is, the formal representation of Hindu architectural elements provide a rich text to be read for the differential degree to which Hindus of both countries negotiate the social and spiritual tensions inherent in resolving these issues with a self-defined dignity under conditions of political and social acculturation.

Acknowledgment

The author is most thankful for the financial support of Slippery Rock University and the National Endowment for the Humanities. In addition, countless Trinidadians and Malaysians made this project possible. I am sincerely grateful for their help. Finally, Sankalpa Nagaraja deserves a special thank you for assisting with data processing and generating the charts.

Selected Bibliography

Abraham, C. 1986. "Manipulation and Management of Racial and Ethnic Groups in Colonial Malaysia: A Case of Ideological Domination and Control." In *Ethnicity and Ethnic Relations in Malaysia*, edited by R. Lee. Northern Illinois University Center for Southeast Asian Studies.

Ackerman, S.E. & R.L.M. Lee, eds. 1988. *Heaven in Transition: Non-Muslim Religious Innovation and Ethnic Identity in Malaysia*. Honolulu: University of Hawaii Press.

Andaya, B.W. and L.Y. Andaya. 1982. *A History of Malaysia*. London: Macmillan Education, Ltd.

Arasaratnam, S. 1970. *Indians in Malaysia and Singapore*. Bombay: Oxford University Press.

Besson, G. 1985. *A Photograph Album of Trinidad at the Turn of the 19th Century*. Port of Spain: Paria Publishing Co.

Biswas, L. 1980. "Hinduism in a Dynamic Urban Setting: The temples and Shrines of Calcutta." PhD dissertation, University of Pittsburgh.

Brereton, B. 1979. *Race Relations in Colonial Trinidad: 1870-1900*. Cambridge: Cambridge University Press.

Clarke, C. 1986. *East Indians in a West Indian Town; San Fernando, Trinidad, 1930-1970*. London: George Allen and Unwin.

Collens, J.H. 1888. *Guide to Trinidad*. 2nd. edition. London: Elliot Stoke.

Crooke, W. 1926. *Religion and Folklore of Northern India*. Oxford: Oxford University Press.

Endicott, K.M. 1991. *An Analysis of Malay Magic*. Singapore: Oxford University Press, reprint.

Forbes, R. H. 1984. "Arya Samaj in Trinidad: An Historical Study of Hindu Organizational Process in Acculturative Conditions." PhD dissertation, University of Miami.

Haraksingh, K. 1981. "Control and Resistance Among Overseas Indian Workers: A Study of Labour on the Sugar Plantations of Trinidad, 1875-1917." *Journal of Caribbean History* 14:1-17.

Hua Wu Yin. 1983. *Class and Communalism in Malaysia: Politics in a Dependent Capitalist State*. London: Zed Books.

Hussain, M. 1990. *Islam and Ethnicity in Malay Politics*. Singapore: Oxford University Press.

Kua Kia Soong, ed. 1987. *Defining Malaysian Culture*. Selangor (Malaysia): K. Das Ink.

124

Jayawardena, C. 1966. "Religious Belief and Social Change: Aspects of the Development of Hinduism in British Guiana." *Comparative Studies in Society and History* 8:211-40.

Jha, J.C. 1974. "The Indian Heritage in Trinidad." In *Calcutta to Caroni*, edited by Laguerre. Bristol: Western Printing.

Kingsley, C. 1871. *At Last: A Christmas in the West Indies*. New York: Harper and Brothers.

Klass, M. 1991. *Singing with Sai Baba: The Politics of Revitalization in Trinidad*. Boulder: Westview Press.

Klass, M. 1961. *East Indians in Trinidad: A Study in Cultural Persistence*. New York: Columbia University Press.

Lee, R.L. & R. Rajoo. 1987. "Sanscritization and Indian Ethnicity in Malaysia." *Modern Asia Studies* 21:2:389-415.

Lewis, J.N. 1983. *Ajoupa: Architecture of the Caribbean, Trinidad's Heritage*. Port of Spain: J.N. Lewis.

Lewis, P. 1994. "Common Houses, Cultural Spoor." In *Re-Reading Cultural Geography*, edited by Kenneth E. Foote and others. Austin, TX: University of Texas Press.

Lowenthal, D. 1961. *The West Indies Federation: Perspectives on a New Nation*. New York: Columbia University Press.

Marriott, M. 1955. "Little Communities in an Indigenous Civilization." In *Village India: Studies in the Little Community*, edited by M. Marriott. Chicago: Chicago University Press.

Mearn, D. J. 1995. *Shiva's other children: religion and social identity amongst overseas Indians*. New Delhi: Sage Publications.

Prorok, C.V. 1998. "Dancing in the Fire: The Politics of Hindu Identity in a Malaysian Landscape." *Journal of Cultural Geography* 17:2:89-114.

Prorok, C.V. 1988. "Hindu Temples in Trinidad: A Cultural Geography of Religious Structures and Ethnic Identity." PhD dissertation, Louisiana State University.

Ramanathan, K. 1995. "Hindu Religion in an Islamic State: The Case of Malaysia." PhD dissertation, Universiteit van Amsterdam.

Ramanathan, K. 1994. "Hindu Temples in Malaysia: Problems and Prospects." Paper presented at the annual meeting of the Association of American Geographers, San Francisco.

Samaroo, B. 1981. "Missionary Methods and Local Responses: The Canadian Mission Presbyterians and the East Indians in the Caribbean." In *East Indians in the Caribbean: Colonialism and the Struggle for Identity*, [edited by?] Millwood. New York: Kraus International.

Sandhu, K.S. 1969. *Indians in Malaya: Some Aspects of Their Immigration and Settlement, 1786-1957.* Cambridge: Cambridge University Press.

Singh, K. 1974. "East Indians and the Larger Society." In *Calcutta to Caroni*, edited by J. LaGuerre. Bristol: Western Printing.

Srinivas, M.N. 1956. "A Note on Sanskritization and Westernization." *The Far Eastern Quarterly* 15 (4):481-96.

Tinker, H. 1990. "Indians in southeast Asia: imperial auxiliaries." In *South Asians Overseas: Migration and Ethnicity*, edited by C. Clarke, and others. Cambridge: Cambridge University Press.

Vertovec, S. 1990. "Oil boom and recession in Trinidad Indian villages." In *South Asians Overseas: Migration and Ethnicity*, edited by C. Clarke, and others. Cambridge: Cambridge University Press.

Vertovec, S. 1993. *Hindu Trinidad: Religion, Ethnicity and Socio-Economic Change.* London: MacMillan Caribbean.

———————————

Photo 7.1. Caret palm temple in northern Trinidad

**Photo 7.2 One of the earliest temples in northern Trinidad (1880s).
The wooden section to the right was added later.**

Photo 7.3. A koutia temple in southern Trinidad.

129

Photo 7.4. Trinidadian style temple in central Trinidad.

Photo 7.5. A *gopura* in Malaysia.

**Photo 7.6. An Amman temple (Mother Goddess temple)
as expressed through ritualized termite
mounds in Malaysia.**

**Photo 7.7. A temple dedicated to a village guardian
known as Maduraiveeran and set in a
rubber grove in Malaysia.**

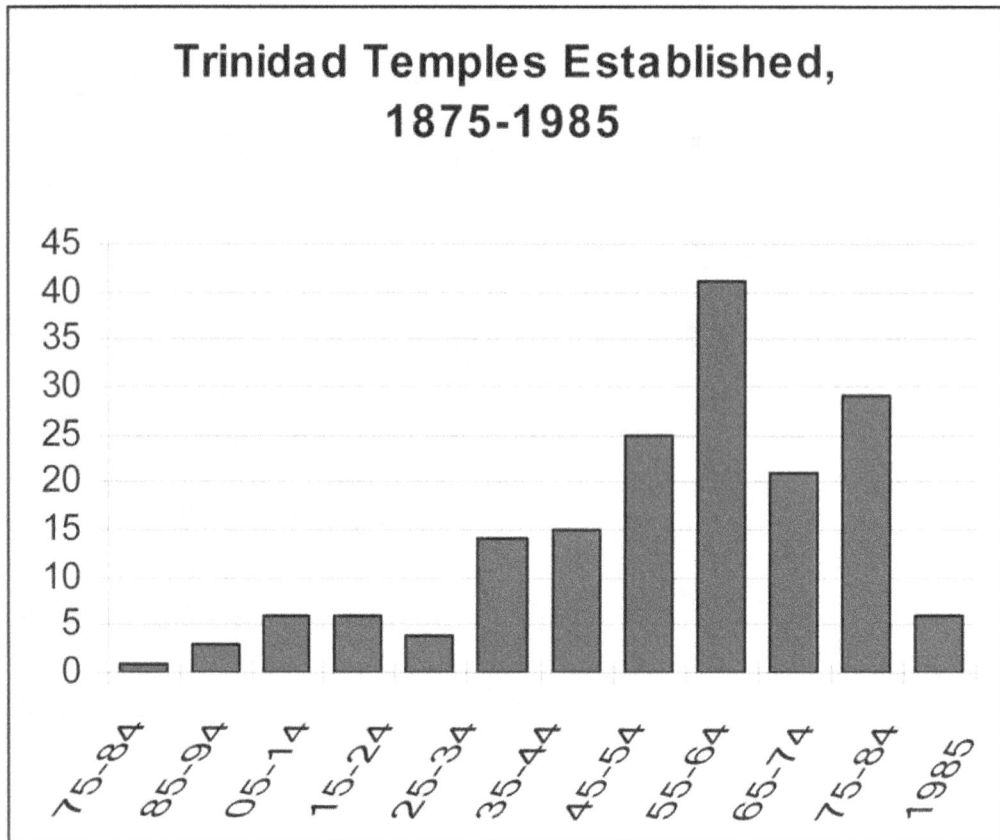

Trinidad Temples Established, 1875-1985

Figure 7.1. Two temples have unknown dates of establishment

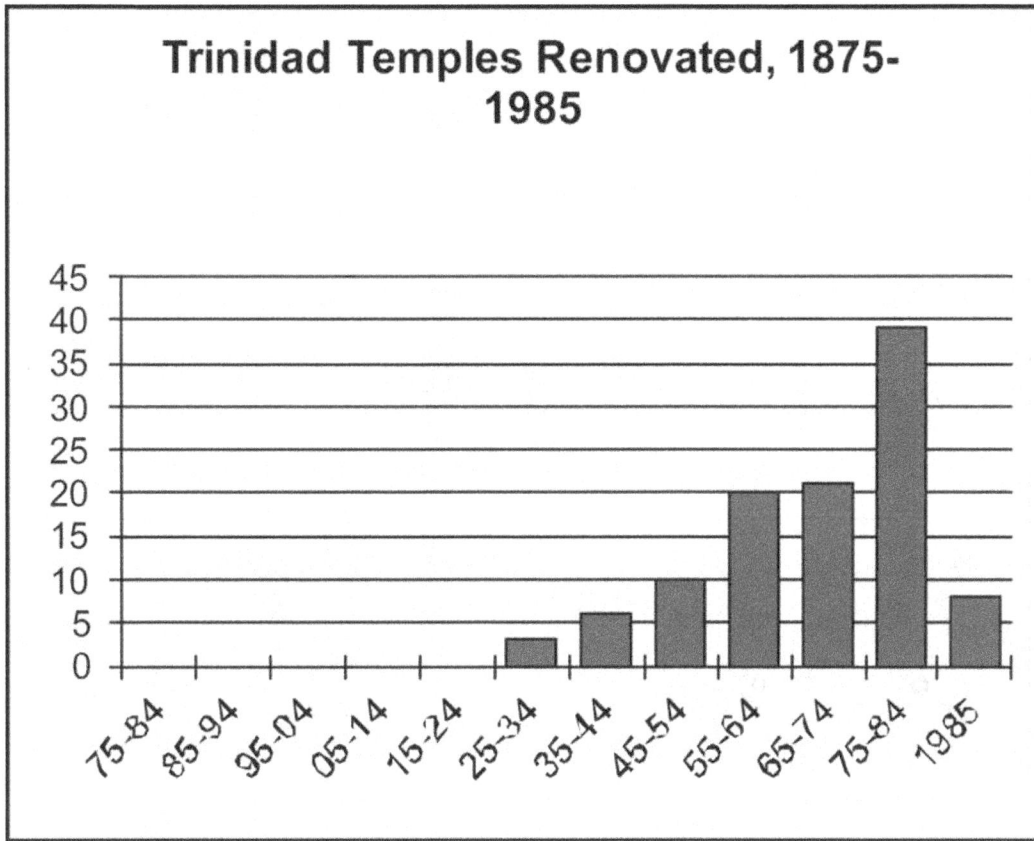

Trinidad Temples Renovated, 1875-1985

Figure 7.2. Twenty temples have unknown dates of renovation

Penang Temples Established, 1790-1994

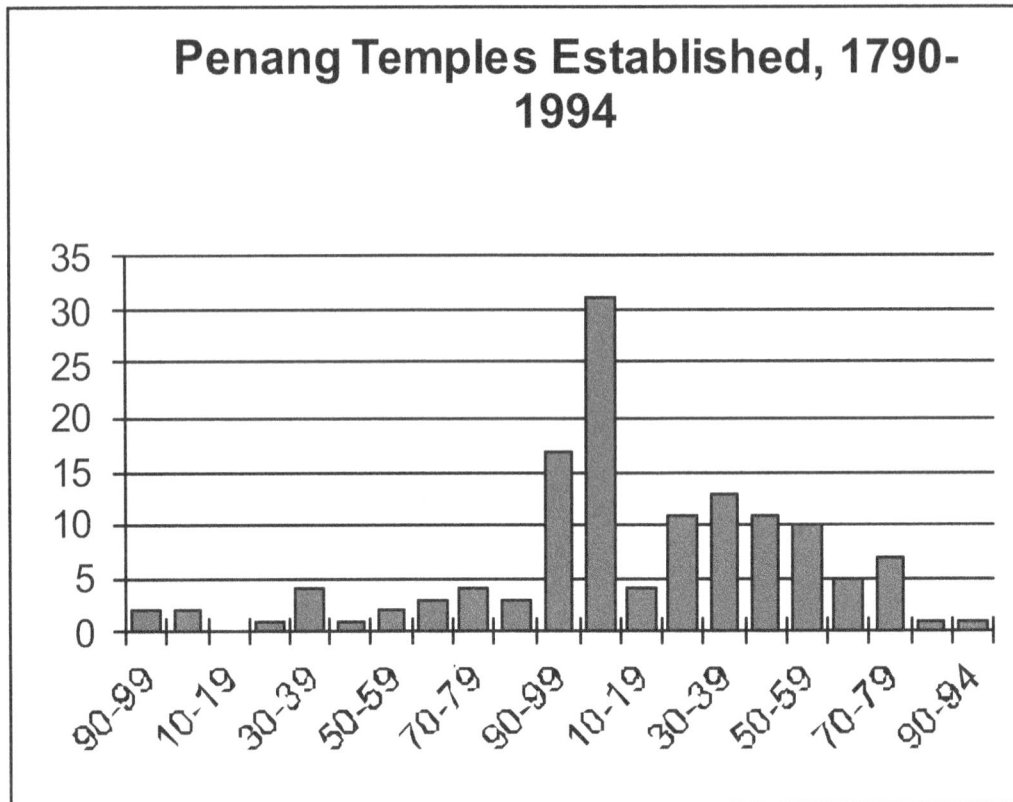

Figure 7.3. Seven temples have no known dates of establishment

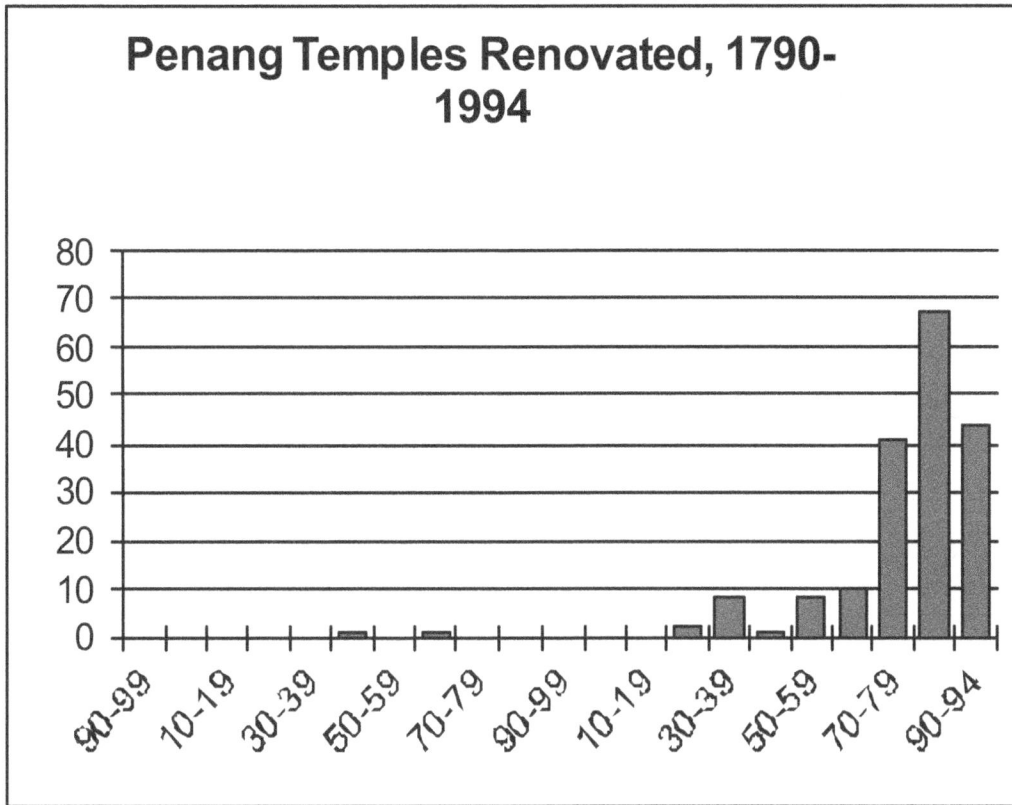

Penang Temples Renovated, 1790-1994

Figure 7.4. Twelve temples have unknown dates of renovation
and four have never been renovated

8

**NON-HAJJ PILGRIMAGE IN ISLAM: A NEGLECTED
DIMENSION OF RELIGIOUS CIRCULATION** [1]

Surinder M. Bhardwaj

Abstract

Emphasis by geographers on the study of the hajj to Mecca has resulted in the neglect of ziarat, or non-hajj pilgrimages to other Islamic holy places. Associated with saints, many of the Sufi order, and martyrs, these holy places attract a vast number of pilgrims. Non-hajj pilgrimages may also be considered symbolic of the regional cultural expressions of Islam, especially in the non-Arab countries. This preliminary study situates ziarat within a typology of Islamic religious circulation. It shows that ziarat is part of the dynamic tradition of religious circulation in Islam in various regions: North Africa, Shia areas of Southwestern Asia, Central Asia, and South Asia.

Pilgrimage studies in Islam, at least those done by geographers, have been primarily focused upon the *hajj* to Mecca because of its pivotal importance in keeping with one of the five pillars of the faith. One of the earliest detailed studies of the hajj from the religious viewpoint was done by C. Snouck Hurgronje in 1880 (Bousquet and Schacht 1957: 171-213). Eldon Rutter (1929) may be credited with perhaps the first explicitly geographic study of hajj, in which he brings out the locational importance of Malaya compared to other Islamic countries, in generating the largest number of hajj pilgrims. Jean-Paul Roux (1958: 175-179) sets the hajj in the context of non-Arab countries with substantial Muslim populations. These early studies on the hajj were followed by Kamal (1961), Al-Naqar (1972), King (1972), Isaac (1973), Sardar and Badawi (1978), Makky (1978,1981), Rowley and Hamdan (1978), Long (1979), and Shair and Karan (1979), to name a few.

---

[1] This paper was originally published in the *Journal of Cultural Geography*, vol. 17, no. 2 (Spring/Summer 1998), pp. 69-87. It is reprinted here with permission from JCG Press.

The establishment of the Hajj Research Centre in 1975 by the government of Saudi Arabia highlights the great importance of hajj-related studies to address the many planning problems of accommodation, health, and transportation. Indeed the large volume of hajj pilgrims, due to the increased ability of more and more Muslims to undertake the once arduous journey, ensures continued emphasis on hajj studies. Central as is the significance of the hajj to Muslims, cultural geographers have neglected to study other Muslim religious journeys, such as visits to sacred shrines of holy men, the graves of saints and Imams, and the tombs of martyrs of the faith. Journey to these places is often termed a *ziarat*, to distinguish it from the hajj. These ziarats, undertaken throughout the Islamic realm, are by no means a substitute for the hajj. Some Muslims may even consider them un-Islamic. Nevertheless, the places of ziarat attract millions of people, who travel substantial distances to these centers, and, therefore, they must be considered an integral but neglected part of Islamic religious circulation.

Focus on the hajj as the preeminent, and the most spectacular, annual event in the Islamic religious calendar has overshadowed the widespread practice of the ziarat to a great number of Muslim shrines. Such scholarly neglect helps to perpetuate a monolithic view of Islam, especially in the West, contrary to the vibrant cultural variety of Islamic societies in the world. Xavier de Planhol (1959) is virtually the only geographer to draw attention to the practice of ziarat. He devoted a section specifically to "the geography of pilgrimages in Islam" in which the hajj is emphasized, but non-hajj pilgrimages are mentioned also. It is surprising that even very recent studies of Islamic religious circulation (Coleman and Elsner 1995; Din and Hadi 1997; Rowley 1997) downplay the significance of the ziarat.

The main purpose of this paper is to draw attention to religious travel undertaken by a large number of Muslims to places other than to Mecca. This research shows that the study of ziarat, as part of the dynamic tradition of Islamic religious circulation, is necessary to understand Islam's variegated cultural manifestations. Numerous *khankahs*, shrines, mosques, tombs and mausoleums of the Muslim saints, martyrs, Sufis, and other holy personages attest to the popularity of ziarat in most of the Muslim countries.

In spite of the non-obligatory nature of a ziarat, probably many more people participate in them every year than in the annual hajj to Mecca. Unfortunately, adequate records of pilgrims participating in ziarats are not available. Planhol (1959: 74), however, gives a few examples of pilgrim attendance at these shrines — namely, over 250,000 pilgrims at the tomb of Ahmed Bamba in Senegal in 1937, several hundred thousand at Tana (Egypt), and about 100,000 at the shrine of Sidi Abed in Algeria. "The visitor to India and Pakistan is always amazed when he discovers the innumerable shrines, saints' tombs, and places of pilgrimage ..." (Schimmel 1980: 126). Shrines continue to play an important role in the life of many rural Muslims.

Various functional aspects of shrines have been briefly discussed by Courtright in the *Encyclopedia of Religion* (1987: 299-302). Non-hajj pilgrimages also may be considered as symbolic of the regional cultural expression of Islam, especially in the non-Arab countries. Whereas the hajj places Islam in a global context, ziarats point up the spatially distinctive cultural traditions of Islamic populations.

In this study, I shall first develop a short typology of Islamic religious circulation, to situate ziarat in the framework of Muslim religious circulation, and then examine the phenomenon of the ziarat in some detail. It is not my purpose to indulge in a debate here on whether ziarat are strictly in keeping with true Islamic principles, but rather to examine this practice in countries which have substantial Muslim populations.

Typology of Islamic Religious Circulation

Muslim pilgrimages may be divided into two broad categories: obligatory and voluntary. This is in contrast with the Christian or Hindu tradition, for example, in which pilgrimage is a non-obligatory religious practice, or Sikhism in which it is discouraged. The obligatory pilgrimage in Islam is, of course, the hajj to Mecca, although the obligation is tempered by the pilgrim's financial and physical ability (Pickthall 1930: 50). The Koran enjoins the believers to "Perform the pilgrimage and the visit for Allah."

The voluntary pilgrimage (ziarat or ziara) may be divided into two distinct types for analytical purposes. First, a religious journey may be undertaken for a purely emotive or sentimental reason. Such a non-obligatory religious journey may be undertaken to listen to a holy discourse of a Sufi saint or any other religious message by or in behalf of an Imam. Such a visit also may be made for personal spiritual uplift. In addition, such a sentimental journey may be made to participate in a periodic festival held in honor of a saint, or to commemorate a special day of martyrdom, passion, birthday, and other such occasions related to religious, or even some especially venerated royal, personages.

A second type of voluntary pilgrimage may be made for reasons related to the problems of mundane existence. Fulfillment of a vow may be a major reason for ziarat. The vows may be made for reasons related to personal health or the health of a loved one. A promise to visit a saint, or a saint's grave or tomb, may be made for chronic non-psychosomatic, as well as for psychosomatic, diseases. Supplications may be made for having an offspring, or good luck in an enterprise. Clearly, some of these pilgrimages are primarily supplicatory, whereas others virtually contractual. But both rely upon the *baraka* (blessing) of the especially esteemed saint (Martin 1987: 116). A ziarat of this type is probably not much different from the pilgrimages undertaken by non-Muslim people. Table 8.1 summarizes the typology encompassing this idea. In addition, Islamic centers of ziarats may be classified as forming levels of an informal hierarchy, such as regional, subregional and local, depending upon the cultural diversity represented at each level.

Table 8.1 Typology of Islamic Religious Circulation

Obligatory
>   Hajj

Voluntary (Ziarat/Ziara)
>   *Emotive/sentimental reasons Spiritual quest*
>>   Participation in festivals (Urs)/commemorations /"jihad"/martyrdom/burial (jihad is used here in its symbolic meaning of "striving")
>>   Dawa (travel for missionary purpose)
>   *Pathogenic (Disease/Health search) reasons*
>>   Psychosomatic ailments
>>   Non-psychosomatic ailments
>   *Desiderative reasons*
>>   Personal (success, achievement, fulfillment)
>>   Loved ones (success, achievement, fulfillment)

Subsystems of Ziarat

The Muslim religious circulation suggested above is composed of two complementary systems, the hajj to Mecca being the overarching, religiously prescribed system, and the ziarat to all other places as the second system. An informal hierarchy of levels of pilgrimage centers in Islam ranges from Mecca at the very apex down to locally venerated shrines of holy people. Ziarats seem to be composed of subsystems that have developed in several cultural contexts, each of which shares the universal characteristics of Islam, but also reflects a cultural distinctiveness. These subsystems of ziarat may be tentatively grouped.

Islamic Holy Places Associated with the Prophet

Muslim holy places usually considered to be immediately below the level of Mecca are: Medina, and al-Aqsa (Dome of the Rock) in Jerusalem. Although the person of Mohammed is not deified in Islam, these two places especially associated with his life are important. Medina was the place where the prophet found security upon his hegira (flight) from Mecca. After the hajj to Mecca, many Muslims visit Medina where the prophet's mosque and tomb, as well as the graves of the famous martyrs, Abu Bakr and Umar, are located (Martin 1987: 345). These visits are not for worship or other religious ceremonies, but rather for showing respect to the martyrs. The three places Mecca, Medina, and al-Aqsa are of pan-Islamic importance, transcending doctrinal or sectarian differences. Ziarat to Medina or to al-Aqsa may be considered extensions of pilgrimage after the hajj has been performed. Considering the political realities of the Middle East, relatively few pilgrims visiting Mecca today extend their sacred journey to al-Aqsa, even though this location is venerated as the place from which Mohammed ascended into heaven.

Shia Shrines in the Middle East

Pilgrimages have a special place in Shia Islam. According to Nasr (1987: 269), the "tombs of all the imams are considered extensions of the supreme centers of Mecca and Medina, and, thus, pilgrimage to these sites ... are strongly encouraged by the jurists and the official religious hierarchy and play a very important role in the Shia religious life."

The Shia Muslims venerate their Imams and saints to such a high degree that sometimes they "allow the obligatory Muslim pilgrimage to Mecca to be substituted by a pilgrimage to the tomb of a Shia saint" (Serjeant 1967: 32). Acceptance of this type of variance or interpretation of Islamic doctrine seems to be symbolic of the

143

difference between the Arab and Iranian culture. Anwar (1960: 141-156) brings out the significance of pilgrimage activity focused on the tombs of the Imams, especially at An Najaf and Yezd. Although Shia shrines such as Mashhad (Iran) may be perhaps as venerated as Medina, and may serve even as an occasional substitute for Mecca by the Shia Muslims, in the context of worldwide Islam they may be, more appropriately, considered specific to the Iranian cultural sphere. Thus, they form part of a subsystem of Islamic religious circulation.

The major Shia shrines in the Middle East/North Africa region (Fig. 8.1) are: the Tomb of Musa el-Khadim (Kazimain) in Baghdad, Iraq; Karbala, Iraq; Mashhad, Iran; An Najaf, Iraq; Qom, Iran; Sammarra, Iraq; the Mosque of al-Khalil at Hebron in the West Bank; Qairwan, Tunisia; Muley Idris, Morocco (Serjeant 1986: 26).

The Sufi Shrines

The Sufi order of Islam has added a large number of shrines to the Islamic religious circulation system throughout the Middle East, North Africa, parts of sub-Saharan Africa, South Asia, Southeast Asia, western China, and the Central Asian countries. Most of these shrines are of regional importance within the framework of the linguistic region of a domiciled saint, but some have a following that cuts across international boundaries, partly due to territorial changes or emergence of new nations. According to Ira Lapidus (1988: 262-263), Sufism became central to the structure of lineage societies after the thirteenth century.

Coleman and Elsner (1995: 69) characterize the Sufi shrines as "alternative routes to the sacred." This, in my view, is only partially true, since these shrines only complement Muslim religious circulation. No site can replace the centrality of Mecca, even though some Shia clerics may argue otherwise, and promoters of a particular shrine, such as Ajmer in India, may speak of it as a "second Mecca" (Coleman and Elsner 1995: 223).

Sufi Shrines of Central Asia

Bennigsen and Wimbush (1985:115-157) have identified and mapped 32 main "working" holy places of the Sufis in the Caucasus (Fig. 8.2), and 59 in Central Asia (Fig. 8.3). They attribute the survival of Islam in this part of the former Soviet Union mainly to this "parallel Islam" rather than the official Muslim establishment, which was loyal to the Soviet regime. As newly independent countries of Central Asia articulate their national identities, it is inevitable that Islam will emerge as a major political force. This process is being already realized by other Muslim countries such as Iran, Pakistan, and Afghanistan, immediately bordering the new

144

Central Asian nations. In this newly developing context, Sufism may no longer be marginalized, and its shrines will become more overtly popular than just a few years ago.

Sufi Shrines of South Asia

Subhan (1960) has listed scores of Sufi shrines in India and Pakistan. These lists include the location of the shrine, and the date of death of the saint associated with each shrine. Although several locations are only vaguely identified (for example, "Bengal"), it is clear that all of these shrines developed during and after the thirteenth century. The largest number of shrines (188) is attributed to the Chishti order of Sufis, although the shrines of Suhrawardi (72), Qadiri (116), Naqshbandi (64), and those of a number of minor or irregular orders (103), are also listed. Some of these shrines are virtually of international importance, for example Ajmer, whereas others are more modest, being patronized in the framework of a local dialect region.

Incorporation of Pre-Islamic into Islamic Religious Circulation

Another component of the Islamic religious circulation system is based on a ziarat to shrines which were holy places in pre-Islamic times, but which were incorporated into more local or national Islamic culture without being associated with the Sufi order. Cuisinier (1960: 251-274) gives some examples of ziarat in the cultural context of Javanese Islam. Ira Lapidus (1988: 261-262) comments on the fusion of Islamic and pre-Islamic identities among village societies focused upon shrine worship. Ikram (1964:124) has suggested that the rapid diffusion of Islam in Bengal after the thirteenth century had its basis in the utilization of a pre-Islamic, Buddhist religious circulation system by the Muslim saints who migrated to Bengal in the wake of Islamic conquest. Wholesale incorporation of the nodes and pathways of a preexisting religious circulation system must have given ready-made access to a vast rural population. Ikram (1964:124) specifically states:

> When the Islamic missionaries arrived they found in several instances that the conquering armies had destroyed both the temples of revived Hinduism and of the older Buddhism; in their place — often on the same sites — they built new shrines. Moreover, they very frequently transferred ancient Hindu and Buddhist stories of miracles to Muslim saints, fusing the old religion into the new on a level that could be accepted by the masses.

Although Ikram's views about Islam's diffusion are not shared by Roy (1983), it seems plausible to accept Ikram's general contention that the religious centers of the pre-Islamic religion served as convenient nodes for the new religion. In this manner the preexisting religious circulation system was simply taken over, though the message and the pilgrims that circulated in the system were Islamic.

Centers of Local Piety: Graves, Mazars, and Tombs

Islam is a vibrant religion intertwined in the daily life of people at the local level. At that level, components of the Islamic religious circulation include tombs, *mazars* (small memorial shrines) and even humble graves of locally respected saints and holy men credited with wisdom, and even miraculous curing. Small periodic gatherings of the devotees on Thursdays, Fridays, or holy occasions may remind the outsiders of their existence. These holy spots are an integral part of the village communities in which they exist. Finally, the local mosque serves as the focus for the affirmation of Muslim beliefs on a continuing daily basis.

Thus, the Muslim religious circulation is composed of several subsystems. No religious hierarchy defines the level of a place, except that all Muslims accept Mecca as Islam's *axis mundi*, and that each local mosque is truly oriented to that focus. Between these levels there are numerous holy places that have developed as Islam replaced other beliefs, and utilized their circulation manifold. Muslim religious circulation may then be considered as a complex system. Within it though there is no single religiously defined hierarchy, except Mecca's unquestioned primacy, but there may be intertwined hierarchies; some based upon the sheer number of pilgrims, others associated with the major branches of Islam or based on sectarian allegiances. Overriding all the above considerations (except the position of Mecca) national political boundaries may influence the development of a system of pilgrimages.

The Ziarat and Regional Cultural Symbolism

The regional cultural variety of Muslims is reflected in the ziarats, not in the hajj. The hajj transcends Islam's cultural mosaic. All Muslims on the hajj, irrespective of their region of origin or social status, must be clad in the *ihram* garb of two white cotton sheets. This dress and the rites of the hajj are visible symbols of the universal Islamic brotherhood.

On the contrary, the non-hajj ziarat reflects the cultural dimensions of Islamic people. There are no uniformly prescribed rules comparable to ihram, and the individual pilgrim in the ziarat follows the rules specific to the place and local culture. The difference between ziarat and hajj is sharply brought out by the fact that

146

many non-Muslims freely participate in the ziarat, but the hajj is exclusive to Muslims.

The behavior of the individuals in the ziarat, moreover, reflects the cultural context, and the individual's existential quest, rather than a universal Islamic canon. In fact, individuals in the ziarat, may be seen expressing behavior not related to Islam as a religion. It is not uncommon to see pilgrims in ziarat singing devotional songs, expressing their frailty, or asking for the intercession of a local saint in personal problems. In some respects the hajj and non-hajj circulation systems may be analogous to the complementarity of the "great" and "little" traditions, which the anthropologist Robert Redfield (1963) developed four decades ago. In such a formulation, the non-hajj religious circulation is reflective of the regional cultural distinctions in Islam. In fact, it could be argued that the non-hajj pilgrimages are symbolic of the distinctive regional/cultural contexts of Islam. Four of these are suggested below, although many other more localized ones could be identified easily.

Sub-Saharan Africa

The ziarat is generally undertaken in most other parts of the world to seek the intercession of the saint based upon a belief in his baraka (divine power emanating from the holy man) (Lapidus 1988: 919). In the context of the sub-Saharan region, however, Trimingham (1980:74-77) makes the point that a true saint cult and asceticism concomitant with the concept of baraka have not become integral parts of Islam because of differences between the world views of the Arabs and the Africans. The concept of baraka is the *sin qua non* of the ziarat in the Middle East, but, according to Trimingham, it did not penetrate in Africa beyond the Sahel. The underlying reasons present a scholarly challenge. Likewise, asceticism, which is fundamental to the lifestyle of Muslim saints and holy men in most other regions of the world, seems life denying to the African cultures (Trimingham 1980: 75). Perhaps due to such reasons the ziarat has had a limited appeal in Africa south of the Sahara.

In Northern Africa, by contrast, the cult of holy men, the marabouts "through whom the supernatural pervades," has a very special place (Eickelman 1976: 10). The marabouts, living or dead, are perceived to have the power to communicate God's power to their clients (Eickelman 1976: 284). Accepting the observations of Trimingham and Eickelman, that asceticism related to sainthood has limited appeal in the life affirming cultures of sub-Saharan Africa, it is not unreasonable to suggest that ziarats are less likely to develop there in contrast to North Africa. This would explain, to some degree, the paucity of pilgrimage shrines in sub-Saharan Africa. The same, however, does not apply to the increasing popularity of hajj among the

Muslims of sub-Saharan Africa. For many relatively recent converts to Islam, to perform hajj is to publicly affirm their conversion. The hajj is likely to intensify as Islamization proceeds in sub-Saharan Africa, but ziarats may take some time to develop.

Iran and the Neighboring Shia Areas

Islam's manifestation in Iran has been very different than in the Arab cultural region, and this has impacted the development of a distinctive pilgrimage tradition in Iran. During the Safavid Period (1502-1736) the state in Iran controlled the religious establishment to an extraordinary degree (Lapidus 1988: 302). The Safavids, who established Shiism in Iran in early sixteenth century, violently suppressed Sunnism (Lapidus 1988: 297). They destroyed many Sunni shrines, and even de-emphasized the pilgrimage to Mecca in favor of ziarats to the shrines of Shia Imams, especially to Karbala (Imam Husayn) and An Najaf (Imam Ali). The practice of pilgrimage to Imam shrines, especially related to martyrdom and the associated effusive ziarat seems to characterize the Persian Shiite cultural region of Islam. This distinctive tradition of ziarat to the Imam shrines has become a national symbol of modem Iran. Upon Imam Khomeini's death in 1989, his golden-domed place of burial has become a national shrine, visited by hundreds of thousands of Iranians from all parts of Iran (*Akron Beacon Journal*, 13 June 1989).

Louis Dupree (1976) has reported a number of ziarat shrines in Afghanistan. He notes that even though saint cults have been forbidden or discouraged in Islam, it has been impossible to eliminate them. Afghans build ziarats around local *malangs*, who are a special class of wandering holy men touched by God (Dupree 1976: 1).

Indonesia

The island world of Indonesia and Malaysia has had a very different system of ziarat. These countries were Islamicized on a base of Mahayana Buddhism and Hinduism, in both of which the practice of pilgrimage to various shrines was a commonplace. Whereas in the coastal areas the influences of Arab Islam and of Indian Muslim merchants from Coromandel and Malabar were considerable due to the trading and commercial connections with the Arab lands and India, in the interior a very modified Islam spread. Drewes (1955: 286) maintains that Indonesian people have retained some of their fundamental pre-Islamic ways including their tradition of visiting shrines. Similarly, according to Planhol (1959: 117-119), conversion of Indonesia to Islam for a long time was very superficial and there was what he terms

148

a "cultural symbiosis." Many Javanese peasants still venerate the rice goddess Dewi Sri (the consort of the Hindu god Vishnu) (Koentjaraningrat 1984: 361). Pilgrimages to pre-Islamic sacred centers continue in Indonesia. In some cases a Muslim saint (marabout) is now the object of pilgrimage in place of a former, but non-Muslim (Cuisinier 1960: 251-273). Lapidus also emphasizes that from the sixteenth to the nineteenth centuries in Ache and Malay villages, people followed both Muslim and non-Muslim practices as well as the practice of visiting holy places and people (Lapidus 1988: 477).

South Asia

The ziarat is a popular aspect of Muslim religious circulation in South Asia (Fig. 8.4). Pilgrimages to shrines of Muslim saints in Bangladesh and India are in a state of considerable revival. The number of pilgrims to such shrines seems to be increasing, though it is not clear whether this increase is simply a function of growing population or increased accessibility. Schimmel (1980:126) has examined the importance of the shrines and places of pilgrimage in the South Asian countries. Major Muslim shrines of South Asia have been mapped in *A Historical Atlas of South Asia* (Schwartzberg 1992: 41, 47). Several places in India and Pakistan are associated with relics of the prophet and of the Sufi saints (Schimmel 1980: 126-127).

The organization of some of the major Muslim shrines, such as that of Muinuddin Chishti at Ajmer (Rajasthan), and of Shah ul Amir Qadir at Nagore (Tamil Nadu) resembles somewhat that of the major Hindu pilgrimage centers. Several organizational similarities between Sufi shrines and Hindu pilgrimage places are well-known (Eaton 1978: 294). Agents of the Muslim *dargah* (sanctuary), just as the *pandas* of Hindu places, conduct the pilgrims to various aspects of the shrines, and ensure that the wealthy patrons, Muslim and non-Muslims, make contributions and record their pilgrimage in the shrines' record books. Pilgrims from Pakistan, and Bangladesh form the largest contingent of foreign visitors at Ajmer. Schimmel (1980:129-138) makes several keen observations regarding the ziarat to these shrines, but the most important motive for the ziarat is supplication for personal problems.

Multireligion pilgrimages to many Muslim shrines (as differentiated from mosques), especially Sufi shrines, have become a characteristic of Indian pilgrimages. Before the emergence of Pakistan and Bangladesh, Hindus frequently patronized Muslim shrines in India, and even today many Muslim shrines attract Hindu pilgrims. This practice occurs at the local, as well as at the national level, despite frequent images of religious discord in the media.

149

The spirit of this type of ziarat is captured in Schimmel's perceptive description of the common elements of ziarat, and of the specific ziarat of Muinuddin Chishti's mausoleum and several other shrines. My own visit to this shrine in 1986 (Fig. 8.5) impressed upon me the fact that religious boundaries are not impermeable, and the "confluence of Muslim and Hindu ideas and forms of asceticism" which Schimmel (1980:137) talks about, occurs particularly at shrines which have become a resource for the human quest for the "ultimate well-being" (Prozesky 1984). A vast number of people undertake ziarat for supplication and many must combine their visit for fulfilling a previous promise along with the day of *Urs* fair held to commemorate the saint's death.

Ziarats in South Asia are undertaken as a matter of individual commitment, obligation, and conviction, not as a result of religious command (Bhardwaj 1987: 457-468). Pilgrims at these places seem expressive. Individual emotions predominate. Perceptible religious diversity rather than total uniformity prevails (since non-Muslims also participate). Inclusion rather than exclusion, intimacy rather than formality, and above all relationship rather than ritual seem to characterize the ziarat. No wonder then that such places have become the symbols of syncretism, so clearly Indian in its essence, and precisely due to this reason, so disagreeable to the religious orthodoxy, both Hindu and Muslim.

Conclusions

Non-hajj religious journeys have received very limited professional attention from geographers. They are an integral part of the Muslim religious circulation in the world even though they are discouraged by the orthodoxy. A variety of focal points exist for such religious circulation, for example, saints, Imams, and martyrs. Their commonality is that pilgrims come to these shrines for supplication, to cope with problems of mundane existence.

In this sense they complement the hajj to Mecca, which Muslims visit due to religious obligation, and where they participate in the "re-actualization" of the momentous formative events of Islam. Thus, the hajj represents the universal aspect of Islam whereas the non-hajj ziarat is the emblem of the regional cultural variety of Islam. These complementary patterns together constitute the Islamic religious circulation. Only further studies can help determine the true nature of this circulation.

Acknowledgments

I am thankful to Dr. Abdullah A. Khan for helpful suggestions on an earlier draft, and to Yichen Zhu for her help in preparation of the maps.

150

References

Al-Naqar, U. 1972. *The Pilgrimage Tradition in West Africa.* Khartoum: Khartoum University Press.

Anwar, A. 1960. "Les Pèlerinages chez les Persans." Pp.139-156 in *Les Pèlerinages. Sources Orientales*, vol. 3. Paris: Éditions du Seuil.

Bennigsen, A., and S. Wimbush. 1985. *Mystics and Commissars: Sufism in the Soviet Union.* Berkeley: University of California Press.

Bhardwaj, S.M. 1987. "Single Religion Shrines, Multireligion Pilgrimages." *National Geographical Journal of India* 33(4): 457-468.

Bousquet, G.H. and J. Schacht. 1957. *Selected Works of C. Snouck Hurgronje.* Leiden: E. J. Brill.

Coleman, S. and J. Elsner. 1995. *Pilgrimage: Past and Present in the World Religions.* Cambridge: Harvard University Press.

Courtright, M. 1987. "Shrines." Pp. 299-302 in *The Encyclopedia of Religion*, vol. 13, edited by M. Eliade. New York: Macmillan.

Cuisinier, Jeanne. 1960. "Les Pèlerinages en Indonesie." Pp. 247-274 in *Les Pèlerinages. Sources Orientales,* vol. 3. Paris: Éditions du Seuil.

Din, A. and A. Hadi. 1997. "Muslim Pilgrimage from Malaysia." Pp. 161-182 in *Sacred Places, Sacred Spaces: The Geography of Pilgrimages*, edited by R.H. Stoddard and A. Morinis. Baton Rouge: Geoscience Publications.

Drewes, G.W.J. 1955. "Indonesia: Mysticism and Activism." Pp. 284-310 in *Unity and Variety in Muslim Civilization*, edited by G. von Grunebaum. Chicago: University of Chicago Press.

Dupree, Louis. 1976. "Saint Cults in Afghanistan." *American Universities Field Staff Reports, South Asia Series* 20(1): 1-26.

Eaton, R. 1978. *Sufis of Bijapur 1300-1700: Social Role of Sufis in Medieval India.* Princeton: Princeton University Press.

Eickelman, D. 1976. *Moroccan Islam: Tradition and Society in a Pilgrimage Center.* Austin: University of Texas Press.

Ikram, S.M. 1964. *Muslim Civilization in India.* New York: Columbia University Press.

Isaac, E. 1973. "The Pilgrimage to Mecca." *Geographical Review* 63: 405-409.

Kamal, A. 1961. *The Sacred Journey: Being a Pilgrimage to Mecca.* London: George Allen and Unwin.

King, R. 1972. "The Pilgrimage to Mecca: Some Geographical and Historical Aspects." *Erdkunde* 26: 61-73.

Koentjaraningrat, R.M. 1984. "Javanese." Pp. 184-191 in *Muslim Peoples: A World Ethnographic Survey*. Edited by Richard V. Weekes. Westport: Greenwood Press.

Lapidus, Ira. 1988. *A History of Islamic Societies*. Cambridge: Cambridge University Press.

Long, D.E. 1979. *The Hajj Today: A Survey of the Contemporary Mecca Pilgrimage*. Albany: State University of New York Press.

Makky, G.A.W. 1978. *Mecca, The Pilgrimage City: A Study of Pilgrim Accommodation*. London: Croom Helm, for Hajj Research Centre.

_____. 1981. *Characteristics of Pilgrim Accommodation in Mecca and Recommendations for Improvements*. Ph.D. dissertation, Michigan State University.

Martin, R.C. 1987. "Pilgrimage: Muslim Pilgrimage." Pp. 338-346 in *The Encyclopedia of Religion*, vol. 11, edited by M. Eliade. New York: Macmillan.

Nasr, S.H. 1987. "Shiism: Ithnā 'Asharīyah." Pp. 260-270 in *The Encyclopedia of Religion*, vol. 13, edited by M. Eliade. New York: Macmillan.

Pickthall, M. 1930. *The Meaning of the Glorious Koran*. London: George Allen & Unwin.

Planhol, Xavier de. 1959. *The World of Islam*. Ithaca: Cornell University Press.

Prozesky, M. 1984. *Religion and Ultimate Well-Being*. New York: St. Martin's Press.

Redfield, Robert. 1963. *The Little Community and Peasant Society and Culture*. Chicago: University of Chicago Press.

Rowley, G. and S.A.S. El-Hamdan. 1978. "The Pilgrimage to Mecca: An Explanatory and Predictive Model." *Environment and Planning A* 10: 1053-1071.

Rowley, G. 1997. "The Pilgrimage to Mecca and the Centrality of Islam." Pp. 141-159 in *Sacred Places, Sacred Spaces*, edited by R.H. Stoddard and A. Morinis. Baton Rouge: Louisiana State University.

Roux, Jean-Paul. 1958. *L'Islam en Asie*. Paris: Payot.

Roy, A. 1983. *The Islamic Syncretistic Tradition in Bengal*. Princeton, N.J.: Princeton University Press.

Rutter, Eldon. 1929. "The Muslim Pilgrimage." *Geographical Journal* 74: 271-273.

Sardar, Ziauddin and M.A.Z. Badawi, eds. 1978. *Hajj Studies*, Volume 1. London: Croom Helm, for the Hajj Research Centre.

Schimmel, Annemarie. 1980. *Islam in the Indian Subcontinent*. Leiden: E.J. Brill.

Schwartzberg, Joseph, ed. 1992. *A Historical Atlas of South Asia*. New York: Oxford University Press.

Serjeant, R.B. 1986. "Islam." In *The Middle East and North Africa 1987.* London: Europa Publications.

Shair, I.M. and P.P Karan. 1979. "Geography of the Islamic Pilgrimage." *Geo-Journal* 3: 599-608.

Subhan, B. 1960. *Sufism, Its Saints and Shrines*. Lucknow: Lucknow Publishing House.

Trimingham, J. 1980. *The Influence of Islam Upon Africa*. London: Longman.

―――――――――――

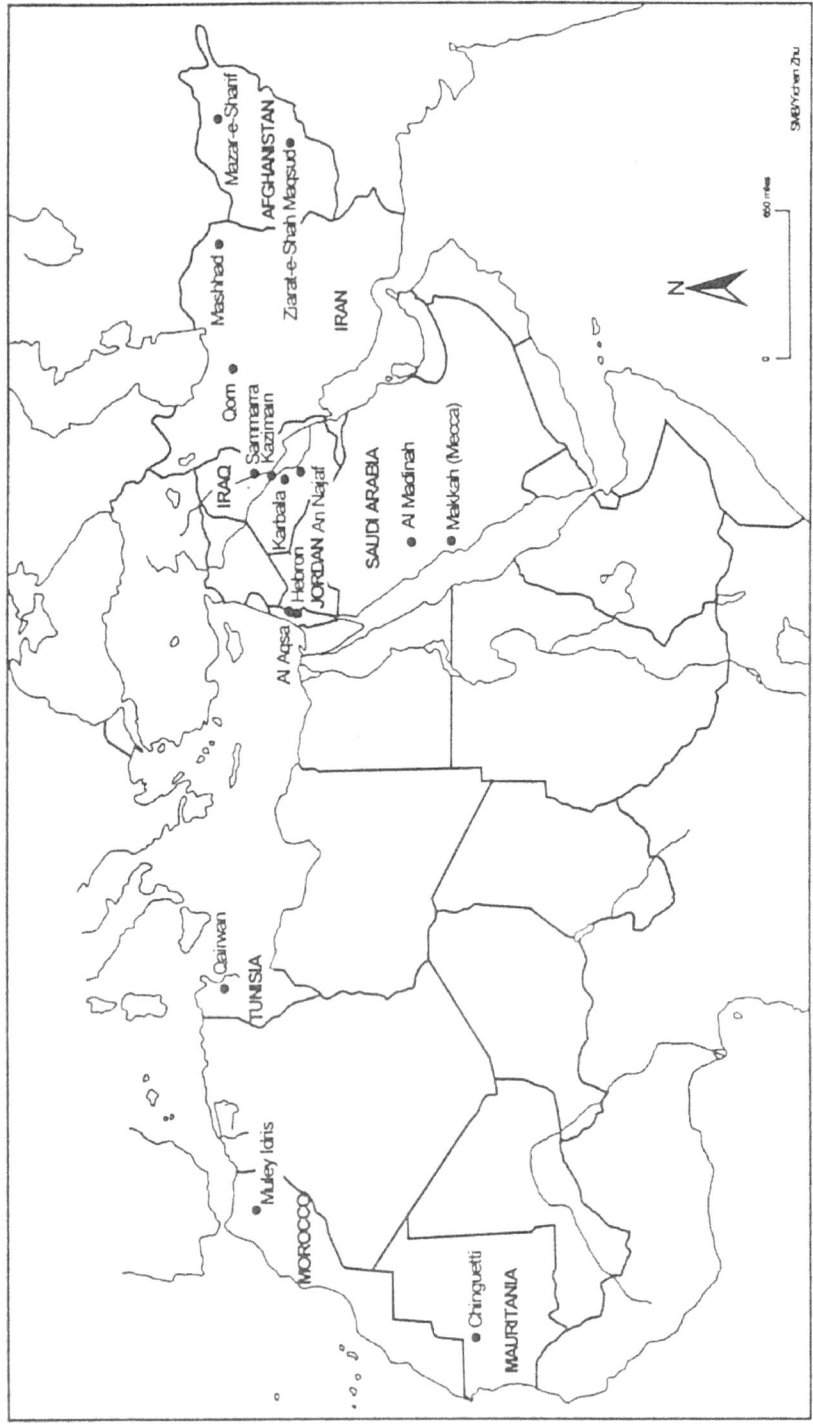

Figure 8.1. Major Muslim holy places in the Middle East and North Africa. Many of these are Shia shrines. Source: based on various authors (see text).

154

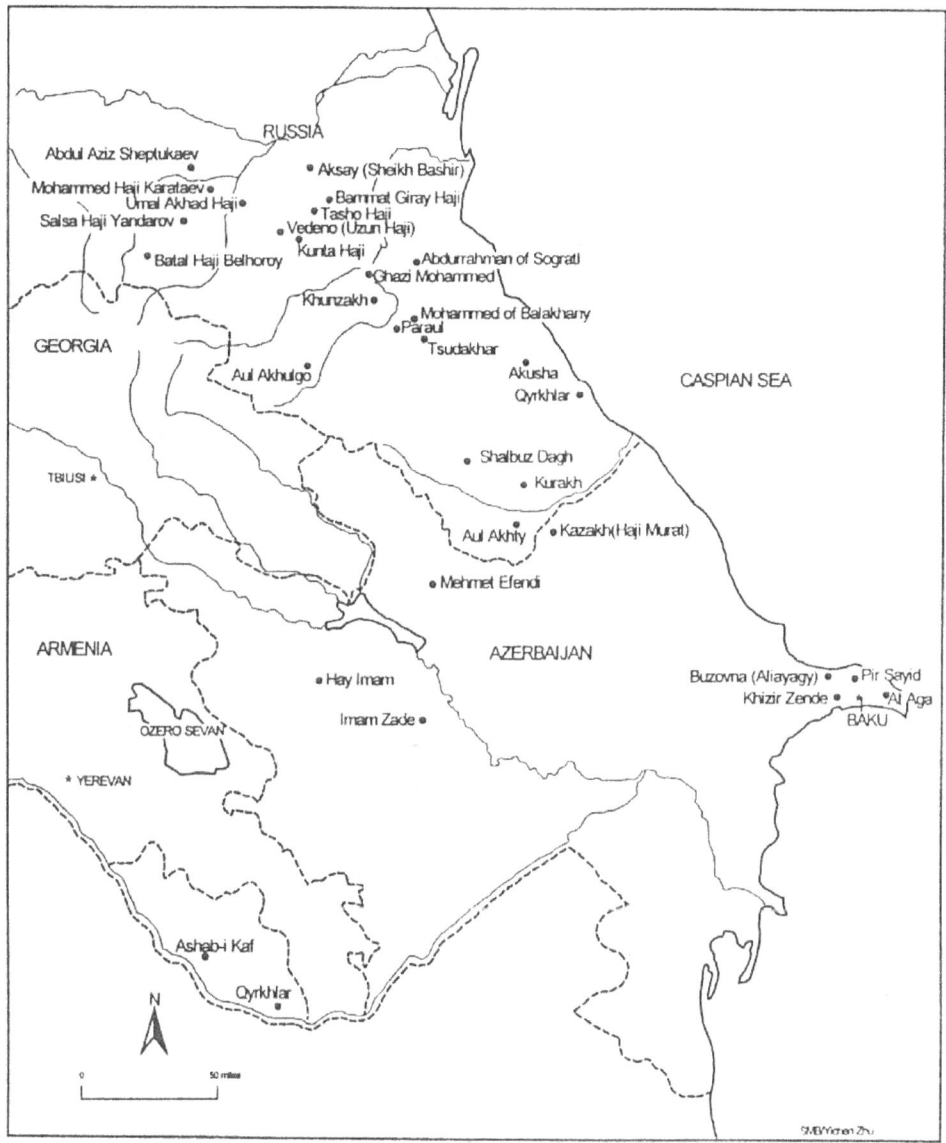

Figure 8.2. Sufi saints and martyrs in the Caucasus region associated with holy places. (Rerawn from Bennigsen and Wimbush 1985: 16).

155

Figure 8.3. Sufi saints and martyrs in Central Asia associated with holy places. (Redrawn from Bennigsen and Wimbush 1985: 130-131).

156

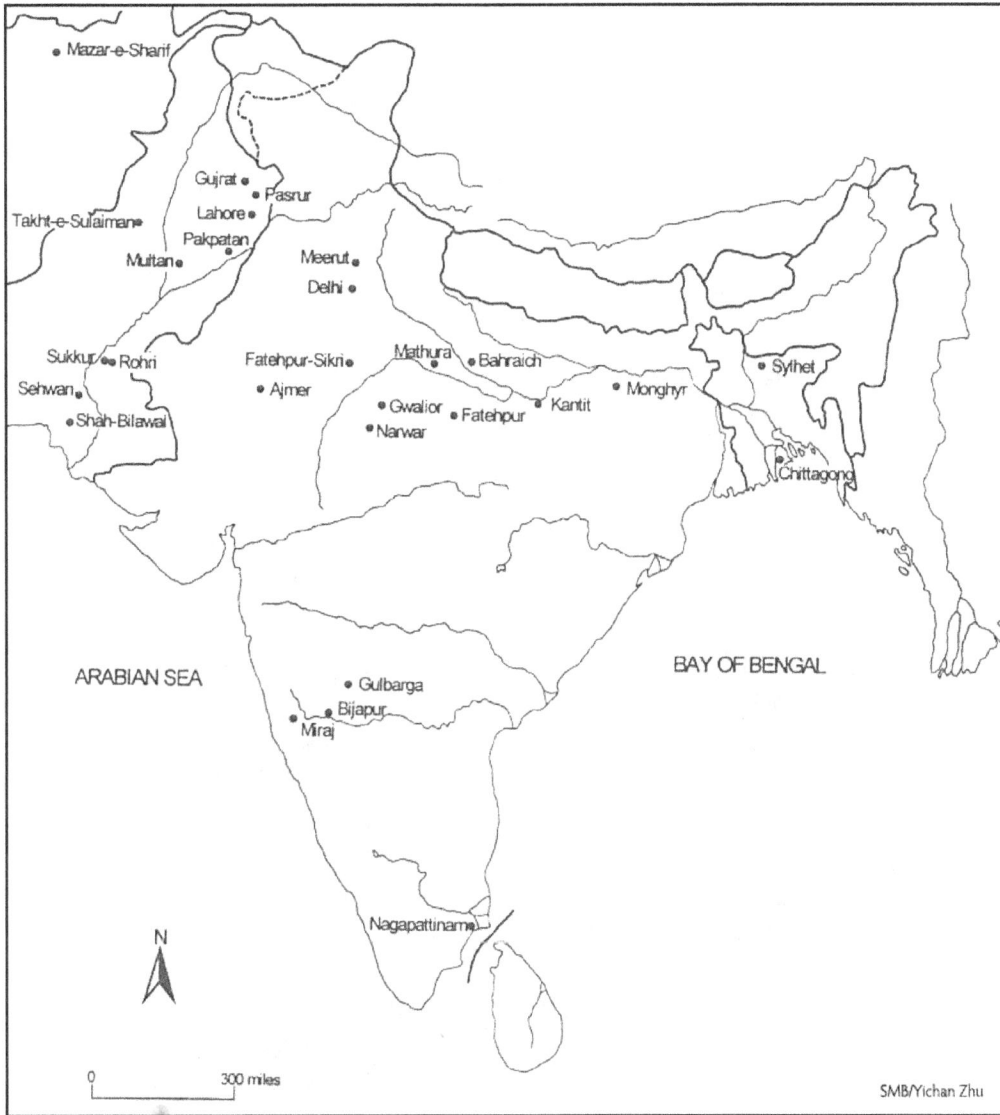

Figure 8.4. Major Muslim non-hajj pilgrimage (ziarat) sites in South Asia.
(Partly based on Subhan 1960).

Figure 8.5. Dargah (shrine) of the Sufi saint Khwaja Muinuddin Chishti (1136-1233 C.E.) at Ajmer in Rajasthan, India. This is the most well-known center for non-hajj pilgrimage (ziarat) in South Asia. Many pilgrims at this holy place are non-Muslims.

9

REGIONALIZATION AND REGIONALISM IN SRI LANKA [1]

Robert H. Stoddard

Abstract

The "ethnic problem" in Sri Lanka today refers primarily to the demand by some Tamil groups for greater autonomy. Much of the current controversy focuses on the degree of autonomy that the various contending groups are willing to accept, such as a separate nation or devolution within the existing state. The issue also involves the delineation of territory and decisions about the criteria applied for establishing boundaries. Regionalization procedures applied to recognized census data can produce various "objective" results, as demonstrated in this paper. However, it is acknowledged that emotional feelings of regionalism are also important in settling boundary disputes.

Introduction

The bombing of an AirLankan plane last spring — just at the time the seven leaders of the major industrial countries at Tokyo economic summit issued their *Statement of International Terrorism* — drew public attention to a situation that scholars of South Asia have known about for several years. I refer, of course, to the ethnic issue of Sri Lanka. The core of the controversy focuses on the degree of autonomy that various contending groups desire, or are willing to accept. On the one side, several Tamil organizations are demanding an independent state, completely separated from the remaining portion of the present day Sri Lanka. On the other side, the Sri Lankan government, although willing to allow more regional autonomy to political

---

[1] Presented at *South Asian Geography: Changing Trends & Patterns I,* 15th Annual Conference on South Asia, Madison, Wisconsin, November 7, 1986.

159

subdivisions where Tamils are dominant, will understandably not agree to the secession of part of the country.

I am not primarily concerned, however, with the political justifications advanced by the various groups for their positions. My purpose here is to discuss the territorial questions related to regionalism and to present various regionalizations based on several criteria and areal units.

Some Territorial Considerations

The *ethnic issue* in Sri Lanka today is a typical illustration of regionalism. This geographic phenomenon occurs where groups of people regard themselves as culturally distinct from other persons living within a particular notion-state and where members of the perceived groups tend to occupy separate areas. Or, at least, many people believe that persons of an identified group *should* be occupying certain regions. This spatial segregation, whether reflecting actual patterns of residency or from idealized occupancy, reinforces feelings of territoriality. Although members of the dominant group may consider certain areas as regions where persons in the subordinate group *belong*, those in control invariably insist that their jurisdiction must extend over the entire country. Often this combination of control with regionalization of ethnic groups is expressed through various forms of spatial discrimination — as illustrated in South Africa.

In contrast, members of the subordinate group, especially if they are in the minority, usually regard territory as an important element in expressing group identity. The desire to exert more self-government contributes to an increased consciousness of a region — that is, regionalism. Ultimately, regionalism may lead to the desire for complete political control over the territory through the formation of a separate nation.

This is essentially the situation in Sri Lanka today (Map 9.1). Although there are varying proposals promoted by the many Tamil groups, most advocate the creation of a new nation, Tamil Eelam. Conversely, the Government agrees there should be greater regional autonomy but certainly not to the extent of complete national separation. Irrespective of decisions about the degree of regional control, the final settlement will necessarily involve a delineation of regional boundaries, which is the issue I am addressing here.

Several Tamils have advocated a boundary coinciding with what is called the Tamil homeland, which is based on territory occupied during selected historical periods (Map 9.2). But obviously, areas of occupancy have shifted through the many centuries of the island's history and they have not necessarily coincided with vague zones of territorial control. Such spatial imprecision means that now the locations

160

of boundaries of so-called "homelands" differ, even among the Tamil groups, as illustrated by the two definitions shown here (Map 9.2). Certainly historians with contrasting allegiance can justify drastically different boundaries. Because of such historical uncertainties and because of the emotions associated with regionalism, an objective delineation of regional boundaries based on ancient settlement patterns or past territorial supremacy is virtually impossible.

An alternative approach to the regionalization of the country is one based on the contemporary distributions of population. This can lead to an objective regionalization, but it will still require political negotiations because ethnic regions are a function of these four criteria: 1. *The definition of the pertinent population.* 2. *The definition of territorial belongingness.* 3. *The size of areal units being grouped.* 4. *The decision about the necessity of regional contiguity.*

For clarification of these criteria, let's first consider the *definition of the group to be regionalized.* Usually, the population is regarded as consisting of those defined by census data as the Sri Lankan Tamils. That is, the area to be regionalized is where the Tamil population is predominately Sri Lankan — not the community regarded as *Indian* (Table 9.1). This is partly because generally the latter have not been politically active, partly because of their uncertain citizenship status, and probably partly because of their caste differences. Nevertheless, for comparative purposes, I have examined the distributions of Tamils as if they were combined into a single ethnic group.

The second condition concerns *how territory is defined as "belonging" to a particular population.* Usually, the definition is based on the existence of a majority, but in a census region where no group exceeds 50%, a case can be made for defining territorial belongingness according to the group having a plurality. In most administrative subdivisions of Sri Lanka, one ethnic group has a large majority so this potential controversy about belongingness occurs infrequently. Nevertheless, it does become an important issue in a few cases, as becomes apparent when looking at the mapped distributions.

The real crux of the territorial problem — which is the third condition — depends on the *size of the areal unit used for identifying and regionalizing the population.* The distributional pattern of Sri Lankan Tamils at the provincial level is quite different from the level of local grama sevekas — as I will show shortly.

The fourth condition is the persistent and troublesome issue of *whether or not a region should be contiguous.* In fact, this has been one of the major controversies in Sri Lanka. The Tamils have insisted that the North and East Provinces should be considered as one region or unit because they have a common boundary, but the national government has maintained that the populations in these two existing provinces do not constitute a single continuous region. Because of these differing viewpoints, the contiguity condition needs to be examined carefully.

Ethnic Regions at Various Scales

With these four conditions of regionalization in mind, let's look at the distributions of ethnic groups in Sri Lanka. The data used for mapping percentages are from the 1981 census, except for the grama sevaka maps.

The first examination here is at the scale of provinces. As can be seen by the tabled percentages (Table 9.2), seven of the nine provinces have a Sinhalese majority, one has a Tamil majority, and one — the Eastern Province — has no ethnic majority. The Sri Lankan Tamils have a plurality with 40% of the total. Locationally, these two non-Sinhalese provinces are contiguous (Map 9.3). Therefore, if the Tamil territory is defined by only a plurality of and if areal units are grouped at the provincial level, then the North and East do, indeed, form a contiguous Tamil region. Conversely, if ethnic regions are delimited by majorities, then the Tamil region consists of just the Northern Province. Furthermore, when both Tamil populations are combined into one category, there are no changes in this map.

The segregation of ethnic groups is also evident at the district level. For example, in over half of the 24 districts, the percentage of the majority exceeds 80 (Table 9.3). In only three districts does the percentage drop below 50%. However, the locations of the districts lacking a majority complicate the task of regionalization (Map 9.4). Two of the three plurality districts are in the Eastern Province, and the district bordering the northern Tamil region. (i.e. Trincomalee) is dominated by Sinhalese. This configuration, therefore, prevents forming a contiguous Tamil region, irrespective of whether the defining criterion is a majority or plurality.

The Tamils are even more geographically fragmented if the *Indian* Tamils are considered a part of the population to be regionalized. This is because, if the percentage of Sri Lankan Tamils is combined with the plurality of Indian Tamils residing in Nuwara Eliya, the total percentage creates a majority in that centrally located district. Using the combined Tamil definition, however, does not alter the tripartite composition of the Eastern Province. Thus, an all-Tamil region (although not mapped here) consists of three widely separated, non-contiguous areas.

The next smaller areal unit is what is commonly called an AGA. Although the AGA is too small a unit for a high level of political autonomy, this does not mean that district or provincial boundaries can not be redrawn to coincide with ethnic differences. So, the patterns generated by this scale need to be examined. As revealed by Map 5, the spatial fragmentation of the Tamils persists at this degree of detail.

162

Not only are the Sri Lankan Tamils not dominant in the Trincomalee District (as already noted), but they form the majority in only one AGA, as well as a plurality in another. Both are isolated from other Tamil regions and from each other. Likewise, the Tamils in the Amparai District are concentrated in one AGA, which is separated from other Tamil areas.

At this geographic scale, the Indian Tamils form a majority on a region consisting of two AGAs (and they constitute the plurality in another). So, like the Moors, they also form district regions within the multi-ethnic country. Consequently, if the two Tamil groups are combined (Map 9.6), the task of forming a contiguous Tamil region would be almost impossible because of the wide scattering of AGAs having Tamil majorities.

It is informative to examine the ethnic distributions in even greater detail because they expose the mosaic of settlement patterns in the Eastern Province. Unfortunately, the data are from the 1971 census; and I obtained them from a source that I suspect contains some copying errors. Irrespective of these limitations, the discontinuity of Tamil concentrations is revealed. In the Batticaloa District (Map 9.7), non-Tamil areas are minor; but in the main portion of Amparai District (Map 9.8), the isolation of Tamil regions is clear. And, in the critical district of Trincomalee (Map 9.9), the impossibility of delimiting a contiguous Tamil region is obvious.

Conclusion

The primary goal of regionalization is to divide an area so that each region is as homogeneous as possible in terms of some specified phenomenon, such as ethnic affiliation. Over much of Sri Lanka, one of the ethnic communities tends to dominate in each administrative unit, so it is fairly easy to delimit the territory *belonging* to the various groups. However, in the Trincomalee and Amparai districts, areas of ethnic homogeneity are very small.

The small size of ethnic areas raises the problem of contiguity. Whether or not a particular region is allowed to consist of more than one contiguous area depends on the reasons for regionalization. In the case of administrative regions, spatially separate parts are seldom favored. Certainly a state having two geographic parts is very rare — as demonstrated by the demise of formerly divided Pakistan. Therefore, the formation of a single political unit consisting primarily of Sri Lankan Tamils seems unlikely because of the many widely separated parts along the east coast.

One alternative, of course, is to give priority to the contiguity goal and to relax the homogeneity constraint. This could be achieved, for example, by joining the existing Northern and Eastern Provinces into a single region and, consequently, sacrificing homogeneity. However, as these maps have clearly shown, the eastern portion would consist only of several minority groups. But this, of course, is the very situation that is being opposed now by those who are dissatisfied with living in a pluralistic society. Thus, this can hardly be regarded as justifiable solution.

Appendix: A Background Summary [2]

Even though my goal is not to examine the sequence of events that have preceded the current controversy, I will provide a very short summary of a few factors contributing to the conflict. Because my summary is very brief, it is highly selective and does not adequately present many aspects of an extremely complex situation.

The ethnic composition of the population during the last decades before independence is typified by data from the 1911 census (Table 9.1). The *Sinhalese* are predominately Buddhist and speak Sinhala. The term *Sri Lankan Tamil* general refers to high-caste Hindus whose ancestors have lived on the island for many centuries but trace their ancient origins to the Tamil speaking area of India. In contrast, the community of *Indian Tamils* originated during the British Colonial period when South Indians were brought to the island to work in plantations. The title *Moor* is almost synonymous with Moslem and relates to persons whose ancestry is mostly rooted in Arabic areas of Southwest Asia. Although many speak Tamil, culturally, they are quite distinct from the other two Tamil-speaking groups.

As indicated by this ethnic classification, in the early 20th century, the Tamils were a minority in a country that was approximately two-thirds Sinhalese. Although ethnic distinctions were reinforced by the Colonial government in the 1920s when indigenous representation was communally based, apparently territorial identification was not an issue until recent decades.

During the later years of the Colonial period, opposition was expressed not only against foreign political rule but also against the domination of the English language and Christian religion. At the time of Independence in 1948, many Sinhalese wanted to regain what they felt had been lost since the arrival of the Portuguese in the early 1500s, the Dutch after 1656, and the British after 1796, especially after the fall of the Kandyian Kingdom in 1815. They wanted to correct the deprivation imposed by foreign rulers by restoring self-rule, their own language, and

---

[2] In addition to the portion presented orally at the South Asian Conference, the following section was included in a written version of the paper. Several aspects of the background were mentioned during the open discussion of the paper.

Buddhism. Sri Lankan Tamils shared similar political, linguistic, and religious aspirations, but obviously they did not want to have one foreign power merely replaced by what some regarded as another alien culture.

By the mid 1950s, many politicians were seeking voted by appealing to Sinhalese chauvinism. Their position can be summarized as follows: Sri Lanka, as an insular country with well defined *natural* borders, is the homeland of Sinhalese culture. Since this is essentially the only area in the world where Sinhala is spoken, this language needs to be protected by giving it a priority status. Also, Sri Lanka has the responsibility — maybe even a sacred obligation — to preserve Theravada Buddhism. And, in a democratic state, the wishes of the majority should be enacted and maintained against outside pressures. The greatest danger to Sinhalese culture is from Tamil Nadu, the source of ancient invasions of the island and the present home of 55 million Tamils.

Many Tamil leaders, in contrast, reflect the perspective of a minority group that fears discrimination by the majority. The island has been their homeland since ancient times, so Sri Lankan Tamils believe their culture should have equal status in a multi-ethnic country. They perceive, instead, discrimination in the following ways: Priority given to Sinhala in the language bill of 1956, government patronage of Buddhism, quotas in higher education and jobs that restrict Tamils who would have succeeded on the basis of merit, and the settlement of other ethnic groups on newly reclaimed — irrigated — lands within the area they consider traditional Tamil territory.

What is known as the *Ethnic Issue* does not date from any particular event. In general, it resulted from a series of actions and reactions by the two groups as they drifted apart. Now, a generation after the passage of the 1956 language bill, the conflict has become bitter, violent, and interrelated with international events and forces.

Domestically, the party in power — UNP — is pressured by the other main Sinhalese party — SLFP — to act more vigorously against Tamil separatist groups. Meanwhile, the relatively moderate Tamil party — TULF — is in jeopardy from most of the over 20 other Tamil groups which oppose any negotiations that do not include a separate state.

Internationally, some of the Tamil groups are supported — to varying degrees — by worldwide leftist organizations and/or drug trading. Almost all of them receive assistance from groups in Tamil Nadu. The Sri Lankan government protests the *harboring of terrorists* by another country. But, any pressure from the central Indian government in New Delhi on the state government of Tamil Nadu feeds the forces of regionalism in India, which endangers the unitary state. Meanwhile, the Indian government accuses the rulers in Colombo of importing Pakistani and Israeli military good and personnel.

It is in this context that the questions about territorial control become especially meaningful.

Table 9.1. Ethnic Groups in Sri Lanka, 1911 & 1981

Year	Sinhalese	Sri Lanka Tamil	Indian Tamil	Moor	Others
1911	2,715,420	528,024	530,983	266.625	65,298
	66.13 %	12.86 %	12.93 %	6.49 %	1.59 %
1981	10,985,666	1,871,535	825,233	1,056,972	110,595
	73.98 %	12.60 %	5.56 %	7.12 %	.74 %

Table 9.2. Ethnic Group Percentages by Providence, 1981

Province	Sinhalese	Sri Lankan Tamil	Indian Tamil	Moor
Western	84.9 **	5.6	1.6	6.2
Central	65.7 **	7.3	18.7	7.6
Southern	95.1 **	0.6	1.3	2.5
Northern	3.0	86.4 **	5.7	4.7
Eastern	25.7	40.3 *	1.2	32.2
North Western	90.0 **	2.7	0.6	6.4
North Central	91.7 **	1.4	0.1	6.5
Ura	75.9 **	4.5	15.7	3.5
Sabaragumuwa	85.4 **	2.2	8.9	3.3

** Majority * Plurality

166

Table 9.3. Ethnic Group Percentages by District. 1981

Province	Sinhalese	Sri Lankan Tamil	Indian Tamil	Moor
Colombo	77.9 **	9.8	1.3	8.3
Gampaha	99.2 **	3.3	0.4	2.8
Kalutara	87.3 **	1.0	4.1	7.5
Kandy	74.3 **	4.9	9.3	10.7
Matale	79.9 **	5.9	6.7	7.2
Nuware Eliya	42.2	12.5	42.4 *	2.5
Galle	94.4 **	0.7	1.4	3.2
Matara	94.6 **	0.6	2.2	2.6
Hambantota	97.4 **	0.4	0.1	1.1
Jaffna	0.6	95.3 **	2.4	1.7
Mannar	8.1	50.6 **	13.2	26.6
Vavuniya	16.7	56.9 **	19.4	6.9
Mullaitivu	5.1	76.0 **	13.9	4.9
Batticaloa	3.2	70.8 **	1.2	24.0
Amparai	37.6	20.1	0.4	41.5 *
Trincomalee	35.8 *	32.0	2.5	28.8
Kurunegala	93.1 **	1.1	0.5	5.1
Puttalam	82.6 **	6.7	0.6	5.1
Anuradhapura	92.1 **	1.0	0.1	6.5
Polonnaruwa	90.9 **	2.2	0.1	6.5
Badulla	68.5 **	5.7	21.1	4.2
Moneragala	92.9 **	1.8	3.3	1.9
Ratnapura	84.7 **	2.3	11.1	1.7
Kegalle	86.3 **	2.1	6.4	5.1

** Majority * Plurality

Map 9.1. Sri Lanka

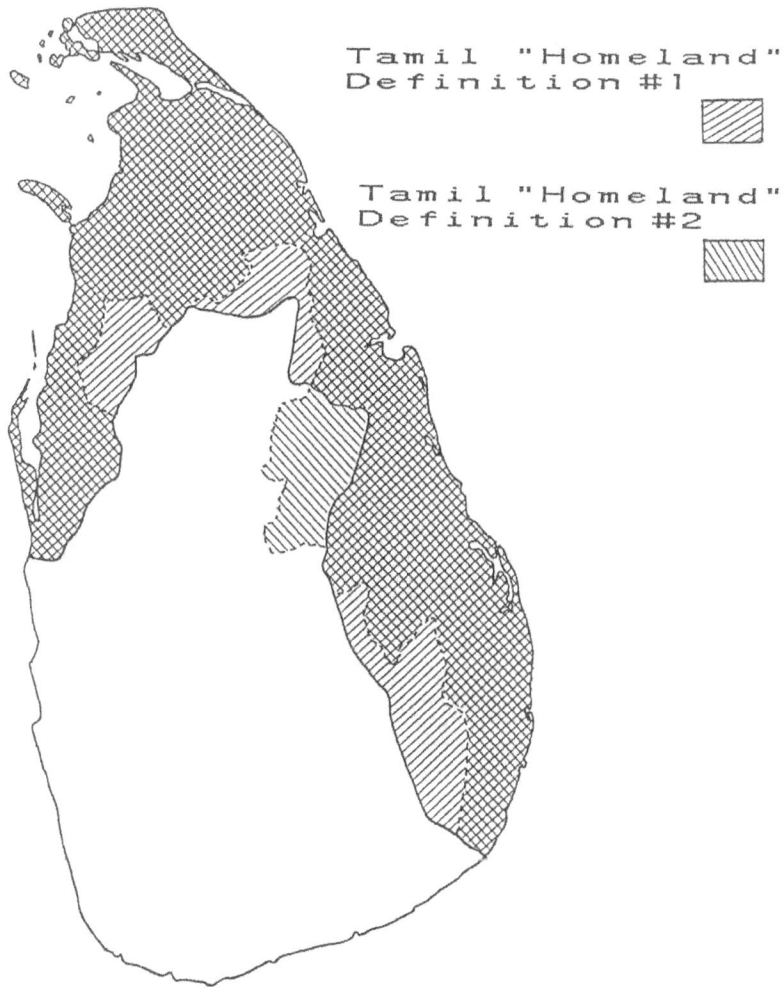

Map 9.2. Tamil Homelands

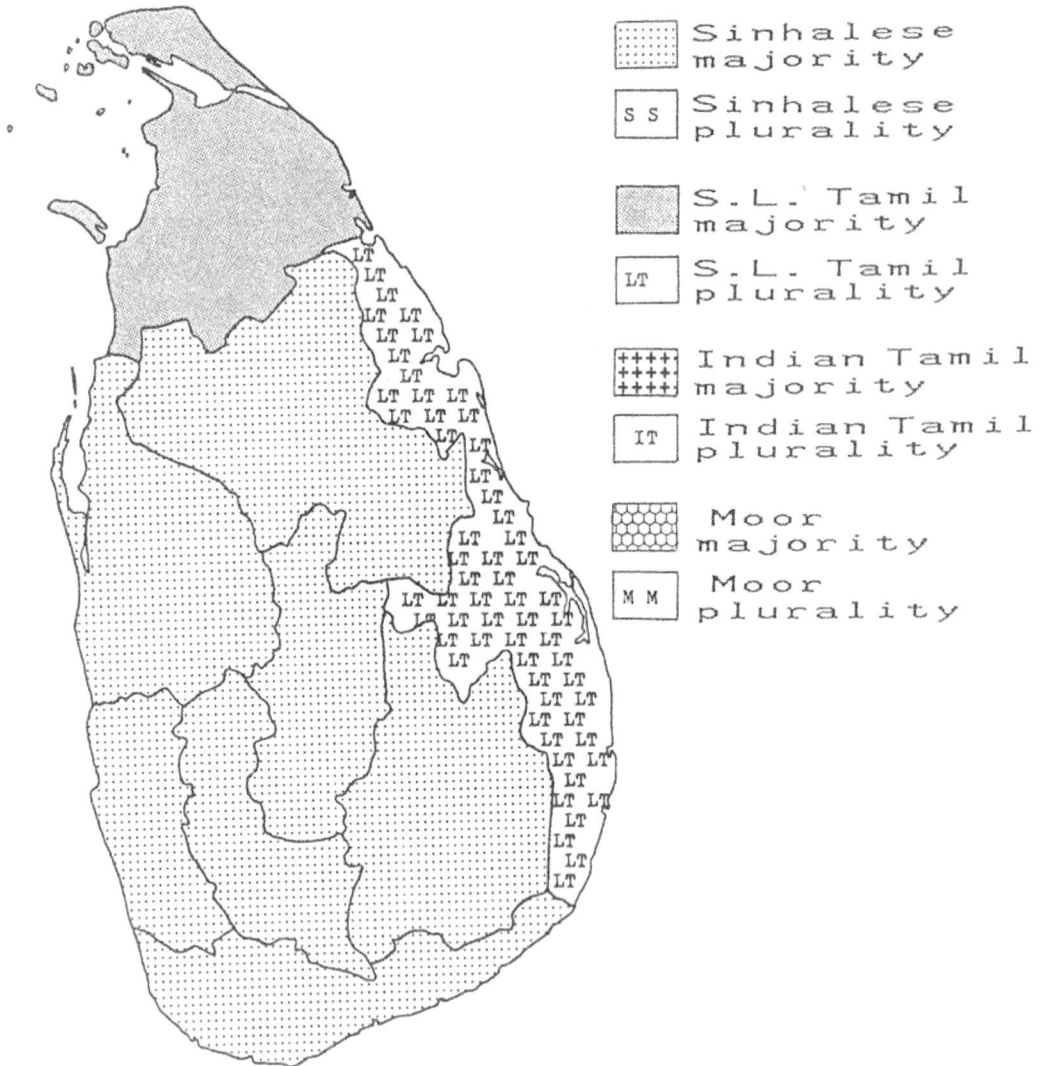

Legend:

- Sinhalese majority
- S S — Sinhalese plurality
- S.L. Tamil majority
- LT — S.L. Tamil plurality
- Indian Tamil majority
- IT — Indian Tamil plurality
- Moor majority
- M M — Moor plurality

Map 9.3. Ethnic Provinces, 1981

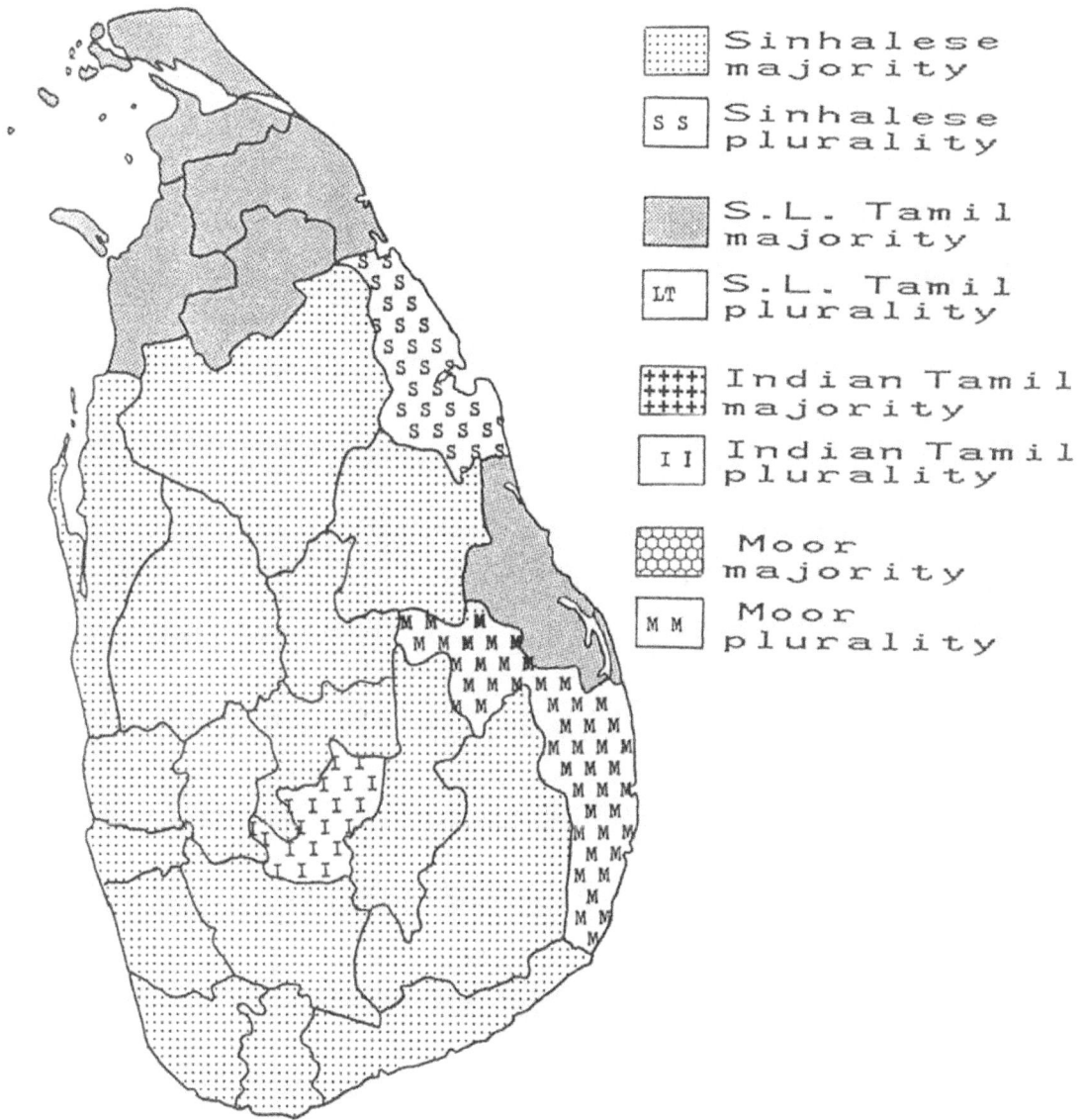

Map 9.4. Ethnic Districts, 1981

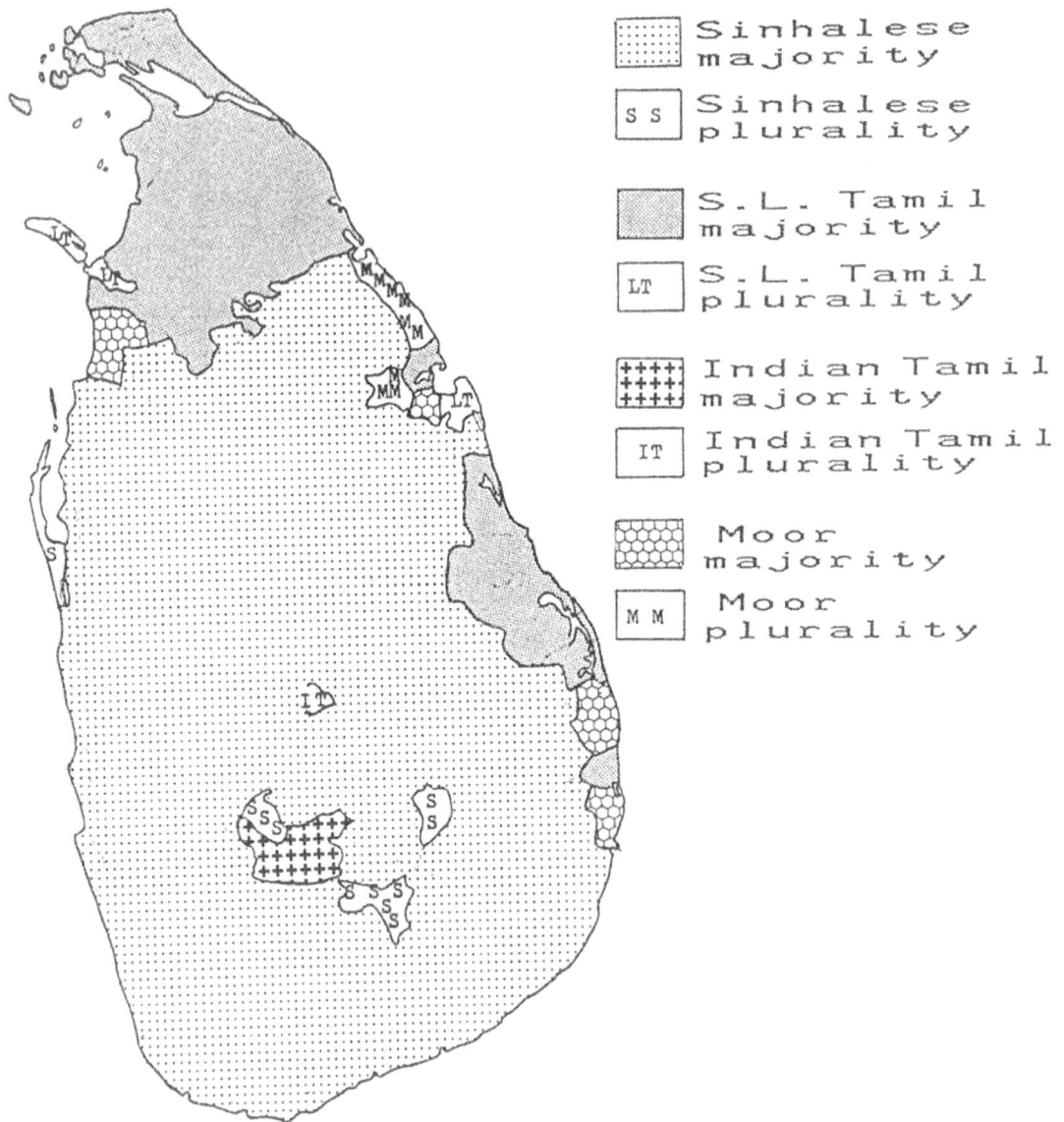

Map 9.5. Ethnic AGAs, 1981

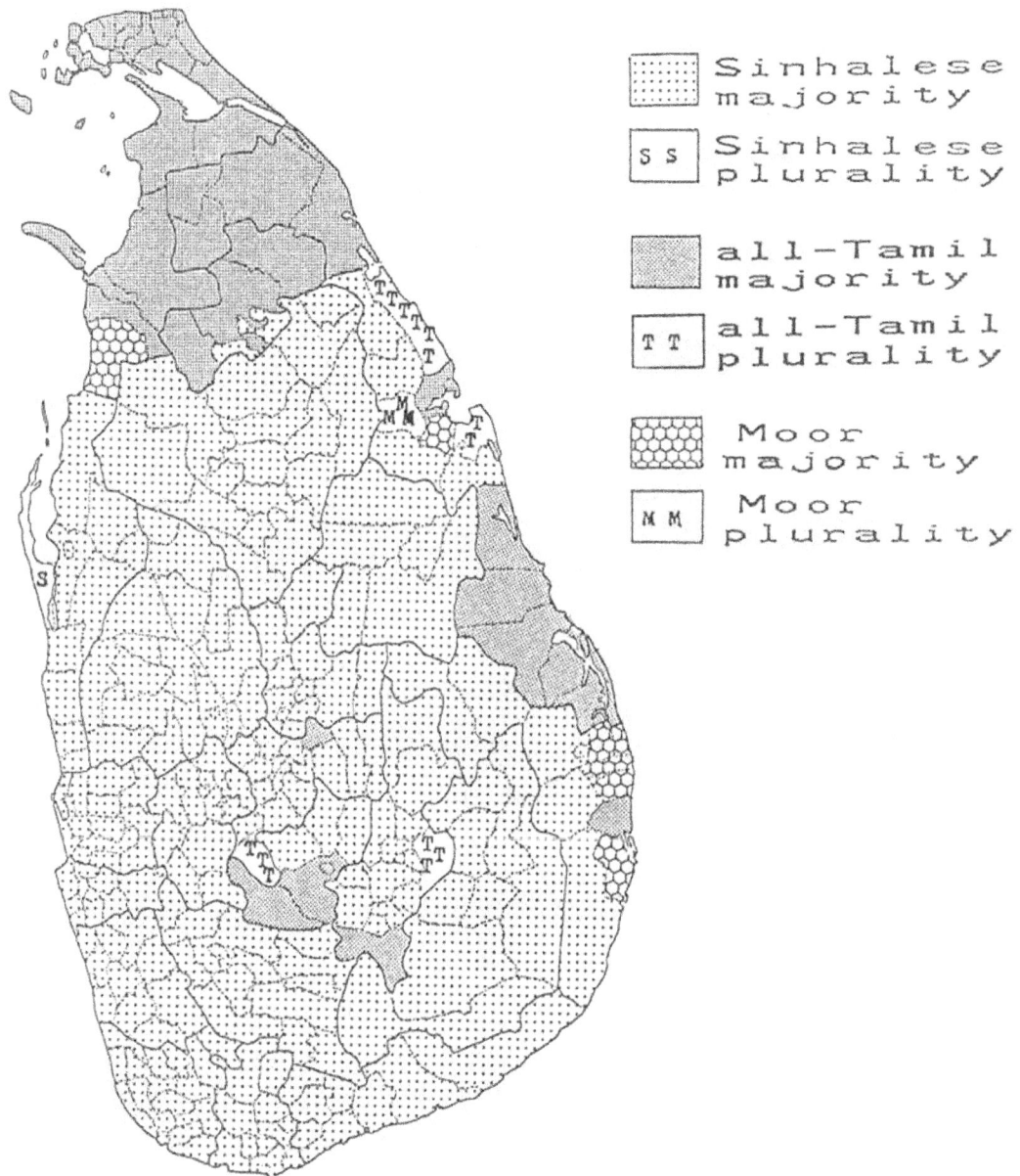

Map 9.6. Combined AGAs, 1981

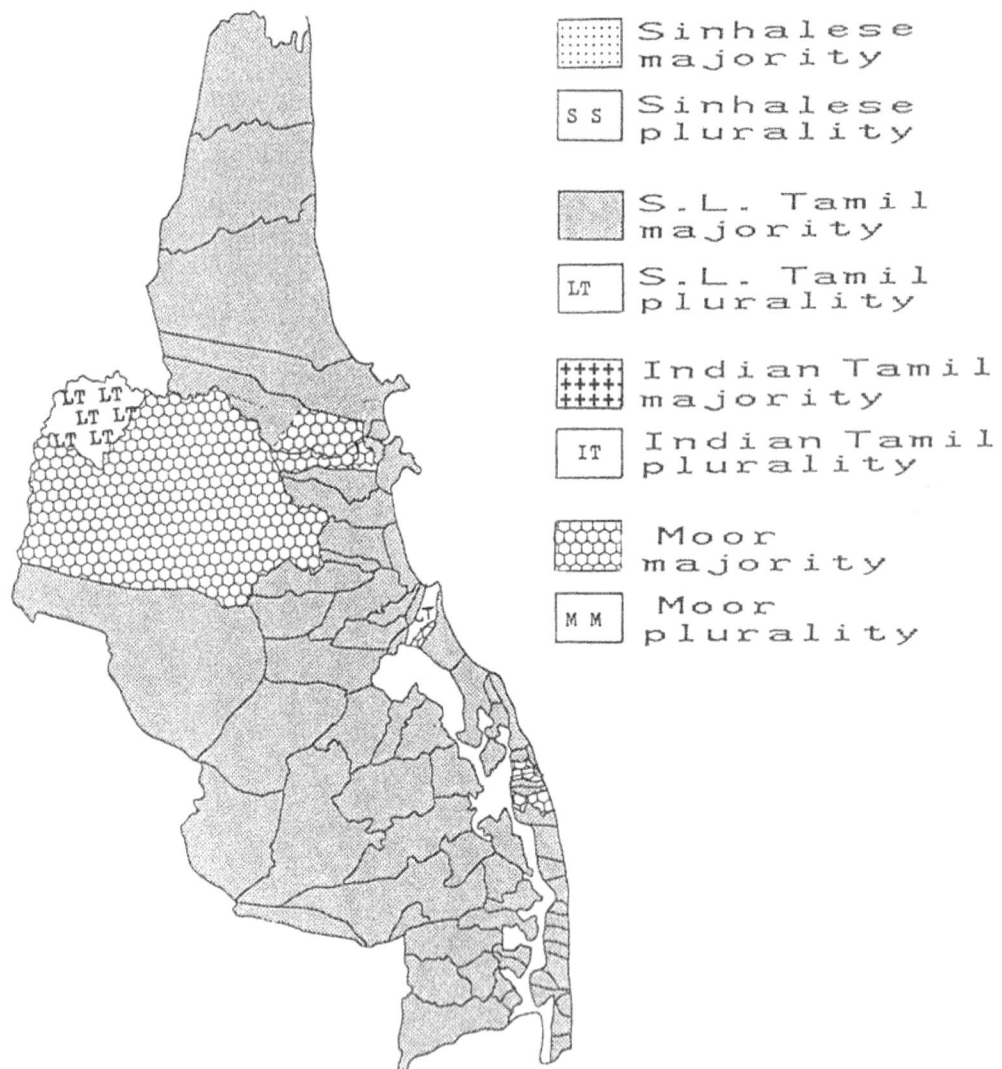

Legend:
- Sinhalese majority
- S S Sinhalese plurality
- S.L. Tamil majority
- LT S.L. Tamil plurality
- Indian Tamil majority
- IT Indian Tamil plurality
- Moor majority
- M M Moor plurality

Map 9.7. Ethnic G.S., Batticaloa

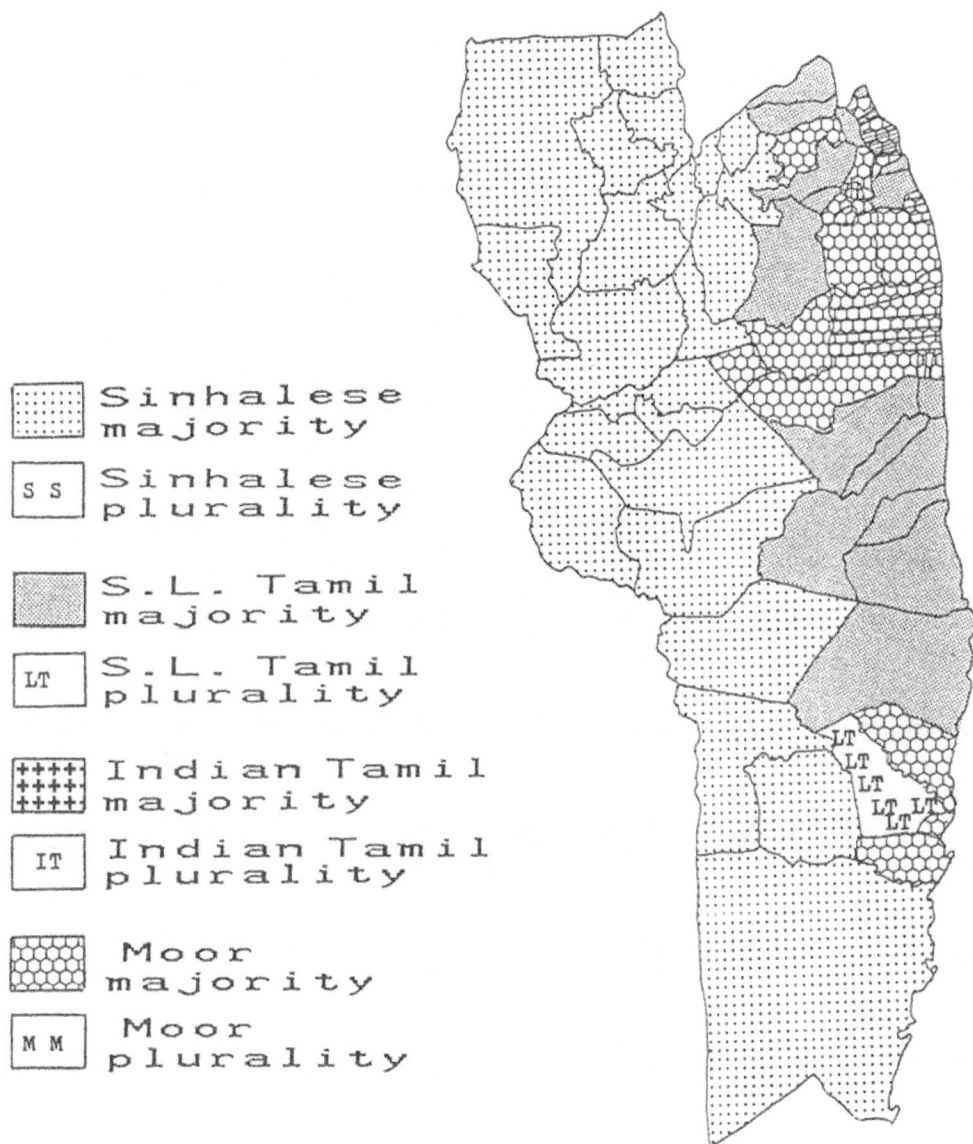

Map 9.8. Ethnic G.S., Amparai

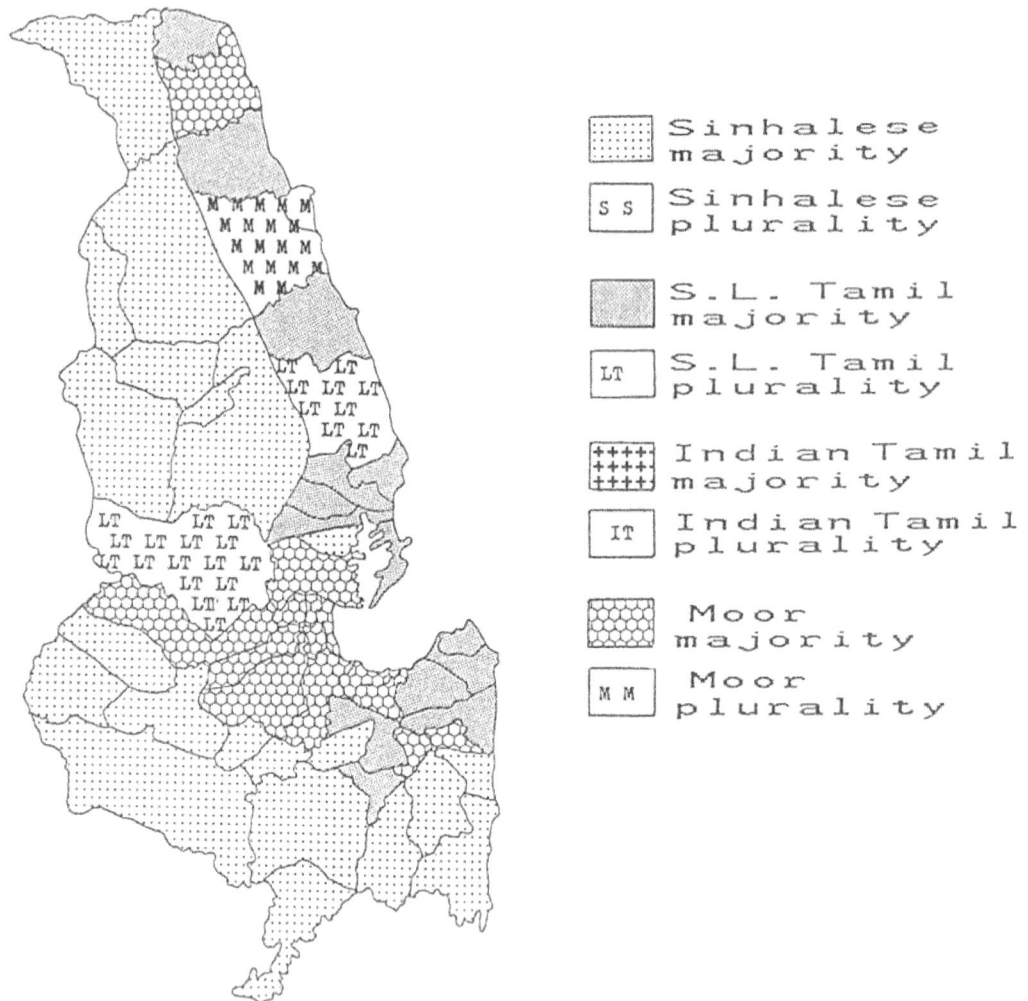

Map 9.9. Ethnic G.S., Trincomalee

Bibliographic Appendices

Writings and Professional Papers by Robert H. Stoddard[1]

Publication Chronology

2011. "Foreword: Holy Places and Pilgrimages: Essays on India." Pp. 1-6 in *Holy Places and Pilgrimages: Essays on India*, edited by Rana P.B. Singh. New Delhi: Shubhi Publications.

2010. "Great Plains Region." Pp. 929-935 in *Encyclopedia of Religion in America*, Vol 2., edited by Charles H. Lippy and Peter W. Williams. Washington, DC: CQ Press.

2010. Review of *The Separist Conflict in Sri Lanka: Terrorism, Ethnicity, Political Economy*, by Asoka Bandarag. *The Professional Geographer* 62 (February): 149–151.

2010. "The Geography of Buddhist Pilgrimage in Asia." Pp. 2-4 and 178 (map) in *Pilgrimage and Buddhist Art*, edited by Adriana Proser. New Haven: Asia Society/Yale University Press.

2010. "Vaishno Devi, the Most Famous Goddess Shrine in the Siwāliks." Coauthored with Georgana Foster. Pp. 109-124 in *Sacred Geography of Goddesses in South Asia*, edited by Rana P.B. Singh. Newcastle upon Tyne (UK): Cambridge Scholars.

2009. "Pilgrimage Places and Sacred Geometries." Pp. 163-177 in *Pilgrimage: Sacred Landscapes and Self-Organized Complexity*, edited by John McKim Malville and Baidyanath Saraswati. New Delhi: Indira Gandhi National Centre for the Arts.

2004. "Geography of Religion and Belief Systems." Coauthored with Carolyn V. Prorok. Pp. 759-767 in *Geography in America at the Dawn of the 21st Century*, edited by Gary L. Gaile and Cort J. Willmott. Oxford (UK): Oxford University Press.

---

[1] The editor bears full responsibility for any errors or omissions in the lists below. Please take special notice that several of Professor Stoddard's publications, including the full text of *Field Techniques and Research Methods in Geography*, are available gratis as PDF downloads via the UNL Digital Commons website maintained by the Libraries of the University of Nebraska-Lincoln.

2004. "Hinduism." P. 746 in *Encyclopedia of the Great Plains*, edited by D. Wishart. Lincoln: University of Nebraska Press.

2004. "The Cultural Geographer's Interest in Regions." Pp. 3-13 in *Cultural Geography: Form and Process (Essays in Honour of Prof. A.B. Mukerji)*, edited by Neelam Grover and Kashi Nath Singh. New Delhi: Concept Publishing.

1997. *Sacred Places, Sacred Spaces: The Geography of Pilgrimages*. Coedited with Alan Morinis. (Geoscience and Man series, Vol. 34). Baton Rouge, LA: Geoscience Publications, Louisiana State University, Department of Geography and Anthropology.

1997. "Introduction: The Geographic Contribution to Studies of Pilgrimage." Pp. Ix-xi in *Sacred Places, Sacred Spaces: The Geography of Pilgrimages*, edited by Robert H. Stoddard and Alan Morinis. Geosciences and Man Series. Louisiana State University, Department of Geography and Anthropology.

1997. "Defining and Classifying Pilgrimages." Pp. 41-60 in *Sacred Places, Sacred Spaces: The Geography of Pilgrimages*, edited by Robert H. Stoddard and Alan Morinis. Geosciences and Man Series. Louisiana State University, Department of Geography and Anthropology.

1997. "The World as a Multilevel Mosaic: Understanding Regions." *The Social Studies* 88: 167-72.

1996. Review of *Losing Asia: Modernization and the Culture of Development*, by B. Wallach. *Journal of Cultural Geography* 16: 113-15.

1996. "The Preservation of Bhutan." *Proceedings* (Nebraska Academy of Sciences) 106: 64.

1995. "South Asia: Summary of Discussion." Pp. 145-48 in *The Challenge of Ethnic Conflict to National and International Order in the 1990s: Geographic Perspectives (A Conference Report)*. Springfield, VA: National Technical Information Service.

1995. "I maggiori pellegrinaggi del mondo." *Annali Italiani del Torismo Internazionale* 1: 101-20. [Translation of the item below].

1994. "Major Pilgrimage Places in the World." Pp. 17-36 in *Pilgrimage in the Old and New World*, edited by S.M. Bhardwaj and G. Rinschede. Berlin: Dietrich Reimer Verlag.

1994. Review of *Nepal: Development and Change in a Landlocked Himalayan Kingdom*, by Pradyumna P. Karan and Hiroshi Ishii. *Journal of Cultural Geography* 14: 107-09.

1994. Review of *Claiming the High Ground: Sherpas, Subsistence, and Environmental Change in the Highest Himalayas*, by S.F. Stevens. *Professional Geographer* 46: 274.

1993. "Where is the Median Center?" *Journal of Geography* 93 (September/October): 234-5.

1992. "Trends in Published Research in India." Pp. 159-66 in *The Roots of Indian Geography: Search and Research; Homage to S. P. Chatterjee*, edited by R.L. Singh and R.P.B. Singh. National Geographical Society of India, Banaras Hindu University.

1992. "The Disaster of Deforestation in the Brazilian Rainforest." Pp. 527-35 in *Natural and Technological Disasters: Causes, Effects and Preventative Measures*, edited by S.K. Mujumdar and others. Pennsylvania Academy of Science.

1992. *Field Techniques and Research Methods in Geography*. (Originally published by Kendall/Hunt, 1982). Reprinted, Marietta, OH: TechBooks.

1990. Review of *Chinatowns: Townms within Cities in Canada*, by D.C. Lai. *Journal of Historical Geography* 16: 364.

1989. *Human Geography: People, Places, and Cultures*. 2nd edition. Coauthored with David J. Wishart and Brian W. Blouet. Englewood Cliffs, NJ: Prentice-Hall. (399 pp.).

1989. "Characteristics of Buddhist Pilgrimages in Sri Lanka." Pp. 99-116 in *Pilgrimage in World Religions*, edited by S.M. Bhardwaj and G. Rinschede. Dietrich Reimer Vertag.

1988. Review of *Regions and Regionalism in the United States*, by M. Bradshaw. *Journal of Cultural Geography* 9: 97-98.

1988. Review of *Refugees: A Third World Dilemma*, edited by J.R. Rogge. *Journal of Geography* 87: 239-240.

1987. "Pilgrimages along Sacred Paths." *The National Geographical Journal of India* 33 (December): 448-456. [Reprinted, see below].

1987. "Pilgrimages along Sacred Paths." Pp. 96-104 in *Trends in the Geography of Pilgrimages: Homage to David E. Sopher*, edited by R.L. Singh and R.P.B. Singh. Research Publication Series 35, National Geographical Society of India, Banaras Hindu University.

1987. "Agents of Change in Rural Sri Lanka." Coauthored with G.M.S. Weerasinghe. *Transition* 16: 2-5.

1986. *Human Geography: People, Places, and Cultures*. Coauthored with David J. Wishart and Brian W. Blouet. Englewood Cliffs, NJ: Prentice-Hall. (341 pp.). This edition also published as a cassette sound recording for visually-impaired students. Seattle, WA: Braille/Taping Service, Washington Library for the Blind and Physically Handicapped, 1986.

1985. "The Formation of Cultural Regions." Pp. 237-249 in *India: Culture, Society and Economy*, edited by A.B. Mukerji and A. Ahrnad. Inter-India Pub.

1985. "The Himalayas." Pp. 9-12 in *Nepal: Nature's Paradise*, edited by T. C. Majupuria. Bangkok: White Lotus Co.

1983. Review of *Patterns of Change in the Nepal Himalaya*, by M. Poffenberger. *Journal of Asian Studies* 42: 996-997.

1983. Review of *Untouchable: An India Life History*, by J.M. Freeman; and *An Exploration of India: Geographical Perspectives on Society and Culture*, edited by D.E. Sopher. *Social Science Journal* 20: 93-96.

1982. *Field Techniques and Research Methods in Geography*. (National Council on Geographic Education Pacesetter Series; Clyde F. Kohn, Consulting Editor). Dubuque, IA: Kendal/Hunt. (234 pp.).

1981/82. "The Mandala as a Geography Model for Sacred Space."*Geography of Religion and Belief Systems* 5: 3-4.

1981. "Comments on the Geography of Pilgrimages in Asia." *Bulletin of Asian Geography* 10: 7-8.

1981. "The Use of Pedestrian Space in a Nepalese City." (Special issue on "Pedestrian Networks," edited by Michael R. Hill). *Man-Environment Systems* 11 (1 & 2): 72.

1980. Review of *A Survey of Research in Geography, 1969-1972*, edited by M. Raza. *South Asia in Review* 5: 5-6.

1979-80. "Perceptions about the Geography of Religious Sites in the Kathmandu Valley." *Contributions to Nepalese Studies* (Journal of the Research Centre for Nepal and Asian Studies, Tribhuvan University, Kirtipur, Nepal) 7: 97-118.

1979. "Spatial Characteristics of Tertiary Activities in Kathmandu." *Himalayan Review* (Nepal Geographical Society) 11: 27-44.

1979. "High School Students' Images of Geography: An Exploratory Analysis." Coauthored with Raymond Hubbard. *Journal of Geography* 78: 181-94.

1977. *Defining Critical Environmental Areas in Nebraska: One Phase of Land Use Planning in Nebraska*. (Occasional Paper No. 3). Lincoln, NE: Department of Geography, University of Nebraska. (117 pp.).

1977. Review of *Quantitative Techniques in Geography: An Introduction*, by R. Hammond and P.S. McCullagh; *Introduction to Quantitative Analysis in Human Geography*, by M. Yeates; and *Statistical Analysis of Spatial Dispersion*, by A. Rogers. *Geographical Analysis* 9: 301-302.

1977. "Educational and Applied Geography in Nepal." *Proceedings* (Nebraska Academy of Sciences) 87: 66-67.

1976. "Comments on Circulation in An Asian Urban Village." *Great Plains - Rocky Mountain Geographical Journal* 5: 63-70.

1976. "A Measure of Highway Expansion in Nepal." *Himalayan Review* 3: 1-9.

1976. "Dissertations and Theses Recently Completed in Geography." Coauthored with Michael R. Hill. *Professional Geographer* 28 (1): 71-93.

1974. *Activities for Spatial Analysis: A Manual of Geographic Methods.* Student manual. Department of Geography, University of Nebraska.

1974. "Recent Geography Dissertations and Theses Completed and In Preparation." *Professional Geographer* 26 (1): 60-99.

1974. "Understanding Map Skills and Spatial Relationships in Primary Grades." *Proceedings* (Nebraska Academy of Sciences) 84: 52-53.

1973. *Planning College Geography Facilities: Guidelines for Space and Equipment.* (Commission on College Geography, Publication No. 12). Washington, DC: Commission on College Geography, Association of American Geographers. (55 pp.).

1972. Review of *Spatial Organization: The Geographer's View of the World*, by R. Abler, J. Adams, and P. Gould. *Professional Geographer* 24: 169.

1971. "Comments on the Contents of Field Work." *Professional Geographer* 23 (April): 152-3.

1971. "The Location of Holy Sites in India." Pp. 268-72 in *Selected Papers: 21st I.G.U. Publication*, Vol. 3: *Population and Settlement Geography and Political Geography.* Indian National Committee for Geography. Calcutta, India.

1970. "Changing Patterns of Some Rural Churches." *Rocky Mountain Social Science Journal* 7 (April): 61-68.

1969. "An Attempted Definition of a Frontier Using a Wave Analogy." Coauthored with David Wishart and Andrew Warren. *Rocky Mountain Social Science Journal* 6 (April): 73-81.

1969. *Introduction to Geography.* (Video-tape); together with a "Course Guide" and "Instructor's Guide." Nebraska Educational Television Council for Higher Education.

1968. "An Analysis of the Distribution of Major Hindu Holy Sites." *National Geographical Journal of India* 14 (June-September): 148-55.

1968. Review of *Geography of Religions*, by D.E. Sopher. *Professional Geographer* 20: 142.

1968. Review of *Bhutan: A Physical and Cultural Geography*, by Pradyumna P. Karan. *Professional Geographer* 20: 136-7.

1967. "The Distribution of Hindu Holy Sites." (Abstract). *Annals of the Association of American Geographers* 57 (December): 805.

1966. *Hindu Holy Sites in India.* Ph.D. dissertation. Iowa City, IA: Department of Geography, University of Iowa. (200 pp.).

1966. "Representing a Spatial Distribution." *Proceedings* (Nebraska Academy of Sciences) 76: 31.

1960. *The Geography of Churches and Their Rural Congregations in Nemaha County, Nebraska.* MA thesis. Lincoln, NE: Department of Geography, University of Nebraska-Lincoln. (150 pp.).

1959. "The Agricultural Geography of Nepal." *Proceedings* (Nebraska Academy of Sciences) 69: 19-20.

Chronology of Professional Papers Presented

2002. "Indians of the East Move West." Coauthored with Bidisha Nag. 26th Annual Interdisciplinary Symposium, Center for Great Plains Studies. Lincoln, Nebraska.

2000. "Spatial Expressions of Religion: The Geographer's Perspective," invited paper for joint meeting of The American Society of Church History and The American Catholic Historical Association. Sante Fe, New Mexico.

1999. "Religions and Belief Systems." Association of American Geographers. Honolulu, Hawaii.

1999. "Sacred Geometries in Contemporary Pilgrimages." International Seminar: Pilgrimage and Complexity. New Delhi, India.

1997. "Characteristics of a Geography Curriculum in the USA." Geography Seminar, Universiiti Kebangsaan Malaysia. Bangi, Malaysia.

1997. "Defining the Geography of Religion: Some Fundamental Issues." Association of American Geographers. Fort Worth, Texas.

1996. "Sovereignty of a Small State: The Case of Bhutan." 25th Annual Conference on South Asia. Madison, Wisconsin.

1996. "Tourism and Religious Travel: A Geographic Perspective." International Conference on Religious Tourism. Milan, Italy.

1996. "The Preservation of Bhutan." Nebraska Academy of Sciences. Lincoln, Nebraska.

1996. "Religion and Necrogeography." Association of American Geographers. Charlotte, North Carolina.

1995. "Religion and Politics." Association of American Geographers. Chicago, Illinois.

1994. "To Bee or Not to Bee." National Council for Geographic. Education. Lexington, Kentucky.

1994. "Geography of Religion: A Taboo Topic?" Association of American Geographers. San Francisco, California.

1993. "Comments on the Ethnic Conflicts in South Asia." The Challenge of Ethnic Conflict to National and International Order in the 1990s: Geographic Perspectives. McLean, Virginia.

1993. "Changing Views of Territorial Sovereignty: Is This Land Really My Land?" National Council for Geographic Education. Halifax, Nova Scotia.

1993. "Regional Muslim Pilgrimages: Marabouts in the Maghreb." Association of American Geographers, Atlanta, Georgia.

1991. "What is Geographic about Religion?" National Council for Geographic Education. St. Paul, Minnesota.

1991. "Religion and Territoriality." Association of American Geographers. Miami, Florida.

1991. "Special Sites and Spatial Styles." Invited speaker. 22nd Annual South Dakota University Geography Convention. Brookings, South Dakota.

1990. "Who Is Destroying the Rainforest?" National Council for Geographic Education. Williamsburg, Virginia.

1990. "Patterns of Religion in Sri Lanka." Association of American Geographers. Toronto, Ontario, Canada.

1989. "Spiritual Magnets for the Multitudes." Association of American Geographers. Baltimore, Maryland.

1988. "Spatial and Environmental Relationships Associated with Major Pilgrimage Places of the World." Interdisciplinary Symposium on Religion and Environment. Eichstatt, Germany.

1988. "Meanings and Measures of Pilgrimage." Association of American Geographers. Phoenix, Arizona.

1987. "Characteristics of Buddhist Pilgrimages in Sri Lanka." Association of American Geographers. Portland, Oregon.

1986. "Regionalization and Regionalism in Sri Lanka." 15th Annual Conference on South Asia. Madison, Wisconsin.

1985. "Patterns of Religious Affiliation in the United States." National Council for Geographic Education. Breckenridge, Colorado.

1984. "Relationship between National Wealth and Linguistic Homogeneity." Great Plains/Rocky Mountain Regional Meeting, Association of American Geographers.

1983. "Negative Geography: Locating Things Elsewhere." National Council for Geographic Education. Ocho Rios, Jamaica.

1978. "To Be Land-Locked and Poverty-Locked." Nepal Studies Association, Association of Asian Studies.

1982. "Simplified Classification for Teaching Human Geography." Association of American Geographers. San Antonio, Texas.

1981. "Pilgrimages Classified by Geographic Characteristics." International Conference on Pilgrimages. Pittsburgh, Pennsylvania.

1981. "The Mandala as a Geographic Model for Sacred Place in South Asia." Association of American Geographers. Los Angeles, California.

1980. "Spatial Relationships Among Religious Sites in the Kathmandu Valley." 9th Annual Conference on South Asia. Madison, Wisconsin.

1980. "Perceptions of Asian Countries Held by American Teachers." National Council for Geographic Education. Des Moines, Iowa.

1980. "Cosmology and the Cultural Landscape of the Kathmandu Valley." Association of American Geographers. Louisville, Kentucky.

1979. "Pedestrian Behavior in a Traditionally Structured Society and Setting." Environmental Design Research Association, EDRA-10. Buffalo, New York.

1978. "Remarks Regarding Religious Routes." Association of American Geographers. New Orleans, Louisiana.

1978. "To Be Land-Locked and Poverty-Locked." Nepal Studies Association, Association for Asian Studies. Chicago, Illinois.

1977. "Small and Landlocked: Geographical Problems of Nepal." Third World Conference. Omaha, Nebraska.

1977. "Spatial Characteristics of Tertiary Activities in Kathmandu." Western Conference, Association for Asian Studies. USAF Academy, Colorado Springs, Colorado.

1977. "Spatial Manifestations of Socio-Religious Values in a Nepalese Town." Association of American Geographers. Salt Lake City, Utah.

1977. "Educational and Applied Geography in Nepal." Nebraska Chapter, National Council for Geographic Education, Nebraska Academy of Sciences. Lincoln, Nebraska.

1976. "A Field Activity for Introducing Geographic Concepts." Great Plains/Rocky Mountain Regional Meeting, Association of American Geographers. Manhattan, Kansas.

1976. "Procedures for the Formation of Regional Units." Seminar on Regional Development and Balanced Growth. Ranikhet, UP, India.

1974. "Communicating the Applicability of Geographic Skills." National Council for Geographic Education. Chicago, Illinois.

1974. "Understanding Map Skills and Spatial Relationships in Primary Grades." Nebraska Chapter, National Council for Geographic Education, Nebraska Academy of Sciences. Lincoln, Nebraska.

1974. "Studying Spatial Interaction: A Field Activity for Synthesizing Information about Human Geography." Association of American Geographers. Seattle, Washington.

1972. "The Location of Trading Posts on the Upper Missouri as Predicted by an Analog Model." Coauthored with David Wishart. Association of American Geographers. Kansas City, Missouri.

1972. "Discussion on the Quality of the Urban Environment." 22nd International Geographical Congress. Montreal, Quebec, Canada,

1971. "The Environment of Residential Space." Great Plains/Rocky Mountain Regional Meeting, Association of American Geographers. Colorado Springs, Colorado.

1967. "The Distribution of Major Hindu Holy Sites." Association of American Geographers. St. Louis, Missouri.

1966. "Representing a Spatial Distribution." Nebraska Chapter, National Council for Geographic Education, Nebraska Academy of Sciences. Lincoln, Nebraska.

1959. "A Bibliography on the Geography of Nepal." Nebraska Chapter, National Council for Geographic Education, Nebraska Academy of Sciences. Lincoln, Nebraska.

Dissertations and Theses Supervised by
Robert H. Stoddard

Connor, Kerry Margaret. 1987. *An Analysis of Residential Choice among Self-Settled Afghan Refugees in Peshawar, Pakistan.* Ph.D. dissertation. 278 pp.

Crump, Jeffrey Randell. 1989. *The Sectoral Composition and Spatial Distribution of Department of Defense Services Expenditures, 1979, 1982, and 1987.* Ph.D. dissertation. 253 pp.

Davidson, Fiona Margaret. 1987. *Role of Producer Services in the Economics of Small SMSAs.* MA thesis. 111 pp.

Hartley, Ralph J. 1989. *Variability in Content and Context of Aboriginal Rock Art on the Northern Colorado Plateau.* Ph.D. dissertation. 245 pp.

Hill, Michael R. 1982. *Spatial Structure and Decision-Making Aspects of Pedestrian Route Selection through an Urban Environment.* Ph.D. dissertation. 276 pp.

Hubbard, Raymond. 1976. *An Analysis of Consumer Spatial Behavior in an Urban Area with Particular Reference to Racial Groups.* Ph.D. dissertation. 475 pp.

Knotwell, James Owen. 1995. *Adaptation to Openings of Discount Retail Centers in Rural Market Centers: The Case of the North Plate, Nebraska, Functional Region.* Ph.D. dissertation. 387 pp.

Louviere, Jordan Joseph. 1968. *Geography of Economic Health in the State of Louisiana, with Special Reverence to Underdevelopment in Red River Parish.* M.A. thesis. 198 pp.

Nag, Bidisha. 2005. *A Journey Across the Black Waters: Female Migration from India to the United States.* Ph.D. dissertation. 112 pp.

Osrunn, Peter Gudmundur. 1971. *Geographic Analysis of Church Lands in Lincoln, Nebraska.* MA thesis. 160 pp.

Richer, Charles Thorne, Jr. 1973. *Flow of Chemical Fertilizer in India.* MA thesis. 175 pp.

Sangeeta, Badal. 1998. *Regional Variations in the Status and Well-being of Women in India.* Ph.D. dissertation. 232 pp.

Wood, Perry S. 1973. *The Growth and Decline of Small Communities in the Southern Allegheny Mountains.* Ph.D. dissertation. 163 pp.

About the Contributors

SURINDER M. BHARDWAJ is Professor Emeritus at Kent State University.

THOMAS DOERING is with the Nebraska Department of Economic Development.

MICHAEL R. HILL, most recently with the Department of Athletics at the University of Nebraska-Lincoln, is a writer/researcher at D&H Sociologists in St. Joseph, Michigan, and editor of *Sociological Origins*.

STEVE KALE, formerly with the Oregon Department of Transportation, passed away in 2013.

CAROLYN V. PROROK is Professor Emeritus at Slippery Rock University.

CARL RITTER was a prominent German geographer at the University of Berlin.

NAINIE LENORA ROBERTSON STODDARD was a longtime resident of Nemaha County, Nebraska, and the mother of Robert H. Stoddard.

ROBERT H. STODDARD is Professor Emeritus at the University of Nebraska-Lincoln.